THE EXECUTIVE MBA IN INFORMATION SECURITY

THE EXECUTIVE MBA IN INFORMATION SECURITY

JOHN J. TRINCKES, JR.

CRC Press
Taylor & Francis Group
Boca Raton   London   New York

CRC Press is an imprint of the
Taylor & Francis Group, an **informa** business
AN AUERBACH BOOK

CRC Press
Taylor & Francis Group
6000 Broken Sound Parkway NW, Suite 300
Boca Raton, FL 33487-2742

International Standard Book Number: 978-1-4398-1007-1 (Hardback)

Library of Congress Cataloging-in-Publication Data

Trinckes, John J.
  The executive MBA in information security / John J. Trinckes, Jr.
    p. cm.
  Includes bibliographical references and index.
  ISBN 978-1-4398-1007-1 (hbk. : alk. paper)
  1. Data protection. 2. Computer security. 3. Information technology--Security measures. I. Title.

HF5548.37.T75 2010
005.8--dc22   2009027900

Visit the Taylor & Francis Web site at
http://www.taylorandfrancis.com

and the CRC Press Web site at
http://www.crcpress.com

Contents

Preface

Information security has become a hot topic over the last few decades and the science behind information security is still being developed. This field is always evolving and growing. It is broad in concept and touches every function or aspect of a business. It is deep, covering the most minute details and technical specifications. It involves everyone in an organization and everyone is responsible for it; however, most individuals, especially executives, have little if any concept of what information security is. They have heard of it in board meetings. They even may sit on committees responsible for the management of the information security program, but how many of these executives are the first to break the rules or policies that they have written? How many of them can name all of the critical business functions and all of the controls in place for the company's assets to protect both the asset and the executive from a security incident? How many, although responsible for managing a security incident, do not have the first inclination of what to do if an incident occurred? Would they know whether some event would be defined as a security incident in the first place?

Because you have taken the first step in reading this book, you have made the effort and have taken the initiative to protect your company's information. You know the value of this information and know the consequences if you do not protect it. You will not be a statistic, but rather the solution to a problem.

This book was written to provide an overview of information security concepts specifically intended for executives. As an executive, you are the individual in charge and ultimately responsible for your company's well-being. You are the primary sponsor and implementer of the information security program. You are the one that can make the difference by setting the example. Overall, you are the one that needs to understand and grasp the concepts of information security.

This book is a manual for developing an effective information security management program for your organization. It extracts concepts from several different sources and combines years of experience and practical applications to allow you, the executive, to formulate a comprehensive program. *The Executive MBA in Information Security* will provide a framework that you can utilize immediately, and it will attempt to provide these concepts in a straightforward and easy-to-read manner. Different sections of this book can be utilized alone or together; they build upon one another in a logical manner. The book will provide you with specific details, hints, traps, and additional resources that will provide all of the information that you will need to know. Although this book will not make you an expert in any one area, as an executive you will definitely obtain a good foundation and understanding of the principles and concepts that information security has to offer.

John J. Trinckes

Acknowledgments

Through faith in God, all things are possible.

I would like to thank my wife for her support on this project and her everlasting love. I would also like to thank my children for their understanding and forgiveness for not spending as much time as I possibly could with them while involved in this project.

I extend my extreme appreciation to Dave Kleiman, Michael Overly, and Chanley Howell, who provided a wealth of information and support along with my editors, Dr. Richard McMonagle and Troy Appling. Without their assistance, this book would have never been up to the standards that I believe it is. I would also like to thank my publisher, Rich O'Hanley, who believed in me and helped title this book, Amy Blalock, project coordinator, and Judith Simon, project editor, who kept me on top of the editorial process.

Finally, I would like to thank all of my associates and friends who have helped me in obtaining the necessary experience and knowledge to make this book a reality.

To follow the path:
look to the master,
follow the master,
walk with the master,
see through the master,
become the master.

Modern Zen poem

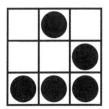

The Author

John J. ("Jay") Trinckes, Jr. (CISSP, CISM, CEH, NSA-IAM/IEM, MCSE, A+) is a Senior Information Security Consultant for CastleGarde, Inc. He conducts internal, physical, and external vulnerability assessments along with specific technical audits such as Bank Secrecy Act assessments. Trinckes has been instrumental in developing audit plans, compliance assessments, business impact analyses, and business continuity and disaster recovery plans for the company's clients. He also conducts security awareness training and other presentations related to information security.

Trinckes is a Certified Information Systems Security Professional (CISSP), Certified Information Security Manager (CISM), and a Certified Ethical Hacker (C-EH). He holds certifications in the National Security Agency (NSA) INFOSEC Assessment Methodology (IAM) and INFOSEC Evaluation Methodology (IEM), along with Microsoft Certified Systems Engineer (MCSE-NT) and Comptia A+ certifications.

Trinckes provides a unique perspective to CastleGarde's engineering team as a result of previous work experience as an Information Security Risk Analyst with a corporate credit union, a Law Enforcement Sergeant, an Assistant Accreditation Manager, and an IT Manager and System Administrator. He holds a current state of Florida law enforcement officer certification, which assists him in providing insight into assessment services through his extensive background in client management, law enforcement, IT support, and information security.

Trinckes graduated with a bachelor's degree in business administration/management information systems from the Union Institute and University in Cincinnati with a 4.0 GPA and is currently working on multiple network- and security-related certifications. He has been a member of numerous highly recognized security industry associations, such as the FBI's InfraGard®, Information Systems Security Association (ISSA), International Association of Technology Professionals (IATP), Information Systems Audit and Controls Association (ISACA®), and the International Information Systems Security Certification Consortium (ISC²).

When he is not working, Trinckes likes to spend his spare time with his family and friends. He can be reached for assistance or comments related to this book at hitechpo@windstream.net

Contributors

Dave Kleiman (CAS, CCE, CIFI, CEECS, CISM, CISSP, ISSAP, ISSMP, MCSE, MVP) has worked in the information technology security sector since 1990. Currently, he runs an independent computer forensics company, DaveKleiman. com, which specializes in litigation support, computer forensic examinations, incident response, and intrusion analysis. He developed a Windows operating system lockdown tool, S-Lok, and is frequently a speaker at national security conferences and a regular contributor to security-related Web sites and Internet forums. Kleiman is a member of many professional security organizations and is also on the certification committee for the National Center for Forensic Science (NCFS) Digital Forensics Certification Board (DFCB), a program of the U.S. Department of Justice's National Institute of Justice.

Kleiman was a contributing author for *Microsoft Log Parser Toolkit* (Syngress Publishing, ISBN: 978-1-932266-52-8), *Security Log Management: Identifying Patterns in the Chaos* (Syngress Publishing, ISBN: 978-1-59749-042-9), and *How to Cheat at Windows System Administration: Using Command Line Scripts* (Syngress Publishing, ISBN: 978-1-59749-105-1). He was technical editor for *Perfect Passwords: Selection, Protection, Authentication* (Syngress Publishing, ISBN: 978-1-59749-041-2), *Winternals® Defragmentation, Recovery, and Administration Field Guide* (Syngress Publishing, ISBN: 978-1-59749-079-5), *Windows Forensic Analysis DVD Toolkit* (Syngress Publishing, ISBN: 978-1-59749-156-3), *CD and DVD Forensics* (Syngress Publishing, ISBN: 978-1-59749-128-0), *Perl Scripting for Windows Security: Live Response, Forensic Analysis, and Monitoring* (Syngress Publishing, ISBN: 978-1-59749-173-0), and *The Official CHFI™ Exam 312-49 Study Guide: for Computer Hacking Forensics Investigators* (Syngress Publishing, ISBN: 978-1-59749-197-6). He served as technical reviewer for *Enemy at the Water Cooler: Real-Life Stories of Insider Threats and Enterprise Security Management Countermeasures* (Syngress Publishing ISBN: 978-1-59749-129-7).

Michael R. Overly, Esq. (CISSP, ISSMP) (moverly@foley.com) is a partner in Foley & Lardner's information technology and outsourcing and privacy, security and information management practices group. He focuses on drafting and negotiating development of technology-related agreements, software licenses, hardware acquisition, disaster recovery, outsourcing agreements, information security agreements, e-commerce agreements, and technology use policies. He counsels clients in the areas of technology acquisition, information security, electronic commerce, and online law.

Overly's numerous articles and books have been published in the United States, Europe, Korea, and Japan. He has been interviewed by a wide variety of print and broadcast media (e.g., the *New York Times, Los Angeles Times, Business 2.0, Newsweek,* ABCNEWS.com, CNN, and MSNBC) as a nationally recognized expert on technology and security-related matters. In addition to conducting seminars in the United States, Norway, Japan, and Malaysia, he has testified before the U.S. Congress regarding online issues.

Overly is a graduate of Loyola Law School (JD, 1989), where he was articles editor of the *Loyola Law Review* and elected to Order of the Coif, and Texas A&M University (MS, electrical engineering, 1984; BS, 1982). He was admitted to the California Bar in 1989. He is a member of the Computer Security Institute, the Information Systems Security Association, and the Computer Law Association.

Chanley T. Howell, Esq. (chowell@foley.com) is a partner with Foley & Lardner in its Intellectual Property Department and a member of the firm's information technology and outsourcing and privacy, security, and information management practices. He represents companies in a variety of technology law areas, such as software agreements, data management and compliance, technology agreements, and the Internet.

Howell is a founder and the former chairman of the intellectual property section of the Jacksonville Bar Association. He is a member of the intellectual property law, business law, and trial lawyers sections of the Florida Bar; a member of the business law, intellectual property, litigation, and construction law sections of the American Bar Association; and on the technology committee of the Jacksonville Bar Association. Additionally, he is a member of the grievance committee for the Florida Bar, which hears and adjudicates grievances filed against attorneys for violating the Rules of Professional Conduct. He is admitted to practice and has practiced before Florida's First District Court of Appeals, the Eleventh Circuit Court of Appeals, and the U.S. Supreme Court. Howell has served on the Fourth Judicial Circuit grievance committee, which investigates allegations of attorney misconduct. He is the professional responsibility partner for Foley's Jacksonville office.

Born in Jacksonville, Howell graduated with honors from the University of Florida College of Law and received his undergraduate degree, cum laude, from Vanderbilt University. He is immediate past chairman of the alumni board and former member of the board of trustees for the Bolles School in Jacksonville.

Chapter 1

Information Security Overview

Objectives

- Understand the steps involved in creating an efficient and successful information security management program.
- Explain corporate governance and how information security relates to corporate governance.
- Understand the goals of information security.
- Explain the difference between information security and IT security.
- Understand the duties inherent to information security and the alignment of information security to business needs.
- List the roles and responsibilities of the chief information security officer.
- Understand the proper organization structure of information security.
- Explain different functional areas related to information security.
- Understand the individual traits, qualifications, certifications, and experience required by an information security professional.
- Explain the steps and process involved in hiring information security professionals.
- Understand the importance of conducting comprehensive background checks on information security personnel.
- Explain the importance of information security.

- Understand information security concepts.
- Understand the laws governing information security.

1.1 Information Security Management

We have to see the big picture...and be able to make out the small details.

ISACA, 2007

The first step in creating a successful information security management program is to determine what the goals and objectives are for an organization. Information security must be aligned with these goals and objectives. It must also take into consideration the overall corporate governance of the organization. We will discuss corporate governance in more detail in the next section.

The second step in creating a successful information security management program is to develop business cases or examples to justify the investment in information security. As economies fall and budgets grow tighter, security is often one of the line items cut from the budget. Security is not cheap and a cost-benefit analysis should be performed to get the most out of limited funds. In its basic form, a cost-benefit analysis is a list of pros and cons related to a specific project. It takes into account what a specific project is going to cost, what that project is meant to do for the business, and, most of all, what the return will be on the investment to move forward with the project.

The third step in creating a successful information security management program is to identify the legal and regulatory requirements for the organization. For example, regulations such as the Gramm–Leach–Bliley Act, the Bank Secrecy Act, and others play a role in the controls that must be implemented in an organization to satisfy regulatory requirements, specifically in financial institutions. Regulators such as the National Credit Union Association and state regulatory agencies play a role in enforcing these regulatory requirements and imposing steep penalties for noncompliance on institutions like credit unions. Other organizations in other industries have specific laws and regulatory bodies that enforce different requirements. As an executive, you are ultimately responsible for following these regulations. You can be personally liable if due diligence is not properly exercised.

The fourth step in creating a successful information security management program involves obtaining senior management commitment to information security. As an executive, you must be totally committed to information security and allocate the necessary resources to obtain an adequate level of protection. You must define roles and responsibilities for information security throughout your organization. Although information security is everyone's responsibility, you must address specific duties and assign specific tasks to certain individuals who are going to take an active role in managing the appropriate information security functions. Along with these roles, communication channels must be developed to support information security and the sharing of information that touches every area of the organization.

Finally, no information security program would be complete without some internal and external reporting mechanism, as well as a way to track the progress of the program. Of course, a lot more elements go into the actual management of the program. We will go into further details later in this book; for now, the preceding steps will definitely get you started in the right direction.

"It is no longer enough to communicate to the world of stakeholders why we exist and what constitutes success[;] we must also communicate how we are going to protect our existence" according to systemic security management (ISACA 2007).

1.2 What Is Information Security?

The goal of information security is to protect the organization's assets.

ISACA, 2007

Before we look at information security, we must understand corporate governance, which is defined as

the set of responsibilities and practices exercised by the board and executive management with the goal of providing strategic direction, ensuring that objectives are achieved, ascertaining that risks are managed appropriately and verifying that the enterprise's resources are used responsibly. (ISACA 2007)

Information security is a part of corporate governance. It provides for the direction of security activities by verifying that specific goals and objectives are achieved. To make information security valuable to the organization, information security must support the business goals.

The goal of information security, as the word implies, is to protect information. Information is defined as data endowed with meaning and purpose. Information may take many forms. It can be in hard copy or paper format, digital format as stored in computers or on digital media, analog format as in audio recordings, or even intangible knowledge format kept within the minds of a few key personnel. No matter what form it is in, this information must be protected. According to the Brookings Institute, an organization's information and other intangible assets account for more than 80% of its market value (ISACA 2007).

Knowledge [or even more apparent, information] is fast becoming the sole factor of productivity, sidelining both capital and labor.

Peter Drucker

Many executives may feel that because the organization has installed firewalls and initiated passwords, the organization is secure. This could not be further from the truth. Information security is concerned with protection of the content, data, and the knowledge based upon this information, regardless of how it is handled, processed, transported, or stored. In the past, security focused on protecting systems that process and store information; however, this approach has proven to be too narrow an approach to accomplish the level of integration, process assurance, and overall security currently required by organizations.

Information security takes a larger view and focuses on the information rather than on the technology to protect. A good information security program addresses this new approach by taking a look at the universe of risks, the benefits that security will provide to an organization, and the processes behind the flow of information. Information security must be driven by executive management and supported by the board of directors. It must be taught and implemented in the organization by making every employee responsible for the protection of the information no matter what form it takes. "Information security provides the essential protective framework in which information can be shared while ensuring its protection from unauthorized users" (ISC² 2008).

Information technology security (or IT security), on the other hand, addresses only the security behind the technology used in business. IT security is usually managed at the Chief Information Officer (CIO) level, with additional resources coming out of network and system administration areas. IT security includes countermeasures to attacks such as firewalls, IDS/IPS systems, MAC filtering switches, harden operating systems, and other hardware or software that assist in protecting the *technology* of the business—not necessarily all the *information* of the business.

1.2.1 Responsibilities

> Some people don't get paid for what they DO; some people get paid for what they CAN DO.
>
> **Author unknown**

Every organization has a Chief Information Security Officer (CISO), whether the person holds that title or not. The responsibilities and requirements to protect sensitive information (no matter what form this information is in) fall upon the individuals at the highest level of the organization. Approximately 30% of all information security managers report directly or indirectly to the CIO. Although this may be functionally adequate, it is not the most optimal structure for several reasons.

The first reason for prudent management to elevate the position of the information security officer to a C-level or executive position is that the broad requirements of information security transcend the responsibilities assigned to the typical CIO. The second reason is that security is often perceived as a constraint on IT operations. It can be in direct conflict with IT enhancements that may cause risks to the organization's information. For example, when IT operation wants to implement a new program being pushed by users in the business, a lot of things must happen before this program goes into production. A lot of this process will be explained later in this book; suffice it to say here that the security of the program has to be considered from the start of the project.

Security may often hamper the progress of the project. It should not be the case that security is preventing organizational progress or change; however, security is an important consideration. Many times program developers are under pressure to roll out programs that may not have been fully tested, or security controls are sidestepped to get their software into production. If proper steps are not followed throughout the process, an organization can be left at great risk. These risks can come in the form of a security breach that can cause the loss of valuable or sensitive data and other damages.

Finally, security must be aligned with business rather than with technology. Technology is not an end in and of itself, but rather a tool to accomplish business. Information security, on the other hand, is a critical business component. To show a high-level commitment to information security, a qualified individual should be appointed as the CISO. As you will notice, a lot of responsibilities fall under the role of the CISO. (See Figure 1.1 for further details.) Appointing a CISO will create a security-positive environment for the whole organization. Information security has to start from the top and work its way down through all organizational levels to be effective. The board of directors and senior management must emphasize the importance of and their support for information security.

1.2.2 Organization

> Security is a process…not a product.
>
> **Phrase coined by Bruce Schneier**

As mentioned earlier, information security can sometimes be a constraint on operations, but it is still a very important consideration. You must never forget that information security must be aligned with the business and not with the technology. Information security deals with all aspects and forms of information. If a security incident were to occur, IT would be concerned with the nature and type of compromise within the boundaries of the technology domain. Information security, on the other hand, would be concerned that a breach occurred in the first place, no matter how it happened or what happened.

Over the last several decades, there has been a separation of security-related activities; however, this has not been conducive to achieving optimal results. It has now become the mainstream concept that security activities must be integrated and centered on information security practices and guidance. For example, it is no longer acceptable to believe that physical security is completely separate from network

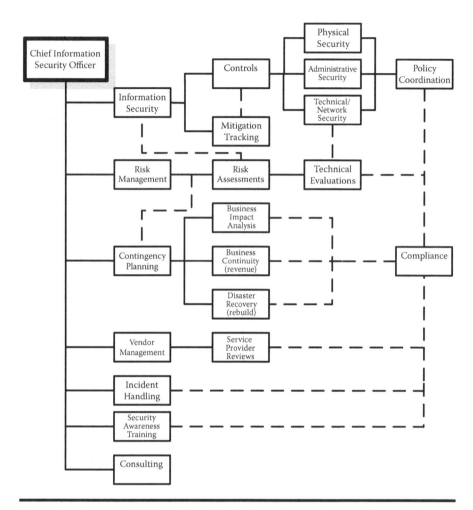

Figure 1.1 Responsibilities of the Chief Information Security Officer.

security activities and vice versa. Although these two areas may have different goals in mind, they ultimately must work together to achieve the ultimate objective of protecting the organization's information and assets.

In designing the company's organizational structure, duties need to be separated between security functions and operational functions. Separation of duties is the concept that operational tasks are separated from approval tasks, which are in turn also separated from review or monitoring tasks. Separation of duties can be achieved through the use of highly isolated and restricted auditing and monitoring of administrative activities. For example, the system administrators can set up a new user on the network; however, they can only do this by authority of the Human Resources Department or the department manager that approves the new user's access level. The Audit Department reviews the new user request document and verifies that the access level is appropriately assigned; however, the Audit Department cannot actually make such changes or additions in the system. Furthermore, the Human Resources Department or management cannot make the actual changes in the system; only the system administrator can make these changes. The system administrator may not approve the changes or audit these changes as being in compliance.

All companies should develop an organizational chart. This chart graphically shows the responsibilities of key positions and how these positions work together in a command and control structure. Each subordinate must report to one and only one supervisor. Each supervisor should report to one and only one department head or senior-level executive. In turn, the senior-level executives should be reporting to one Chief Executive Officer (CEO) and the CEO should be reporting directly to the board of directors or directly to the owner of the company. There are a few exemptions to these general rules. An example of this is for audit. To keep with the principle and independence of separation of duties, it is important that the Audit Department report to the board of directors or owner of the company directly, outside the chain of command of the chief executive officer. A check and balance system must be integrated into the organization to protect it and ensure that the business is operating as it was intended to operate.

In the specific context of information security, an ideal organizational structure would be for the chief information security officer to report directly to a security committee made up of executive-level managers. This security committee would report to the board of directors and be assigned the authority to prioritize information security-related projects, approve information security controls, approve information security mitigation efforts, and direct the chief information security officer in the alignment of information security strategies with business needs. Allowing the CISO to report to a security committee enables him or her to carry out his or her duties most effectively and limits some of the conflict of interest pressures that may be present in an organization. The concept of developing a security committee also enables flow of communication between organizational groups. It provides for clear understanding and enterprise-wide information security management. (See Figure 1.2 for further details.)

1.2.3 Functions

Technology is a tool to accomplish business, not an end in itself.

ISACA, 2007

As discussed earlier, information security governance can only be accomplished by senior management involvement in approving policies and providing strategic direction. The board of directors and senior management must establish appropriate monitoring and metrics combined with reporting and trend analysis to assess

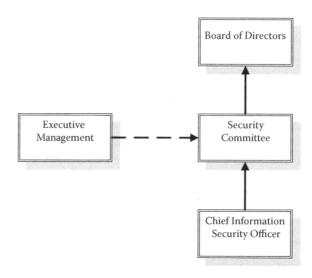

Figure 1.2   An example of an organization chart related to information security reporting.

information security effectively. The board of directors and senior management must support information security executives, implement security governance activities, and define the strategic security objectives of the organization. To achieve consensus on priorities, executives may choose to set up a steering committee to include all key personnel from across all aspects of an organization. Because information security covers all aspects of the organization, the committee would be able to provide input on trade-offs and resource management of projects with different priorities.

We have already discussed the specific differences between CIO responsibilities and CISO responsibilities. Each position is very important and both need to work together to reach the goals set by the organization. Many other different roles are related to information security—for example,

■ forensic specialist;
■ security architect;
■ information assurance manager;
■ IT security manager;
■ certification and accreditation specialist;
■ risk manager; and
■ compliance officer.

As the scope of traditional security roles has expanded, so have the expertise and extensive technical background required of the information security professional.

Not only do information security professionals need to be adept technically, but they also need to be knowledgeable of business. They need to be professionals in business risk analysis and security control integration. Information security professionals need to be well versed in many areas to develop an adequate security framework aligned to business functions and strategic goals.

Information security professionals and, more specifically, CISOs need to be able to function within their assigned duties. Chief information security officers need the resources, support, and authorization to carry out an effective information security program adequately.

1.3 Ideal Traits of an Information Security Professional

The old cliché that says that "good things happen to those who wait" is false. Instead, I would argue that good things happen to those that MAKE THINGS HAPPEN.

John J. Trinckes, Jr.

Executives seeking information security professionals should be looking for individuals who

- are versed in information security and all of its job functions, duties, and responsibilities;
- understand technology and are experienced in implementing effective security solutions;
- understand the regulatory and legal requirements of the specific industry;
- have good communication skills and can correlate security initiatives to business goals; they must understand the value of security and be able to express this value to senior management;
- are well versed in risk management;
- can be team players and work with all key stakeholders of the organization;
- can see the overall security requirements of the organization;
- have a positive attitude and high ethics; and
- pursue continuing education to stay current on the latest security trends.

Information security professionals also need to be good leaders. They need to know how to manage the wide array of responsibilities that they have, how to delegate appropriate duties, how to organize and prioritize, and how to talk "business" to get the funding required to carry out the necessary security projects. Information security professionals need to be motivators and set the tone of the entire information security program.

1.3.1 Certification Requirements

> A man's judgment cannot be better than the information on which he
> has based it.
>
> **Arthur Sulzberger Hays**

Although certifications may not be required, they do show a level of competency that all information security professionals should possess. One of the most respected certifications in the information security industry is the Certified Information Systems Security Professional (CISSP®) certification. The CISSP is governed by the International Information Systems Security Certification Consortium (ISC²). This certification was developed in the early 1990s by pioneers in the information security industry. The vendor-neutral certification tests the candidate's broad knowledge in information security-related domains. A certificate holder must pass a 6-hour exam and possess at least 5 years of experience in at least two information security-related domains. A candidate must also be endorsed by a certified ISC² professional and subscribe to the ISC² code of ethics. To maintain certification, the professional must annually complete continuing professional education requirements.

Other highly respected professional security certifications include the Certified Information Security Manager (CISM) and Certified Information Security Auditor (CISA). Both of these credentials are governed by the Information Systems Audit and Control Association (ISACA). Again, the candidate must pass a written exam, have the necessary years of experience in the related field of study, subscribe to a code of ethics, and maintain continuing education requirements.

The credentials listed previously primarily concentrate on higher level concepts of information security such as aligning information security to business needs. If an individual wants to get more technical experience, he or she may want to look into the certified ethical hacker curriculum sponsored by the EC-Council or other technical security programs developed by the SANS Institute. Some other organizations have also started to push some entry-level certifications, such as Comptia through its Security+ program.

More vendor-specific certifications include those developed by Microsoft through its Microsoft Certified Systems Engineer (MCSE) and Microsoft Certified Professional (MCP) programs and Cisco through its Certified Cisco Network Associate (CCNA), Certified Cisco Network Professional (CCNP), and Certified Cisco Internetwork Expert (CCIE) tracks.

Each of these certifications has its own degree of difficulty and concentration. They vary in their requirements, maintenance, fees, continuing education, and scope. There are many more certifications and organizations that are not discussed here, but these are just a few to give you an example of the level of professionalism with which these organizations are going to bring information security to the forefront of executives' minds.

Because information security is a fairly new industry, it is important to take a look at the overall qualifications of a prospective employee. It is important that prospects have some real-world experience and be able to translate "book learning" into tangible real-world actionable items. Job candidates should be willing to learn and place their emphasis on education. Information security is a dynamic environment that changes on a daily basis. An information security professional must be able to adapt to changes, forecast trends in vulnerabilities or mitigation efforts, and think outside his or her normal comfort zone.

1.3.2 Recruiting

Information security professionals are in high demand, so to avoid losing qualified candidates, the Human Resources Department should work closely with the hiring manager and possibly a specialized recruiter to speed up the hiring process. If you decide to work with a recruiting firm, it is important to research this firm thoroughly. You should check references and verify that the firm has an established and successful track record of hiring individuals specific to your industry. You may also want to check out professional organizations' job boards and online career centers. You will find a wealth of resources that are usually free of charge.

The Internet allows for free communication between individuals around the world. It may be a good course of action to see how your company's image is portrayed through the different types of social networks and Web2.0 systems. Some of the places where you may want to look would be searches through Google, Facebook, LinkedIn, MySpace, Yahoo, and others. This should allow you to take a look into the company's online persona to see if you can find any negative comments, blogs, or interesting information that is publicly available about your company. You may be very surprised at what you may find and what people are saying about your company.

It can be very beneficial to check your company's image. That is, it is important to emphasize your strong points to make your company more attractive to prospective candidates. If your company is known to take care of its employees, the company's reputation, will precede it. Unfortunately, it will be hard to overcome a bad reputation and you may miss out on recruiting the best talent if your company is not known to treat its employees fairly.

Although the Internet has been very helpful in recruiting new talent, it also comes with some drawbacks. First, the Internet is still assumed to have some anonymity. Sometimes recruits may overstate their qualifications and experiences to get themselves in the door. This can cause a company to waste a lot of resources recruiting individuals who look good on paper, but are not actually right for the job.

Second, there are several recruiting job boards on the Internet. With the number of job boards available and the number of individuals looking for jobs, to find the right candidates can be a daunting task. It is a good idea to place your job advertisements on those boards that specialize in your industry.

Finally, you should make sure that your job postings are of a general nature. It is important that you do not provide too much specific information about your software and hardware, especially when posting for technical jobs. This is a security risk that we will discuss in more detail in Section 4.3.4 in Chapter 4.

1.3.3 Screening

Because information security is a relatively new discipline, educational institutions have only been offering degrees within this area for about the last 5 years. Many colleges and universities are now developing graduate-level courses in information security and the different fields of studies related to it. As the demand increases for information security professionals, so will the program offerings, certifications, and skill sets for these professionals. Here is a list of some general requirements or suggestions broken down by general skills, education, and technical skills as revised from the ISC² *Hiring Guide to the Information Security Profession:*

general skills
- ability to achieve and maintain vendor-specific and vendor-neutral high-level professional certifications
- excellent leadership skills
- strong conceptual and analytical skills covering a wide range of areas
- excellent oral and written communication skills along with good presentation skills
- good team-building abilities and the ability to operate effectively as a team member
- the ability to manage projects and understand how subcomponents interrelate within the project
- strong multifunctional skills, organization skills, and the ability to use sound judgment in prioritizing assigned tasks
- strong interpersonal skills and the ability to manage conflicts
- the ability to demonstrate security-related concepts to nontechnical and technical staff across a broad range of organizational units

education
- doctorial degrees for professors, researchers, and other advanced developer positions in information security-related areas
- master of science in information security-related areas or master of business administration with an emphasis in information security-related areas (Note: These may now become standard requirements for directors or executive-level information security positions.)
- bachelor of science in information security-related areas
- bachelor of arts in information security-related areas
- associate degree in information security-related areas

technical skills
  - knowledge and understanding of security best practices, standards, regulations, and procedures to develop an effective information security program
  - knowledge and understanding of security programs, implementations, and analysis of the results given by these systems
  - knowledge and understanding of computer, network, and security systems and protocols

1.3.4 Interviewing

When interviewing a prospective candidate, the Human Resources Department should work closely with the hiring manager and/or recruiter to develop specific evaluation criteria. All members of the interviewing team should have an insight into the position's responsibilities, skills requirements, reporting structure, title, compensation, and other details of the job. Although the hiring manager may focus on the technical side, Human Resources should be mindful to check for the "softer" skills side. Candidates should be rated on how well they communicate and articulate a value-added approach to the business. Asking "how" questions and using real-world examples will provide some insight into the thought processes of the candidate. These questions may deal with the candidate's experience in handling certain situations or solving certain problems. Because the information security field is always evolving, an appropriate question may identify the type of professional literature the candidate reads or the types of professional Web sites he or she visits for research purposes.

Other important areas that should be reviewed are areas involving the prospect's personal life. Of course, these questions have to be crafted carefully; however, it should be important to know what prospects do to decompress, hobbies they may have, and other interests that motivate them. Answers to these questions help assess the type of individual that you may be working with on a daily basis. Information security can be very stressful and a lot of responsibility is placed on individuals who have chosen this profession. It is essential that this be kept in mind as you go through the interview process. For example, if an individual has no extracurricular activities and only wants to work, it may be a sign that he or she may get burnt out or stressed out. During times of high stressors, employees must be counted on to do what they are called upon to do. It is imperative that these individuals have an outlet of some kind so that these stressors can be diverted instead of being bottled up and potentially causing problems later.

It is important that expectations of the job are fully disclosed. These expectations should coincide with the job description. This is why it is essential that all job functions have a specific and detailed description of what they entail. These details should also be in line with management expectations. For instance, if you are looking to hire a senior-level manager on salary who is expected to work 40–50 hours a week, the salary should be commensurate to the 50-hour-a-week pay and the prospective employee should be made aware of this up front. Issues will definitely arise if this manager is putting in 60–70 hours a week when he or she was told they it was only necessary to work 40–50 hours a week. There has to be a mutual understanding, term, or contract between the employer and the employee, and it needs to be discussed during this interview process.

1.3.5 Reference Checks

The truth is the truth until you add to it.

ISACA, CISA, 2007

Due to the sensitive role that information security professionals play in an organization, a thorough background check should be conducted on all candidates applying for information security-related positions. All prospective job candidates should successfully pass a security check that includes reviews of professional references, personal references, education, certifications, criminal records checks, and credit reporting checks. Any candidate that intentionally omits, falsifies, or misstates the truth should not be permitted to continue in the application process. Applicants should be given the opportunity to dispute the information contained in the background check report if they deem the information to be inaccurate or incomplete. Special care should always be taken in choosing the best candidate for the position.

In addition, more and more companies are now looking into candidates' online profiles. As described earlier with the company's Internet profile, a lot of individuals are now utilizing the Internet for more social activities. The Internet can be a great source to determine what type of personality the potential candidate has. Searches on Google, LinkedIn, MySpace, Facebook, and others can offer a lot of information about an individual. Individuals involved in blogging may reveal the type of person they are or the type of work ethic they may have. This information should not be utilized alone; rather, the combined information obtained from all sources should give you a decent overall perspective of the applicant.

Why is finding the right candidate so important in information security? The American Society of Industrial Security (ASIS) reported in a survey in 1996 that more than 75% of the computer security breaches reported were due to the actions of insiders. FBI statistics also back the ASIS survey by showing that more than 60% of the computer crimes reported originate from inside the organization. Although these are just some statistics, it does give a fair assessment of the importance of bringing trustworthy and dependable individuals into your company. Remember that these individuals, for the most part, will have unabated access to your information, systems, and other sensitive assets.

1.3.6 Retention

As mentioned earlier, the demand is high for qualified information security professionals, so companies should strategically plan out a formalized career progression and retention plan. Along with good benefits and pay, companies should look at providing educational and training opportunities. Companies should also look for ways to have their information security professionals network with their peers and other established external support resources. It is important that these professionals stay current and updated on the ever evolving information security industry.

1.3.7 Trust and Loyalty

Above all else, companies should appreciate their employees' hard work. All too often, employees will become disgruntled if they are not shown appreciation or respect that they feel they deserve. If this occurs, it can definitely increase the company's chances of becoming a victim of information theft or some other sort of computer-related crime. Your company does not want to become another statistic. Appreciation can be shown in small ways and will not cost the company much, but the return on investment will be seen in many areas. It will be seen as an increase in productivity and may lower the risks associated with insider criminal activities.

Two important elements that go along with appreciation are trust and loyalty. As part of retention, companies need to realize that one of the most important assets that a company has is its people. You must trust in your employees and make them feel appreciated for the work that they do.

Most individuals are motivated by at least one major factor: *being happy.* Sometimes it does not matter how much money you make: If you are not happy with what you are doing, you will not stay around to do it.

As an executive, it is important to listen to your employees because they are usually on the front line in the day-to-day operations of your business. Many times we forget that we may have in-house experts, and instead go out and hire consultants at huge per-hour rates. This may be necessary due to independent audit regulations or a company's lack of expertise in a particular area. It may also be more cost effective in the long run to hire a consultant instead of hiring an employee. I would caution you to make sure that these consultants have your best interest in mind.

As a consultant, I want to preserve my reputation and provide the best possible professional services to my clients. Unfortunately, a lot of individuals who call themselves "consultants" have no professional experience, education, training, certification, or other items to back up their claims. It is important to get references on these individuals and do your due diligence in conducting background checks. We will talk more of some specific steps you can follow in selecting service providers and to conduct a review of these providers in Section 6.9 in Chapter 6.

For right now, I would like you to think about trust and loyalty because your security posture can depend heavily on these two items.

> When we are debating an issue, loyalty means giving me your honest opinion, whether you think I'll like it or not. Disagreement, at this stage, stimulates me. But, once a decision has been made, the debate ends. From that point on, loyalty means executing the decision as if it were your own.

> **Colin Powell**

1.4 Why Is Information Security Important?

> There are two kinds of companies: those that have [experienced a security breach], and those that will.

> **Paraphrase of quote from Robert J. Scott, managing partner of legal and technology services firm Scott & Scott**

You may have already realized the importance of and emphasis placed on information security, but you may not know that information security plays a key role in other areas of your business. Information security addresses civil or legal liability that the company and its management may be exposed to as a result of the information provided to the public. It also addresses due care for the protection of private information and the information provided to regulators. As already discussed, information security's goal is to protect information. In many industries, regulations require and mandate that certain information be privately kept. If this information is leaked or provided to unauthorized individuals, civil and legal actions may be brought against the company and its management.

Information security provides policy compliance assurance. Through the methodical process that is formed by the information security framework, policies are developed, reviewed, and audited or tested. Business units, systems, users, and other elements are assessed to ensure that they are in compliance with documented policies. When discrepancies or exceptions are noted, policies or the activities they govern are revised so that compliance can be achieved.

Through the risk assessment process, the uncertainty of business operations is reduced. Formal risk assessments increase predictability of operations by lowering the risks to an acceptable level. Businesses have inherent risks. At times, the higher the risk is, the higher is the payoff; however, if a business becomes too risky, it can fail. There are many examples of this and the economic state of the real estate markets in 2009 is a perfect example of risks not being properly managed. It is important that a definable level of risk be maintained; this can be achieved through the information security process.

Information security provides a plan to optimize resources. Through the information security framework and structure, limited security resources can be optimally allocated. Information security will determine the level of security that will be required to protect a specific asset. For example, if an asset costs $100,000, but the controls required to secure that asset cost $200,000, it may not be prudent to have this asset protected. Instead, resources may be allocated to protect other aspects of the asset with which it integrates, or management may decide to take the risk of not protecting the asset due to the costs involved. In either case, information security will justify and document the decision. It will alleviate undue burdens and allow for the proper allocation of resources. In this way, information security also provides assurance that critical decisions are based on the best information available.

Information security provides efficient and effective risk management. As already alluded to, risks are determined and mitigated to predefined acceptable levels. This can also improve business processes or activities. If a certain activity is found to be too risky, the activity can be changed and, in turn, improved. Information security also lays out the structure for rapid responses to incidents. We will discuss this in further detail under Section 6.3 in Chapter 6.

A few of the most critical business activities are mergers and acquisitions, business recovery, and responses to regulations. Information security provides for the safeguard and accountability of information during these activities. As discussed earlier, one of the major assets to a company is information. During mergers and acquisitions, it is essential to secure and protect this information. A major element of information security is the business continuity and disaster recovery function. It is essential that a business continue and survive a catastrophic event. Information security will provide the steps necessary to recover critical business functions after a disaster and will assist in the continuation of business activities.

Information security protects the company's reputation and improves the trust in customer relationships. It provides a level of confidence and assurance that the company cares about its business. More importantly, the company can demonstrate its commitment to excellence and care that it provides to its customers through information security. This due diligence can also contribute to an increase in interactions with trading partners. Companies like to work with other companies that have a level of commitment to excellence that is the same as or better than what they have.

Information security can provide new and better ways to handle electronic transactions. More and more companies are conducting their business online. This can provide huge boosts in revenue and other opportunities that may have not been available to the company in the past. Information security may be able to provide alternative revenue streams that were overlooked or may not have been otherwise possible without it.

In the annual study of the *cost of security breaches* conducted by the Ponemon Institute, the average data breach cost in 2008 was $202 per record. In 2007, the average data breach cost was $197 per record and, in 2006, it was $182 per record. This represents about an 11% increase over the last 2 years of the average cost of a data breach.

If you have not yet figured out why information security is so important, let me throw some statistics in the mix:

■ Approximately 80% of the national critical infrastructures in the developed world are controlled by the private sector (ISACA 2007).
■ According to the Identity Theft Resource Center, 2007 was a year of record data breaches. There were a total of 431 reported incidents and 128,250,494 records were affected. In addition, there were 32.2% of incidents with unknown numbers of affected records.
■ The average security breach can cost a company between $90 and $305 per lost record, according to a new study from Forrester Research (Internet Security Alliance 2008).
■ The security breach at TJX Companies, Inc. could cost the company $100 per lost record, or a total of $4.5 billion, according to the calculations of a database security company (Gaudin 2007). The breach caused the disclosure of over 94 million individual records.
■ According to the Web Application Security Consortium 2007 Annual Report, 67% of the attacks they recorded were motivated by "profit." Ideological hacking came in second (Web Application Security Consortium 2008).
■ Over 44% of Web attack incidents were tied to noncommercial sites such as government and education. On the commercial side, Internet-related organizations (that include retail shops composed mostly of e-commerce sites, media companies, and pure Internet services such as search engines and service providers) top the list (Web Application Security Consortium 2008).
■ The average number of records affected by an incident where records were leaked or stolen in 2007 was 6,000 records (Web Application Security Consortium 2008).

Another set of statistics published in *eWeek* magazine on June 16, 2008, shows that data breaches were probably avoidable. "Your Data Breach Was Probably Avoidable," an article by Roy Mark, detailed a study conducted by Verizon Business over a 4-year time span with more than 500 investigations involving 230 million records. I wanted to share the following:

■ Seventy-three percent of breaches resulted from external sources.
■ Nine out of ten breaches could have been prevented with reasonable security measures.
■ Sixty-two percent of the breaches were attributed to "significant internal errors" that directly or indirectly contributed to the breach.

- Of the deliberate breaches, 59% were the result of hacking and intrusions.
- Nine out of ten breaches involved some type of "unknown" (includes systems, data, network connections, and account user privileges).
- Seventy-five percent of the breaches were discovered by third parties, rather than by the victim company.
- In 59% of the data breaches, the company had security policies and procedures in place, but not implemented.
- Over 40% of the breaches were caused by remote access and control attack pathways.

The overall summation of this article was that it is imperative to know what assets are and where data are located. If you do not know what you have and where it is, you cannot protect it.

You have probably seen headlines in the newspaper or in magazines or have heard of major security breaches such as these:

- "Rogue Trader Simply Sidestepped Defenses." Jérôme Kerviel, a stock trader working at the French bank Société Générale, placed fraudulent trades circumventing security controls that were in place for such trading. The bank lost $7.2 billion and may have contributed to the decline in the European markets on January 21 and 22, 2008. This event preceded a three-quarter-point cut in interest rates by the Federal Reserve. Kerviel's trading position was estimated at approximately $75 billion (Lemos 2008).
- In January 2008, a sophisticated network intrusion caused a compromise of a database storing 226,000 records at Davidson Companies, a financial services holding company.
- In May 2008, Walter Reed Army Medical Center and other military hospitals fell victim to a security breach involving sensitive information on about 1,000 patients.
- In June 2008, an application-level compromise of Cotton Traders' (a UK clothing retailer) Web site exposed up to 38,000 customers' credit card details.
- In July 2008, LPL Financial had 10,219 clients' information stolen when hackers obtained log-in passwords of employees and gained access to customer account information. This was the second data breach within 1 year for this company.
- "Revealed: 8 Million Victims in the World's Biggest Cyber Heist." An Indian hacker breached the Best Western Hotel group's online booking system and sold details of the attack to the Russian mafia. The criminals stole identities of an estimated eight million people and may have netted nearly £2.8 billion in illegal funds (*Sunday Herald* 2008).
- "World Bank under Cyber Siege in 'Unprecedented Crisis.'" Since the summer of 2007, the World Bank has had at least six major intrusions. It is not

known how much information was stolen, but the attacks appear to be originating from China (Behar 2008).

■ "Hacking the Presidential Campaigns." Both the Republican and Democratic presidential campaigns' IT systems were hacked. They were reported to have experienced a sophisticated cyberattack originating from an unknown foreign entity (Hines 2008).

Baseline Magazine (2008) recently came out with its top 10 most disastrous security breaches for 2008. This is a summary of their results:

1. *Central Collections Bureau.* This company had a theft of eight computers in March of 2008 that comprised the loss of 700,000 records. This was the largest reported data breach in Indiana.
2. *Bank of New York Mellon.* A box of backup tapes was lost on their way to storage in February of 2008. The tapes contained 12.5 million customer records and the loss could not be tracked due to the transport truck having multiple stops on its way to storage and a broken lock on the truck.
3. *Countrywide.* An employee stole 2 million customer records in increments of 20,000 by downloading them on weekends from an unprotected computer.
4. *Sarah Palin,* Alaska governor and 2008 vice-presidential candidate. The alleged suspect, David Kernell, son of Tennessee Democratic State Representative Mike Kernell, broke into Mrs. Palin's personal e-mail account and posted it online.
5. *Best Western.* This breach was noted earlier; however, there is some question as to the extent of the damages. Best Western claims that only 10 customers were affected; however, Scotland's *Sunday Herald*, which reported the breach, claimed to have a screenshot of a database that contained eight million records.
6. *Alaska Airlines and Horizon Airlines.* Although a call center employee only stole 1,500 credit card records, these records were all specifically targeted for fraud.
7. *Colorado Department of Motor Vehicles.* Approximately 36 former employees had access to as many as 3.4 million records up to a year after they left the department.
8. *University of Utah Medical.* A courier delivering a tape containing 2.2 million patient records stopped at home prior to delivering the tape to storage. The tape was stolen from the courier's vehicle.
9. *U.S. Army.* Although no information was reported stolen, the U.S. Army banned the use of USB devices in November to fight an outbreak of the worm "W32.SillyFDC," a malware program that steals confidential information.
10. *Jefferson County.* Jefferson County, West Virginia, released a new online search tool in November that exposed personal information of about approximately 1.6 million citizens.

1.5 Information Security Concepts

Security by obscurity—IS NOT SECURITY!!

Author unknown

Moving forward through the rest of this book, it is important to understand some of the terms and concepts involved in information security. Definitions given here are short and concise. We will talk about specific details of each later in this book and give practical examples of how each is used:

- *access control:* limiting authorized access to authenticated entities
- *architecture:* the design of the structure and relationships of its elements
- *attacks:* types and nature of security compromises
- *auditability:* ability to enable reconstruction, review, and examination of sequence of events
- *authentication:* providing proof of identity; this can be something you know (password), something you have (security token), or something you are (fingerprint)
- *authorization:* what is allowed when access has been granted
- *availability:* a resource that is accessible and usable when required
- *business dependency analysis:* determining the extent to which the business relies on a resource
- *business impact analysis:* evaluating the results and consequences of a compromise
- *compliance:* ensuring that all laws and industry regulatory requirements are met
- *confidentiality:* prevention of unintended disclosure
- *control:* any action or process that is used to mitigate risk
- *countermeasure:* any action or process that reduces vulnerability
- *criticality:* the importance to the business of a resource
- *data classification:* the process of determining the sensitivity and criticality of information
- *exposures:* areas subject to impact by threats
- *gap analysis:* the analysis between the difference in what is actually taking place in an organization and what the organization is actually trying to achieve
- *governance:* providing control and direction to activities
- *identification:* verification of a person or thing; recognition of such
- *impact:* the results and consequences of a risk materializing
- *integrity:* assurance that data have not been subject to unauthorized modification
- *layered security:* "defense in depth" so that compromise is contained
- *management:* overseeing activities to ensure objectives are met
- *nonrepudiation:* cannot deny an event or transaction
- *policy:* high-level statement of management's intent and direction
- *residual risk:* risk remaining after countermeasures and controls
- *risk:* the exploitation of a vulnerability by a threat

- *security metrics/monitoring:* measuring security activities
- *sensitivity:* the level of impact from an unauthorized disclosure
- *standards:* allowable boundaries of actions and processes to meet policies
- *strategy:* the steps required to achieve an objective
- *threats:* any action or event that may cause adverse consequences
- *vulnerabilities:* weaknesses that may be exploited by threats

1.6 Laws of Security

Your security is only as strong as your weakest control.

John J. Trinckes, Jr.

One of the best articles I have found on the basic laws of security is paraphrased here from "10 Immutable Laws of Security," written by the Microsoft Security Response Center:

Law #1: If a malicious individual persuades a user to run his or her program on the user's computer, it is no longer the user's computer.

Law #2: If a malicious individual can alter the operating system of a user's computer, it is no longer the user's computer.

Law #3: If a malicious individual has physical access to a user's computer, it is no longer the user's computer.

Law #4: If a user allows a malicious individual to upload programs to his or her Web site, it is not the user's Web site anymore.

Law #5: Strong security is always undermined by weak passwords.

Law #6: Treat your system administrators well and make sure they can be trusted because a computer is only as secure as the administrator makes it.

Law #7: The decryption key determines how securely your data are encrypted. (If you use a weak encryption algorithm or do not secure the keys, encryption is worthless.)

Law #8: Keep your virus scanners up to date because an old .dat file is just slightly better than having no virus scanner installed at all.

Law #9: It is very difficult to be anonymous in the real world and on the Web. (Your behaviors will determine the level of privacy you will have.)

Law #10: "Security is a process…not a product" (phrase coined by Bruce Schneier).

We have already touched on a few of these laws through some of the examples provided earlier in this book. These laws should be taken to heart because they are fundamental to understanding the principles of good information security management.

1.7 Summary

Throughout this chapter we discussed and provided an overview of information security. As you have already determined, many functions and responsibilities fall under the information security management purview. An information security manager and, more specifically, a chief information security officer have a wide range of duties that touches every aspect of the organization. For this reason, we discussed the important traits of an information security professional, giving some examples of different certification requirements, screening processes, and interviewing techniques.

We discussed some reasons why every company needs to place importance on information security. With increases in security breaches, identity theft, and other types of criminal fraud activities, information security is probably one of, if not the, most important business activities of any organization. We discussed some of the concepts related to information security and elements involved in implementing an effective information security management program. We finished this chapter discussing some of the security laws, with an emphasis on protecting physical access to your organization's business assets.

References

Baseline Magazine. December 2008. Top 10 security breaches in 2008. Retrieved December 19, 2008, from Baseline Magazine: http://www.baselinemag.com/c/a/IT-Management/Top-10-Security-Breaches-in-2008/?kc=BLBLBEMNL12152008STR1

Behar, R. October 10, 2008. World Bank under cyber siege in "unprecedented crisis." Retrieved October 10, 2008, from FOXnews.com:http://www.foxnews.com/printer_friendly_story/0,3566,435681,00.html

Drucker, P. 1999. *Management challenges for the 21st century.* Oxford: Butterworth-Heinemann, Ltd.

Gaudin, S. May 2, 2007. Estimates Put T. J. Maxx security fiasco at $4.5 billion—T. J. Maxx. Retrieved January 29, 2008, from Information Week: http://www.informationweek.com/news/showArticle.jhtml?articleID=199203277

Hines, M. November 10, 2008. Hacking the presidential campaigns. eWeek, p. 8.

Internet Security Alliance. 2008. Internet security alliance—Enterprise Integration Program on Security Incident Handling. Retrieved January 30, 2008, from Internet Security Alliance: http://www.isalliance.org/content/view/55/197/

ISACA. 2007. *CISM review manual.* Rolling Meadows, IL: ISACA.

ISC². 2007. Hiring guide to the information security profession. Retrieved January 27, 2008, from ISC² Web site: https://www.isc2.org/Documents/HiringGuide/HiringGuide08.pdf

Kabay, M. E. September 11, 2000. From product to process: Bruce Schneirer's take on security. Retrieved May 22, 2009 from NetworkWorldFusion: www.networkworld.com/newsletters/sec/2000/0q11sec1.html

Lemos, R. January 29, 2008. Rogue trader simply sidestepped defenses. Retrieved January 30, 2008, from Security Focus: http://www.securityfocus.com/brief/671?ref=rss

Pavel, C. Colin Powel Quotes. Retrieved May 22, 2009 from Thinkexist: http://thinkexist. com/quotation/when-we-are-debating-anissue-loyalty-means/338170.html

Ronsvalle, J. and S. June 3–10, 1998. Giving to Religion: How Generous Are We? Retrieved May 22, 2009 from Religion-online: http://www.religion-online.org/showarticle. asp?title=242

Scott, J. June 12, 2006. Software audits: not a case of if, but when. Retrieved May 22, 2009 from computerworld: http://computerworld.co.nz/news.nsf/0/6FDD949C856F7018 CC257188001AAE56?OpenDocument

Sunday Herald. August 23, 2008. Revealed: 8 million victims in the world's biggest cyber heist. Retrieved August 24, 2008, from Sunday Herald: http://www.sundayherald. com/news/heraldnews/display.var.2432225.0.0.php

Web Application Security Consortium. 2008. Web Hacking Security Consortium—Web hacking incidents database (WHID). Statistics. Retrieved February 8, 2008, from Web Application Security Consortium: http://www.webappsec.org/projects/whid/statistics.shtml

Chapter 2

Information Security Requirements

Objectives

- Understand the interrelationship of regulations, policies, procedures, standards, and guidelines.
- Explain certain industry regulations and understand how these regulations or other regulations may affect your industry.
- Understand the penalties for noncompliance.
- Understand the common elements of compliance.
- Explain the different types of guidelines, standards, and measurement techniques that can be utilized in developing a security framework.
- Describe the different types of security controls.
- Understand the pitfalls to an effective information security program and how to overcome them.
- Understand the "defense in depth" concept.
- Conduct an evaluation using the deter, prevent, detect, prosecute (DPDP) steps.

2.1 Interrelationship of Regulations, Policies, Standards, Procedures, and Guidelines

To understand the interrelationship of regulations, policies, standards, procedures, and guidelines, we must first know what each of these terms means. It is a misconception to think that these terms are all the same and interchangeable; they are not. Regulations, for instance, are laws and requirements placed on an organization by government regulators. Regulations are mandated. They must be followed or implemented or there can be severe consequences to the company or the executives in charge. These consequences can come in the form of penalties, fines, loss of revenue, or even jail time. The Sarbanes–Oxley Act (SOX), Gramm–Leach–Bliley Act (GLBA), and Health Insurance Portability and Accountability Act (HIPAA) are examples of regulations that are discussed in further detail in Section 2.2.

Policies are formal documented statements of high-level requirements and management intentions. Policies are also mandated by certain regulations. Policies outline the expectations of executive management. Most regulations dictate that companies are required to have certain policies implemented in their organizations. Examples of policies can be found in Appendix A and Appendix B in the back of this book.

Standards provide execution-level instructions based on policies and other compliance-related standards. Standards attempt to tie policies into procedures. An example of a standard is the International Organization of Standardization (ISO) 27001, which concentrates on the area of information security. Other examples can be found in Section 2.4.2.

Procedures are instructions for important processes that may or may not be mandatory, based on their purpose. Procedures are usually more detailed than policies and provide step-by-step instructions on how to carry out a specific policy. Several procedures may be used to carry out one specific policy.

Guidelines are examples of how certain procedures are implemented in real-life terms. They are a set of common good practices that are followed under given circumstances in given situations.

All of these terms are interrelated in some form. An example of their interrelations is seen in Figure 2.1 as follows: regulations dictate policies, policies set standards, standards tie procedures into policies, procedures are specific instructions for individual processes that produce the guidelines that are considered best common practices to follow.

2.2 Regulations

As an executive, you are required to know the laws and regulations that your specific industry must follow. To understand how information security ties into your organization, you must first assemble the requirements. The many possible

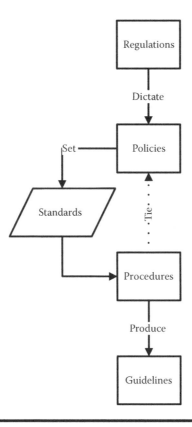

Figure 2.1   Interrelationship of regulations, policies, standards, procedures, and guidelines.

compliance objectives include SOX, GLBA, HIPAA, Federal Financial Institutions Examination Council (FFIEC) regulations, contractual requirements such as the Payment Card Industry (PCI) Data Security Standards (DSS), and others.

2.2.1 Sarbanes–Oxley Act (SOX)

In response to the high-profile financial scandals of companies such as Enron and WorldCom, the United States passed several pieces of legislation to protect company shareholders and the general public. The Sarbanes–Oxley Act of 2002 was one of these legislative efforts to protect against fraudulent practices and accounting errors. The act publishes rules on requirements and sets deadlines for compliance administered by the Securities and Exchange Commission (SEC). Sarbanes–Oxley defines the type of records that are required to be stored and how long they should be stored. The act states that all business records, including electronic records, must be stored for "not less than five years."

However, the act does not set business practices or tell companies how they should store these records. This legislation had major impact not only on the accounting departments of corporations, but also on IT departments because most corporations' records are stored in electronic format. Storage of electronic records can be a challenging task for IT departments. IT managers have to take into consideration the cost of electronic storage and make sure that the archiving system not only is cost effective, but also satisfies all regulatory requirements. Companies and executives that do not comply with this act can face fines, imprisonment, or both (Spurzem 2007).

Additional information on SOX can be obtained by looking up *IT Control Objectives for Sarbanes–Oxley* from ITGI.

2.2.2 Gramm–Leach–Bliley Act (GLBA)

The Financial Services Modernization Act of 1999, better known as the Gramm–Leach–Bliley Act, prevents the sale of private financial information. It also protects against obtaining personal information through false pretense, an activity known as *pretexting*.

The intent of the GLBA legislation was to upgrade the financial services. More specifically, as more banks, stock brokerage companies, and insurance companies merged together, these new institutions had unrestricted access to large amounts of personal information. Before the GLBA legislation was enacted, insurance companies, for example, maintained health records that were unique from the banks that kept mortgage information and stockbrokers that kept stock information. Once these companies began to merge, they were able to consolidate, analyze, and even sell this personal information to other companies.

Due to the risks involved with the disclosure of such information, the GLBA protects this personal information with three requirements:

All banks, insurance companies, and brokerage firms must store personal financial information in a secure manner. You may think that securing information should be an assumed good business practice, but this is not necessarily the case. For example, prior to this regulation, an insurance company may have merged with a bank. We may assume the bank would have good security controls over its information; however, this may not necessarily have been the case for the insurance company, which may not have had the most stringent controls over its information. As the entities merged, the companies would have had to decide on common practices and policies that they might not have been accustomed to following in the past. An example of one of these practices is when employees of these companies go home at night. These employees should place any files that contain personal financial information in a locked filing cabinet or secured records room. The insurance company, for example, may not have had this requirement in place prior to the merger.

These organizations must notify their customers of their privacy policies. You see an example of this requirement in action when you go to open a bank account, and you are given a form that describes how the information you share with the bank will be used. You can also see how these companies comply with this regulation by reviewing the privacy policies published on their Web sites.

These organizations must provide their customers with the option to opt out. Banks, insurance companies, and brokerage firms must allow their customers the opportunity to exercise their right of not sharing their personal financial information with other companies (Electronic Privacy Information Center 2005).

Additional information related to GLBA regulations can be found in the *Interagency Guidelines Establishing Information Security Standards.*

2.2.3 Health Insurance Portability and Accountability Act (HIPAA)

A regulation known as the Health Insurance Portability and Accountability Act (HIPAA) of 1996 affected the health care industry. This law is primarily composed of two legislative actions. The law first attempts to reform the provisions of health insurance, and then it requires the simplification of administrative tasks. These two actions significantly changed the legal and regulatory environment of the health care industry by governing health care benefit provisions, payment and delivery of services related to health care, and the security of protected health care information.

This law has many aspects that require providers to make several changes. Almost all types of entities (including research facilities) within the health care industry will be required to comply with HIPAA. These requirements will affect the organizations' operational policies, procedures, and business practices. It will also change the information systems that are currently utilized.

The Civil Rights Division of the Department of Health and Human Services (DHHS) is the regulator involved in compliance enforcement. The HIPAA regulation carries steep penalties for noncompliance. Civil fines of up to $25,000 per standard per year can be issued to those providers that do not comply with any of the electronic data, security, or privacy requirements. Criminal fines of $50,000–$250,000 and 1–10 years' imprisonment can be imposed on those covered entities that violate the privacy regulations for commercial or malicious purposes. Failure to comply can also carry uncalculated impacts by a provider running the risk of violating the public trust (UCSF Campus and UCSF Medical Center 2001).

Additional information on HIPAA can be obtained from the National Institute of Standards and Technology (NIST) special publication 800-66, *"An Introductory Resource Guide for Implementing the Health Insurance Portability and Accountability Act,"* or from cms.hhs.gov.

Although HIPAA regulations were enacted almost 3 years prior to the GLBA regulations, it has taken the health care industries longer to comply with these security requirements. From my assessment, the health care industry is about 10 years behind the financial industry in terms of providing adequate security for personally identifiable health information. I attribute this to the resources that have been allocated to the enforcement of these regulations. The Civil Rights Division of the DHHS has just recently started to take a closer look at health care providers and has levied some hefty fines on providers that are not compliant.

I also believe, in some ways, that individuals assume that health care providers are not targets for financially related crimes, whereas criminals know that financial institutions keep records on individuals that contain account numbers, credit card numbers, and other related information concerning monetary instruments. I believe that individuals do not place the same importance on health care information.

Let us take a second to think about the information that health care providers maintain on an individual. If you remember the last time you went to the doctor, you probably received a stack of papers that you had to fill out. These papers probably asked for your name, address, phone number, and social security number. They may have also asked for your driver's license number or other type of identification. In fact, the provider probably made a copy of your license along with your insurance card. When you left, you may have had to pay for the service. You may have used a credit card or written a check.

If you think about it, what information did you provide to your health care provider that was different from what you provided to your financial institution? I can answer that for you: not much. In fact, your health care provider has even more sensitive information about you than your financial institution. Your provider has sensitive health-care-related information, probably along with a family health history. Although you might have felt like you were signing your family away when you took your last loan out or received a mortgage from the bank or you might have felt like you were giving away a kidney, the financial institutions still do not care too much about your health history, at least not yet.

2.2.4 Federal Financial Institutions Examination Council (FFIEC)

The Federal Financial Institutions Examination Council (FFIEC) was established under Title X of the Financial Institutions Regulatory Rate Control Act (FIRCA) of 1978 (Public Law 95-630) on March 10, 1979. Ten years later, the Appraisal Subcommittee (ASC) within the Examination Council was established pursuant to Title XI of the Financial Institutions Reform, Recovery, and Enforcement Act (FIRREA) of 1989.

Several governing bodies make up the regulators of financial institutions: the board of governors of the Federal Reserve Bank (FRB) system, the Federal Deposit

Insurance Corporation (FDIC), the National Credit Union Administration (NCUA), the Office of the Comptroller of the Currency (OCC), and the Office of Thrift Supervision (OTS). In an effort to promote and recommend uniform supervision of financial institutions, these regulators utilize the FFIEC to set principles, standards, and reporting for the federal examination of financial institutions.

Under Section 340 of the Housing and Community Development Act (HCDA) of 1980, the FFIEC was given more statutory responsibilities. Under the Home Mortgage Disclosure Act (HMDA) of 1975, depository institutions must disclose certain data. The FFIEC facilitates the public access to these data, along with aggregating the data by census tract for each Metropolitan Statistical Area (MSA). To accomplish this task, the advisory State Liaison Committee was established. This committee is composed of five representatives of state supervisory agencies (FFIEC 2007).

Additional information on the FFIEC and its requirements related to information security can be obtained from the *IT Security Examination Handbook* located on its Web site at www.ffiec.gov.

2.2.5 Payment Card Industry (PCI) Data Security Standard (DSS)

Although the payment card industry DSS is titled as a "standard," it is placed under regulations because it is a formal contractual requirement between card payment providers and retailers. The founding payment providers, including American Express, Discover Financial Services, JCB, MasterCard Worldwide, and Visa International formed the PCI Security Standards Council. The council's goal is to facilitate the adoption of standard data-security measures on a broad scale throughout the global markets. The council created the PCI data security standard, which is a comprehensive set of requirements to provide an enhancement to security of payment account data (PCI Security Standards Council 2006).

The PCI DSS version 1.2 provides a proactive approach to organizations for the protection of customer account data. The PCI DSS consists of 12 mandatory requirements pertaining to the storage, transmittal, and processing of payment cards. These requirements are additionally subdivided into sections that cover security policies, procedures, management, network architecture, software design, and other security controls. PCI DSS describes activities with which organizations must comply in regard to managing and administering their information systems. Overall, the PCI DSS is intended to protect the payment card data that are entrusted to these organizations (Mackey 2008).

Additional information on PCI DSS can be obtained from the "Payment Card Industry (PCI) Data Security Standard," "Self-Assessment Questionnaire," "Security Audit Procedures," and "Security Scanning Procedures" located at www.pcisecuritystandards.org.

2.3 Common Elements of Compliance

Once your industry's specific regulations are determined, a framework of compliance needs to be developed. All of these regulations require some form of controls to be implemented to satisfy compliance. These controls can be classified as administrative, management, operational, or technical, among others. For instance, the NIST SP800-53 details a security baseline with three general classes of security controls (management, operational, and technical). Each family of controls contains security controls related to the security function of that family. A two-character identifier is assigned to identify each family. See Table 2.1 for additional information (National Institute of Standards and Technology 2005).

Table 2.1   Security Control Classes, Families, and Identifiers

Class	Family	Identifier
Management	Risk assessment	RA
Management	Planning	PL
Management	System and services acquisition	SA
Management	Certification, accreditation, and security assessments	CA
Operational	Personnel security	PS
Operational	Physical and environmental protection	PE
Operational	Contingency planning	CP
Operational	Configuration management	CM
Operational	Maintenance	MA
Operational	System and information integrity	SI
Operational	Media protection	MP
Operational	Incident response	IR
Operational	Awareness and training	AT
Technical	Identification and authentication	IA
Technical	Access control	AC
Technical	Audit and accountability	AU
Technical	System and communications protection	SC

All compliance guidelines describe similar requirements. The common elements are as follows:

■ information analysis (ownership, custodianship, use, and sensitivity);
■ risk assessment;
■ policy, process, and technical control establishment;
■ measurement of effectiveness;
■ adjustment and adaptation for improvement;
■ repeatable steps; and
■ methodology to implement the process (such as the PDCA process—plan, do, check, act).

2.4 Security Controls

Many things that can improve security cost nothing.

ISACA, 2007

Security controls consist of (1) policies, (2) procedures, (3) practices, (4) technologies, and (5) organizational structures. Their purpose is to provide a reasonable level of assurance that the objectives laid out by executives to conduct business are achieved. Security controls also attempt to prevent certain undesirable events. If these events do occur, security controls are meant to detect them. Corrective actions can then be taken to mitigate any additional damage caused by the event.

Controls come in the form of physical, technical, and procedural controls:

■ Examples of *physical controls* are locks, fixed windows, or employee ID tags.
■ Examples of *technical controls* are software that controls network access, use of badge systems to prevent unauthorized access, or screen savers that are password protected after a period of inactivity on a workstation.
■ Examples of *procedural controls* consist of policies, procedures, or standard practices such as escorting visitors into nonpublic areas at all times.

One of the primary methods of managing risks is by implementing effective controls. Determining the types of controls to implement in an organization is a major responsibility of information security management. Controls have to be implemented properly for the type of asset being protected. It is also important to get buy-in from employees who will be utilizing these controls on a daily basis because the controls are not of value if they can be circumvented (ISACA 2007).

Control frameworks are a collection of controls based on a consensus of best practices that are used in steering, controlling, or measuring the way in which

Table 2.2   Best Practices and Areas of Concentration for Industry Best Practice Guidelines

Best Practices	Areas of Concentration
Australian Standard for Corporate Governance of ICT (AS8015)	Corporate governance
Control Objectives for Information and Related Technology (COBIT)	IT governance
Committee of Sponsoring Organizations of the Treadway Commission (COSO)	Corporate governance
Dynamic Systems Development Method (DSDM)	Agile development
Information Technology Infrastructure Library (ITIL)	IT service management
IT Service Continuity Management. Code of Practices (PAS-77)	Service continuity
Central Communication and Telecommunication Agency (CCTA) Risk Analysis and Method	Risk management
Projects in Controlled Environments (PRINCE2)	Project management
Skills Framework for the Information Age (SFIA)	Competency framework for IT

organizations work. The three broad types of control frameworks are best practice guidelines, standards, and measurement techniques. We will cover each of these in the following sections.

2.4.1 Industry Best Practice Guidelines

Industry best practice guidelines created as a cross section of experts with practical experiences are recognized and used widely within the industries. Guidelines can be implemented selectively and are not certified by governing bodies as compliant to specific regulations. See Table 2.2 for further examples.

2.4.2 Standards

Standards are widely used and created on behalf of standards organizations by a cross section of experts representing relevant companies and organizations. Standards are

Table 2.3   Standards and Areas of Concentration

Standards	Areas of Concentration
British Standards Institution (BSI):BS25999	Business continuity
International Organization for Standardization (ISO):20000	IT service management
International Organization for Standardization (ISO):27001	Information security
International Organization for Standardization (ISO):19770	Software asset management
International Organization for Standardization (ISO):9000	Quality management
TickIT	Application development/quality management for software
International Organization for Standardization (ISO):14001	Environmental management

supported by reference materials and/or by a certification scheme and qualifications are usually available. See Table 2.3 for further examples.

2.4.3 Measurement Techniques

Measurement techniques are also widely used within the industry. These are often created by experts within one organization, such as academia, and then widely adopted. They are supported by reference materials and can often be certified for partial compliance. See Table 2.4 for further examples.

2.5 Control Objectives for Information and Related Technology (COBIT)

Control Objectives for Information and related Technology focus on information technology-related processes from the perspective of IT governance, management, and controls. When dealing with information security, control objectives need to be broadened beyond just IT activities.

As discussed earlier, security controls attempt to prevent certain undesirable events by defining organizational structures designed to provide assurance that objectives are met. These control objectives are normally defined by executives and

Table 2.4 Measurement Techniques and Areas of Concentration

Measurement Techniques	Areas of Concentration
Capability Maturity Model® Integration (CMMi) (Maturity scale of 1–5)	IT application development and project management
European Foundation of Quality Management (EfQM)/Malcolm Baldridge	Organization-wide excellence model
J. D. Power/Software Support Professionals Association (SSPA)	Certified technology service and support program
Six-Sigma/Lean Management	Process improvement methods

state the desired intent of certain control procedures governing a particular process (ISACA 2007).

There are four domains of COBIT:

- *Plan and organize.* This domain covers strategies and tactics and is concerned with the best way in which IT can contribute to business objectives.
- *Acquire and implement.* To realize the IT strategy, IT solutions must be identified, developed, or acquired. They must also be integrated into the business process and implemented in the organization.
- *Deliver and support.* This domain is concerned with the delivery of services.
- *Monitor and evaluate.* All IT processes need to be assessed regularly over time for their quality and compliance with control requirements (ISACA 2007).

2.6 ISO 27002 Overview

The International Organization of Standardization (ISO) has developed the "Code of Practice for Information Security Management." It is a comprehensive set of controls comprising best practices in information security and is internationally recognized. The ISO control set needs to be interpreted according to your organization's needs; however, every major section is included in virtually every regulation in place today. It has become the de facto standard and some countries have required their companies to become compliant with ISO standards. This standard framework allows organizations to integrate multiple regulations into an effective compliance program.

ISO 27002 is specifically a security standard. It contains a comprehensive list of security practices that can be applied to all organizations. Depending on the level or extent of controls required by your organization, ISO 27002 can be customized to your needs. It emphasizes the need for a cooperative effort among business, management, human resources, and technology representatives working together to create an efficient information security management program. ISO 27002 also covers policies surrounding data classification, handling, and access. It requires organizations to address areas such as policy and procedure management, network and system administration/configuration, and software development.

> The beauty of using the ISO standard with specific regulations is that the regulations fill in the necessary details that the framework lacks while the framework provides structure to address multiple sets of requirements consistently. The two concepts work hand in hand and provide effectiveness, efficiency, and auditability. (Mackey 2008)

ISO has 11 major sections:

■ security policy;
■ organizational security;
■ asset classification and control;
■ personnel security;
■ physical and environmental security;
■ communications and operations management;
■ access control;
■ systems development and maintenance;
■ incident response;
■ business continuity; and
■ compliance.

2.7 Capability Maturity Model (CMM)

The capability maturity model is a measurement technique that defines a desired state of security with a specific level. The six levels range from zero to five and are defined as follows:

■ *Level 0:* Nonexistent—there is no recognition by the organization of security needs.
■ *Level 1:* Ad hoc—risks are considered on an ad hoc basis and there is no formal process in place.
■ *Level 2:* Repeatable but intuitive— understanding of risk and the need for security is emerging; however, processes are done more out of intuition than formality.

- *Level 3:* Defined process—the company has a defined risk management policy, and security awareness is spread throughout the organization.
- *Level 4:* Managed and measurable—there is a risk assessment standard procedure and information security roles/responsibilities are assigned. Formal policies and standards are in place.
- *Level 5:* Optimized—the entire organization has formal processes that are implemented, well managed, and monitored on a continuous basis.

2.8 Generally Accepted Information Security Principles (GAISP)

Originally known as the Generally Accepted Security System Principles (GASSP), GAISP was developed to provide a clear and articulate set of principles for essential security features, assurances, and practices. The following are the principles identified under the GAISP as paraphrased here from ISACA (2007):

- The *pervasive principle* states that there must be clearly defined information security responsibilities.
- The *awareness principle* says that all employees should be made aware of information security policies and have the required access to these and other items necessary to the security of the data. They should also be informed of security threats to data.
- The *ethics principle* requires users and administrators to use the information in an ethical manner.
- The *multidisciplinary principle* calls for all essential personnel across multiple business units to be involved in the information security program.
- The *proportionality principle* states that risk assessments are essential to determining the adequate protection of information assets and the proper portion of the resources allocated to these assets.
- The *integration principle* says that there should be an enterprise-wide information security program coordinated and integrated with each business unit.
- The *timeliness principle* requires security breaches to be handled in a timely and efficient manner along with responding to other security threats as they may arise.
- The *assessment principle* states that risks should be assessed on a periodic basis or when the need arises due to changes in the systems environment or advancement in technology.
- The *equity principle* says that personal feeling should not interpret the handling of information security, which should be unbiased to all parties responsible for the information.

2.9 Common Pitfalls of an Effective Information Security Program

There are many reasons why an information security program may not be as effective as it should be. The following is a list of some common pitfalls and some suggestions to overcome them:

- *Overconfidence.* This is the tendency of individuals to be overconfident in their ability to make accurate estimations. For example, an individual may overestimate the risk involved in carrying out a certain business practice. This is dangerous in that a lot of the components that go into having an effective information security program deal with the ability to make accurate judgments or estimates. A way to overcome this pitfall is to get second opinions of estimates and make sure to look at all things involved in the calculations. Having an independent person look over these estimates can assist in providing other aspects that may not have been originally considered.

- *Optimism.* This pitfall deals with forecasts that are too optimistic. Everyone wants things to go right and sometimes people will exaggerate the positive and downplay the negative. It is important to keep a conservative outlook on the future. Always overestimate the costs and underestimate the benefits.

- *Anchoring.* This deals with individuals focusing on the first number presented. Even though a subsequent estimate of a totally unrelated subject involving numbers is provided, individuals tend to "anchor" on the first number. To solve this pitfall, numbers should be used as a last resort and should be accurately presented. Numbers should be checked, rechecked, and then checked again before presenting them so that, when anchoring occurs, decisions can be made on sound estimates. It may also be prudent to hold discussions of certain matters at different times so as not to confuse issues, especially when a lot of numbers may be utilized.

- *The status quo bias.* No one likes change, and change is sometimes hard to accept. Individuals tend to stick with that which they know and with which they are familiar—even if the way in which they currently do things is inadequate or ineffective. *Who Moved My Cheese?*, by Spencer Johnson, is a good read on the topic of managing change.

- *Mental accounting.* This pitfall deals with "colored" money, a term that describes how budgets may be set up with different amounts going to different areas or expenses. Some individuals tend to treat money differently depending on where it comes from, where it is kept, and how it is spent. Most of the time, money coming in and going out is really all the same, no matter the sources from which it comes. Priorities need to be assessed and considerations need to be made to ensure that the proper resources are going to certain areas of the organization, especially with information security.

■ *The herding instinct.* A fundamental human trait deals with conformity and validation of others. Individuals have a hard time disagreeing with others and will tend to follow the "herd" even if it is not really for the good of the entire organization. To overcome this pitfall, it is important that an organization recognize new ideas and keep an open mind.

■ *False consensus.* Individuals sometimes overestimate the extent to which others share their views, beliefs, and experiences. They may seek only opinions and facts that support their own beliefs. This is known as confirmation bias. Individuals may remember facts and experiences that only reinforce their current assumptions. This is known as selective recall. Some individuals will have a biased evaluation of a topic and will easily accept any evidence that supports their beliefs while challenging contradictory evidence. Others will be duped into "groupthink" and pressured into agreement normally found in a team-based culture. All of these can hinder an effective information security program that is often in direct conflict with innovation. It is important that perceptions are reasonable and communications are open between key personnel.

2.10 Defense in Depth

As you have noticed, there is a lot to the effective management of information security. As we discussed earlier, security basically means to protect from danger. The term "defense in depth" is used to refer to a layering tactic used in security. This idea is not so much about totally preventing an attack because this is never or rarely the case; rather, it is about weakening an attacker over time by deploying defensive mechanisms into an attacker's way. These mechanisms are objects that attackers have to overcome to get to their target.

This tactic began as a military strategy and can be described by using an analogy of a castle. When a castle was built, it was normally built in a large, open area surrounded by little houses or farmlands. On the outskirts of these houses were outposts. The first line of defense for the villagers would be the observation of attackers from these posts, which would send alarms back to the castle. This would allow the defenders to get prepared for an attack. These attackers would then have to travel some distance across open fields to get to the castle. The castle was normally built with a moat surrounding it and a drawbridge. The only way across the moat was across the drawbridge, which would automatically be lifted prior to an attack. The castle was also built with reinforced walls and towers to observe the surrounding areas. From the first wall to the castle, there was usually a large courtyard that could offer refuge for the fleeing villagers or could be used to funnel attackers into a small concentrated area to be killed. Throughout the area were armed guards, catapults, archers, and other defensive weapons to keep the attackers at bay. The structures contained spiral staircases, long hallways, and multiple rooms to confuse or entrap the attackers and, ultimately, protect the king and queen.

All of these defensive mechanisms were utilized to weaken the attackers as they overcame each of the obstacles laid before them prior to their ever reaching the doors of the king's chambers. These same concepts are used and have proven to be effective in the information security realm. A company's network is protected by multiple layers of protection, including firewalls, switches, routers, VLANs, secured operating systems, encryption, and many other advanced technologies. In addition, this equipment is secured in dedicated server rooms with other physical security controls such as badge systems, alarm monitoring systems, CCTV surveillance systems, cipher punch code systems, fingerprint systems, retina scan systems, facial recognition systems, voice activation systems, and other advanced physical access control systems.

All of these elements make it more difficult for a determined attacker to gain access to the information. In addition, they give the defender time to process the attack vectors and possibly intercept or stop the attacker from gaining access or damaging the systems.

Zones are usually used to describe and practice the "defense in depth" idea. I like to utilize the acronym "DPDP"—deter, prevent, detect, and prosecute. I utilize this train of thought when evaluating the security controls in place for a certain asset. I pretend that I am a criminal that has targeted the organization I am evaluating. I then attempt to walk in the shoes of the criminal while looking at the controls that are in place. Let me first explain what each zone comprises and then I can give you an example of how you can use this train of thought to test your own security controls.

The first zone we look at is the deterrent zone. This zone of defense does not restrict access, but makes it clear that the resource is restricted and permissions to the access are denied. This zone is implemented to discourage security violations. Controls in this zone may consist of warning signs or well-lit parking lots. Although they may not prevent criminal activity, they may deter such activity from occurring. They can also prevent some of the more opportunistic types of attacks, but will not stop a determined attacker.

The next zone is the prevention zone. Systems in this zone are meant to force restrictions on resources that individuals do not have the right to access. Controls in this zone may consist of badge access on doors or password log-ins on workstations. Again, this zone is meant to stop an attack; however, an attacker can bypass or negate such controls that may be in place. If unauthorized use of a restricted resource is obtained, some mechanism needs to be in place to generate an alarm.

This is where the detective zone of defense comes into play. This zone does not stop the access; however, if access is obtained, it will detect such activity and notify the appropriate authorities. Controls in this zone may consist of burglar alarms or intrusion detection systems on the network.

If the system is compromised, you may want to prosecute the attacker. For prosecution, you may have to determine the identity of an attacker. This may be accomplished by video surveillance equipment or other types of monitoring devices such as event monitoring on network devices. Along with prosecution, there are two subset zones: corrective and recovery zones, which are used to restore the system, capabilities, and resources. I consider these a subset of the prosecution zone because they do not have any true effect on stopping an attack; however, they are still important to consider in mitigating damage that may have been caused by a security breach.

One final zone is known as the compensation zone. It is utilized to provide alternative forms of controls. Compensating controls may not fall into any of the specific zones, but can be utilized to further enhance other types of controls—for instance, the integration of the alarm system with the access controls system. If an unauthorized attempt is detected by the access controls system, then the alarm system should be activated or vice versa. Each of these systems may work on separate processes, but when integrated together, they can implement more effective control measures.

Throughout the remainder of this book, we will go into detail for each area of concentration and provide tips on what can be done to strengthen the security of your organization. See Table 2.5 for additional control examples of each of the zones.

Now that we have some idea of what the zones are, we can go through an example of how we can use this train of thought to test our security controls. Let

Table 2.5 Defense-in-Depth Examples

Defenses against System Compromise Zones	*Policies, Standards, Procedures, Technology*
Deterrent zone	Parking lot lights, warning signs, separate and independent networks, data classification policies, access control procedures, security awareness training
Prevention zone	Badge access, locks, virus and spyware programs, procedures on handling data, firewalls, intrusion prevention systems, encryption, MAC filtering solutions
Detection zone	Intrusion detection systems, burglar alarms, network logging, network monitoring, forensic analysis program, software integrity programs
Prosecution zone with subzones of correctives/recovery	Surveillance cameras, auditing programs, system backups, tapes, disaster recovery solutions, incident response procedures
Compensation zone	Integrated systems, new technology, proper change management procedures, added security

us say that we are going to test the security of our office, which is in a single-story building owned solely by our company. Only our employees should have access to the office. In conducting an evaluation of the facility, we would go through the "DPDP" process. Keep in mind that this is a scaled-down example and a lot more goes into an evaluation of this type; however, this scenario should be able to illustrate the concepts that are presented here.

Starting with deterrent, we would look at and ask some of the following questions: Are our parking lots lit up at night? Do we have floodlights on the building? Do we have warning signs in the area to indicate that it is private property? Are we located in a well-populated area? Is the office always open? We would take together all of the security controls that we see in place to determine if a criminal element would want to target this facility.

Next, we move on to prevention. If the security controls are not adequate to deter the criminal or make him or her want to attack another business in the area, what other controls are in place at the facility that would prevent the criminal from getting in? Do we have locks on the doors? Are they functional? Do the windows open? Do we have security guards patrolling the office or the nearby areas?

Next, we look at detection. If the doors or windows can be broken, what controls are in place to detect such an intrusion? Do we have an alarm system? Do we have motion detection? Do we have glass-break sensors? Are all of these systems adequately placed and monitored on a continuous basis?

Finally, we look at the prosecution. If the alarm systems work as they are supposed to, how long will it take for law enforcement to arrive? Do we have security cameras in the office that can capture a picture of faces?

As mentioned earlier, we cannot forget about the corrective and recovery zones. How long would it take to fix the door or window that is broken? Will we have someone stand by until it can be fixed? If computer systems were stolen, how will they be replaced? Will there be information stored on them that could be retrieved by the attacker? Do we have current backups in place?

As you may notice, some of the controls looked at may cover multiple zones. This is where the compensation zone comes in. In this example, we may not have glass-break sensors in place; however, we may use motion detection alarms all over the facility. Thus, even though the attacker may break the window and get into the office, the motion detection will discover the intrusion and get law enforcement on its way.

2.11 Summary

In this chapter, we discussed the interrelationships of regulations, policies, standards, procedures, and guidelines. Although it is a common misconception that these terms are interchangeable, they are distinctly separate. As you may recall, regulations dictate policies; policies, in turn, set standards; and standards tie procedures back to policies. Guidelines are best common practices that are produced by procedures or specific instructions for individual processes.

We discussed the different regulations that require an information security management program to be implemented in different industries. We also discussed the different components of compliance and security controls that need to be implemented in the information security management program. Related to security controls, we discussed industry best practice guidelines, standards, and measurement techniques that we can use to measure how effective our controls are implemented. We detailed some specific information security frameworks that can be utilized such as COBIT and ISO. In addition, we discussed some pitfalls and how to overcome some of the obstacles that can be put in the way of implementing an information security program at your organization. Finally, we discussed the defense in depth principle and explained why it is important to provide layers of protection for your processes and systems.

References

Board of Governors of the Federal Reserve System. 2008. Integrity Guidelines Establishing Information Security Standards. Retrieved May 22, 2009 from Federal Reserve: http://www.federalreserve.gov/bankinforeg/interagencyguidelines.htm

Electronic Privacy Information Center. January 1, 2005. Epic Gramm–Leach–Bliley Act page. Retrieved January 28, 2008, from EPIC: http://epic.org/privacy/glba/

FFIEC. July 26, 2007. About the FFIEC. Retrieved January 28, 2008, from FFIEC: http://www.ffiec.gov/about.htm

ISACA. 2007. *CISM review manual.* Rolling Meadows, IL: ISACA.

Johnson, S. 1998. *Who moved my cheese? An amazing way to deal with change in your work and in your life.* New York: G. P. Putnam's Sons.

Mackey, R. January 28, 2008. How to apply ISO 27002 to PCI DSS compliance. Retrieved February 6, 2008, from SearchSecurity.com: http://searchsecurity.techtarget.com/tip/0,289483,sid14_gci1295905_tax309647,00.html?track=NL-430&ad=621581&asrc=EM_NLT_3012889&uid=6549743

National Institute of Standards and Technology. 2005. *Recommended security controls for federal information systems.* Gaithersburg, MD: Technology Administration/U.S. Department of Commerce.

PCI Security Standards Council. 2006. About the PCI DSS—PCI Security Standards Council. Retrieved January 28, 2008, from PCI Security Standards Council: https://www.pcisecuritystandards.org/tech/index.htm

Spurzem, B. September 20, 2007. What is Sarbanes–Oxley Act? A definition from Whatis.com. Retrieved January 28, 2008, from searchcio.techtarget.com: http://searchcio.techtarget.com/sDefinition/0,,sid182_gci920030,00.html

UCSF Campus and UCSF Medical Center. 2001. What is HIPAA? Retrieved January 28, 2008, from UCSF: http://www.ucsf.edu/hipaa/whatis.html

Chapter 3

Managing Risks

Objectives

- Explain and understand risk management.
- Understand the steps involved in setting up an efficient risk management system.
- Understand how to conduct a risk assessment.
- Describe the eight steps to risk management.
- Explain how the Technical Evaluation Plan (TEP) fits into the risk assessment and the importance of conducting a technical evaluation.
- Describe the methodology of the technical evaluation plan.
- Describe the different sections of the executive summary and explain the importance of including these sections within the risk assessment report.
- Understand the importance of follow-up.
- Explain the importance of tracking risk mitigation efforts.
- Describe steps to take in order to resolve conflicts.
- Understand test plans.

3.1 Risk Management

One of the most important aspects of information security is to manage risk in your information systems. The mission of risk management is to create value through the balance of risk taking and reward. Companies normally make profits by taking calculated risks. This same concept applies to developing a risk management system. You must be able to align risk taking with the risk appetite of the organization. It makes no sense and will eventually lead to the demise of the company if you spend $2 million to protect a system that houses information worth only $1 million. Efficient risk management can provide reasonable assurance that the organization's goals and objectives are being achieved.

Although there are numerous risk management methodologies, the one I like to use is the one explained in the National Institute of Standards and Technology (NIST) Special Publication 800-30, "Risk Management Guide to Information Technology Systems." The next section will detail the steps involved in setting up a risk management system, how to conduct a risk assessment, and how to track mitigation efforts. This section will provide a practical guide with detailed examples that you can utilize right away to implement or maintain your risk management efforts.

> The objective of performing risk management is to enable the organization to accomplish its mission(s) (1) by better securing the IT systems that store, process, or transmit organizational information; (2) by enabling management to make well-informed risk management decisions to justify the expenditures that are part of an IT budget; and (3) by assisting management in authorizing (or accrediting) the IT systems on the basis of the supporting documentation resulting from the performance of risk management. (Stoneburner, Goguen, and Feringa 2002)

The NIST methodology takes into account the system characteristics, user access controls, vulnerabilities, threats, and security controls implemented on the system. The steps in the methodology build on to each other and the end result is normally the production of a risk assessment report.

We will discuss each of the following steps involved in producing a risk assessment report (with some modifications to assist in practical use) further throughout the rest of this chapter:

- system characterization;
- threat identification;
- vulnerability identification and categorization;
- control analysis;
- likelihood rating;
- impact rating—premitigation;
  - traceability matrix development—financial, regulatory, and operational risks;
  - loss of confidentiality, integrity, and availability;
  - mitigated risk, residual risk, and adjusted impact rating;

■ risk determination;
  - impact rating—postmitigation;
  - effort matrix; and
■ recommendations.

3.1.1 Step 1—System Characterization

In the context of conducting a risk assessment, a system is considered to be a component or a process of a business function. The depth to which you break down a process is determined by the objectives of the risk assessment. During the system characterization step, the system under review is comprehensively understood and the underlying technology base for the risk assessment is identified. This step will define the organization's systems and identify the system boundaries, elements, users, and network infrastructure, if applicable. This step will also assess the value of the asset and classify the asset under the company's information asset or data classification policy.

The risk assessment report will normally include the following:

■ *Purpose* of the risk assessment—what are the predefined objectives that this risk assessment is supposed to achieve?
■ *Description* of the technology base of the system or what the system is composed of—depending on the depth of the risk assessment, this can be a single component or a list of components that make up the system to include hardware, software, and other assets such as personnel.
■ System *boundaries* may include routers, firewalls, switches, or other types of physical or network access control devices. System boundaries are where systems or components of that system integrate or "touch" each other. The point at which they "touch" is considered the boundary point. Boundary points are usually seen at the network devices such as firewalls or routers, but they can also be at the software level, where one software application integrates with another software application.
■ *Inventory* sheets of the systems included in the assessment include all of the actual devices, computers, hardware, software, etc. that make up the system under review. The inventory sheet should also include a classification of the component based on the organization's data classification scheme.
■ The list of *users* and their roles within the system contains the names of personnel that utilize the system and a description of how they utilize it. For instance, one employee may just use the system in his or her job functions, while another may be responsible for administering and maintaining the system.
■ *Processes* and/or documentation related to the system include policies, procedures, standards, and other documentation that directly or indirectly affects the system.
■ *Diagrams* may include network diagrams, flow charts, process diagrams, etc.

3.1.2 Step 2—Threat Identification

Threats, as you may recall, are any actions or events that may cause an adverse consequence. Threat identification defines and identifies threats to the system under review. Furthermore, it identifies threat sources and their impact on the system under review. Threats are identified in many ways. One way is to research them in existing documentation from agencies like NIST, a Computer Emergency Response Team (CERT), and others. Other methods include brainstorming with the business owners and identifying threats from a business point of view and reviewing system documentation and comparing it against best practices.

A threat can more specifically be defined as the potential for a threat source to exploit a specific vulnerability. A threat source is defined as the intent and method targeted at the intentional exploitation of vulnerabilities or a situation and method that may accidentally trigger vulnerabilities. Several vulnerabilities are inherent to a system at any point in time. Your concern should be focused on when a threat source may have a high probability of exploiting these vulnerabilities. For instance, you would want to pay close attention to a known exploit that is publicly available for one of your systems. If this happens, you would want to update your system to patch this vulnerability or implement some other countermeasures, depending on the risk involved with this exploit.

The risk assessment report will normally contain a threat statement, which is basically a summary and description of the possible threats or threat sources pertaining to the system under review. I have conducted careful research into threats and have determined that there are essentially five different broad categories of threats: human threats, environmental threats, software/hardware threats, regulatory threats, and emerging threats. Each of these categories can be broken down into subcategories such as accidental, criminal, internal, external, etc. The following threat sources can be utilized in your threat statement:

Human threats consist of accidental and premeditated threats. Accidental threats occur when loss or damage is caused to the organization's assets. This also includes errors and omissions by employees. Under accidental threats are internal sources that include employees and external sources that include vendors and consultants. Premeditated threats consist of any threat that is criminal, malicious, or possibly done with a political motive. These include terrorist acts, theft, fraud, sabotage, kidnapping, ransom, and espionage. These threats can also be subdivided into internal sources that include employees and external sources that include hackers, cyberterrorists, vendors, and consultants.

Environmental threats are related to the loss of physical and infrastructure support involving natural threats, man-made threats, and supply system threats. Natural threats include tornadoes, hurricanes, floods, earthquakes, and fires. Man-made threats include environmental accidents, intentional attacks, and wars, and they may also include fires. Supply system threats include any disruption in utilities such as water, electricity, or air-conditioning (HVAC systems).

Software/hardware threats deal with specific IT equipment or programs. This may include illegal computer operations or software. Malicious code, hardware problems, programming errors, and even software vendor updates can be a threat source. Malicious code can include viruses, malware programs, Trojans, and worms.

Regulatory threats deal with laws and regulations from governing bodies. Although these threats are not necessarily threats in and of themselves, if requirements are not met, they can cause adverse effects upon an organization. Regulations can be internal and external. Internal regulations include policies, procedures, and those individuals responsible for assuring that these regulations are followed within the organization. External regulations involve statutory laws, regulatory agencies, fines, and the negative image of an organization when it does not comply with certain requirements.

Emerging threats are a catchall for any unforeseen or future threat that may come about as technology advances. A current threat that is becoming more of an issue is the threat to personal privacy through the use of new techniques to monitor online activities.

3.1.2.1 Threat Source References

Some sample references can be obtained from the following sources:

- corporate network—information security risk assessment workgroup operational and technical threat sources;
- National Institute of Standards and Technology risk management guide for information systems; and
- CERT.

3.1.3 Step 3—Vulnerability Identification and Categorization

Vulnerability is defined as a flaw or weakness in system security procedures, design, implementation, or internal controls that can be exercised (accidentally triggered or intentionally exploited) and result in a security breach or a violation of the system's security policy, a disruption in operations, or a compromise of data integrity. Vulnerabilities are the paths that a threat source can take that may result in a loss. As mentioned earlier, several vulnerabilities can be inherent to a system; the threat occurs when exploits become available.

Vulnerability identification and categorization is where the vulnerabilities are identified for the system under review. Included in this step are technical vulnerabilities as well as process vulnerabilities. Vulnerabilities are paired with threats that are further detailed by threat source and threat action. The goal of this step is to develop a list of system vulnerabilities that could be exploited by potential threat sources.

The report may include a table of vulnerabilities with potential threat actions. This table summarizes vulnerabilities determined from interviews and questionnaires. Each of the vulnerabilities is matched to possible threat sources and threat actions from step 2. For example, maybe you are working a risk assessment for your company's database. You know that a vulnerability of your database may be that data can be copied without your knowing about it. The threat source matched to this vulnerability may be employees that are considered human internal threats. The threat action can be the loss or theft of the data.

Over 100 different threat actions can be matched to 22 different threat sources discussed earlier. There can also be well over 100 different vulnerabilities for any given system. As you can see, risk assessments can get very complicated very quickly. Do not despair, however; risk assessment programs have been developed to make these types of correlations easier. I discuss one such program in Appendix F.

Remember that we are primarily concerned with threats that have a high probability of succeeding by exploiting known vulnerabilities and that can cause serious damage to a system. We will discuss how this can be figured out as we progress through the rest of this chapter.

3.1.4 Step 4—Control Analysis

Through control analysis, all controls within the environment are identified and documented. As discussed earlier, security controls are implemented against threats. Numerous control sets can be utilized by organization, such as the NIST Special Publication 800-53, "Recommended Security Controls for Federal Information Systems" or the "Information Technology—Security Techniques—Code of Practice for Information Security Management" (ISO/IEC 27002, formerly ISO/IEC 17799:2005). A combination of these controls and others can be utilized to establish your overall security framework.

One advantage of utilizing a standard industry control list is that each control is organized by a control type, control number, and subcontrols. The control number is the baseline for the control and the subcontrols are options depending on the risk rating.

Depending on the detail required by your industry, these controls may need to be paired with each individual system component identified in step 1. In most cases, your report will include a table identifying current controls in place and planned controls that may be required to be implemented. In essence, this is similar to a gap analysis.

A gap analysis is a review of your security controls. Once you have figured out what type of control framework is required to protect a certain system, you must then find out what types of controls you already have in place. When conducting a gap analysis, you will map or correlate what is existing to what is required. Any requirement not met is considered the gap that the organization must fill or with which it must come into compliance. To perform a gap analysis, first codify and list out all requirements. Then, list out all controls or elements under review. Finally, match these elements to the requirements and see what is left out. A gap analysis works well in developing policies and procedures by figuring out requirements and existing policies. After going through a few gap analyses, you will see how effective they are in determining the actual state of the company.

3.1.5 Step 5—Likelihood Rating

Likelihood rating is the possibility of occurrence to all vulnerabilities identified in step 3. To complete this step, the organization must define certain ratings. Some methodologies use a subjective scale of low, medium, or high, while others may attempt to quantify the ratings. This quantification can become very tedious in some instances and can create an undue burden. I have found that combining a subjective scale along with a well-defined rating can give better, rationally quantified ratings. Table 3.1 provides an example of a possible rating scale and definitions that apply to each rating.

Again, this is a little subjective; however, if you follow the defined rating scale, there is less room for opinions and more documented rationale.

3.1.6 Step 6—Impact Rating (Premitigation)

3.1.6.1 Traceability Matrix Development

A traceability matrix takes all vulnerabilities and lists the financial, regulatory, and operational risks from low to critical for each. The Requirements Traceability Matrix (RTM) is used to capture threats and vulnerability pairs and to document the likelihood of occurrence along with the residual risks.

Two methods are used to evaluate impact: quantitative and qualitative. The quantitative method attempts to express impact in dollar amounts. Although that process may have some applicability to certain operations, it does not appropriately measure the overall risk. Dollar calculations cannot accurately reflect the risk impact involved in loss of service or trust in the corporation.

Qualitative measurements, on the other hand, clearly identify the nature of the risk and assist management in establishing priorities. For example, loss of system access for a short time, in dollar terms, is relatively small compared to the impact of the loss of service. Continued service degradations will erode the customer base and member confidence. These measures are the benchmarks for impact analysis. Table 3.2 and Table 3.3 show examples of defined ratings for each, respectively. As a point of reference, numbered scores can be added to quantify the ratings a little more as opposed to using high, medium, or low.

Financial risk can be quantified in the same manner, based on monetary loss. This is best determined by the organization because each organization has varied levels of risk that it is willing to accept.

Table 3.1 Likelihood Rating

Ratings	Title	Definitions
1	No credible chance of occurring	Events that are within the realm of possibility; however, they have no credible chance of occurring; these could include such events as meteor strikes and volcanoes
2	Almost no credible chance of occurring	Events that have an extremely low possibility of occurrence, but are not inconceivable; these could include such events as nuclear explosions and earthquakes
3	Very unlikely	Events that have a low, but still possible chance of occurring; these could include such events as chemical explosions or biological incidents
4	Unlikely	Events that have a low to medium chance of occurring, but they are doubtful to occur; these could include such events as burglary or other violent acts
5	50/50 Chance of occurring	Events that have just as good a possibility of occurring as not; these could include such events as bomb threats or water failures
6	Likely	Events that have more chance of occurring than not; these could include such events as data theft or targeted IT attacks
7	Very likely	Events that have more than two chances in three of occurring; these could include such events as Web page defacement or other types of vandalism
8	Extremely likely	Events that have more than three chances in four of occurring; these could include such events as denial of service or malware attacks
9	Almost inevitable	Events that have a surety of occurring, but have some minimal chance of not occurring; these could include such an event as having severe weather
10	Inevitable	Events that will definitely occur; these could include such events as incorrect data entry or power outages

Table 3.2 Regulatory Risk

Rating	Definitions
Low	Informal recommendation from an auditor or regulator
Medium	An auditor's or regulator's finding that may lead to a compliance requirement
High	An auditor's or regulator's finding that requires compliance attention
Critical	A statutory or regulation violation

Table 3.3 Operational Risk

Ratings	Definitions
Low	Will not disrupt system availability
Medium	Disruption less than or equal to 3 hours
High	Disruption longer than 3 hours or up to 24 hours (1 business day)
Critical	Disruption greater than 24 hours (1 business day)

3.1.6.2 Loss of Confidentiality, Integrity, and Availability

When developing a traceability matrix, you will also take into consideration the loss of confidentiality, integrity, and availability, which are considered the CIA triad of information security. One of the primary goals of information security is to protect the CIA triad. During this step of a risk assessment, you will assign values for the impact of the loss to the business if security failed to protect the confidentiality, integrity, and availability of the information:

The impact of the loss of confidentiality looks at what the loss would be if information were to be released to unauthorized individuals. This loss can be measured in dollar amounts, but to keep it standard with the rest of our concepts, we may want to classify this loss using the low, medium, or high method. One cautionary note: you must clearly define what each of these levels is prior to rating them.

The impact of the loss of integrity looks at the loss to the business if information was modified in an unapproved manner. Again, this can be measured in dollar amounts; however, consistency throughout the rating process will reveal better results. As already discussed, it is important that a standard be used and definitions defined prior to rating.

The impact of the loss of availability looks at the loss associated with the resource being destroyed or otherwise unavailable. You may think that this is the same as the operational risks areas we looked at earlier; however, this is a little more specific. We are primarily looking at the specific resource, such as a server or a database, rather than the process or operation in which this resource is involved.

3.1.6.3 Mitigated Risk, Residual Risk, and Adjusted Impact Rating

After completing the traceability matrix, we will now determine the percentage of risk mitigated and the percentage of residual risk left. The Percentage of Risk Mitigated (PRM) is a perceived amount of threat realization impact that has been mitigated by the current controls in place. The Percentage of Residual Risk (PRR) is the perceived amount of threat realization impact remaining after the current mitigating controls in place have been considered.

To explain these terms, let us use an example of a workstation that has no battery backup power. The risk in this scenario is that information being worked on can be lost if a power failure occurs and hard drives can possibly be corrupted due to the sudden power loss. The PRM under this scenario would be equal to 0%: No risk has been mitigated. The PRR is calculated by subtracting the PRM from 100%—in this case 0%, leaving a PRR of 100%. Now, if a backup power supply were added to the workstation, the PRM may be considered at around 75%. We may not consider it 100% because some form of risk is always inherent to technology. For instance, the battery backup may not work or be configured properly to keep the computer running when there is a sudden loss of power all the time. Thus, the PRR would then be calculated to be pretty low at around 25%. Table 3.4 shows an example of a possible rating scale and definition for the PRR.

The Adjusted Impact Rating (AIR) is a method of quantifying threat realization before and after mitigating controls have been applied. It allows for the line-across viewing of the threat to the organization, the effects that threat realization would have on the organization, and the mitigating strategies the organization already has in place to decrease these effects. The products of this method are percentages of risks mitigated, risks remaining, and a number from 1 to 10 that translates into a level of impact that is defined in the adjusted impact rating key listed in Table 3.5.

The adjusted impact rating table can be divided into nine columns, as seen in Table 3.6, and constructed as follows:

■ Column one is the vulnerability identified in Section 3.1.3.
■ Column two is the impact of the loss of confidentiality (rated as low, medium, or high) as discussed in Section 3.1.6.2.
■ Column three is the impact of the loss of integrity (rated as low, medium, or high) as discussed in Section 3.1.6.2.
■ Column four is the impact of the loss of availability (rated as low, medium, or high) as discussed in Section 3.1.6.2.

Table 3.4   Key to Percentage of Residual Risk Remaining

Residual Risk Remaining	Definitions
10%	No credible risk remains
20%	Very little risk remains
30%	Some risk remains
40%	More than one third of the risk remains
50%	Half of the risk remains
60%	More than half of the risk remains
70%	More than two thirds of the risk remains
80%	More than three quarters of the risk remains
90%	Almost all of the risk remains
100%	All of the risk remains

Table 3.5   Key to Adjusted Impact Rating

Adjusted Impact Rating	Definitions
1	No real impact on the organization
2	Very little impact on the organization
3	Little impact on the organization
4	Some impact on the organization
5	Midlevel impact on the organization
6	Significant impact on the organization
7	Serious impact on the organization
8	Severe impact on the organization
9	Crippling impact on the organization
10	Continuing business functions become untenable

Table 3.6 Adjusted Impact Rating

Vulnerabilities	C	I	A	P of O	IR	PRM	PRR	AIR

Notes: C = confidentiality; I = integrity; A = availability; P of O = possibility of occurrence; IR = impact rating; PRM = percentage
of risk mitigated; PRR = percentage of residual risk; AIR =
adjusted impact rating.

■ Column five is the Possibility of Occurrence (P of O). This is a numeric rating
of the likelihood that a threat will occur and is expressed in a range from 1 to
10. (Refer to Section 3.1.5 for more information.)
■ Column six is the impact. This is the perceived impact before mitigating factors have been considered and is rated from 1 to 10. (Refer to Section 3.1.6
for more information.)
■ Column seven is the PRM. This is the perceived amount of threat realization
impact that has been mitigated by the controls in place as listed in the previous column. (Refer to Section 3.1.6.3 for further information.)
■ Column eight is the PRR. This is the perceived amount of threat realization
impact remaining after mitigating controls in place have been considered.
(Refer to Section 3.1.6.3 for further information.)
■ Column nine is the AIR. This is a number from 1 to 10 that translates into
the level of impact remaining after mitigating controls have been applied.
(Refer to Section 3.1.6.3 for further information.)

3.1.7 Step 7—Risk Determination

Now that we have completed the adjusted impact rating table, we are ready to make
a risk determination of the vulnerabilities that we have documented. In this step,
we will list all vulnerabilities for any observations ranked medium or higher. This
step will also provide a postmitigation impact rating and effort matrix that includes
how much effort it will take to mitigate the vulnerability along with the benefit that
the mitigation will provide. In the next few sections, we will see how we have made
the risk determinations. Please pay special attention to the risk determination key
as you review the following sections:

F = financial risk;
R = regulatory risk;
O = operational risk;
C = confidentiality;
I = integrity;
A = availability;

P of O = possibility of occurrence;
IR = impact rating;
PRM = percentage of risk mitigated;
PRR = percentage of residual risk; and
AIR = adjusted impact rating.

3.1.7.1 Impact Rating—Postmitigation

In our methodology, risk is determined by the value calculated from the Adjusted Impact Rating (AIR) utilizing the following formula:

$$AIR = (P \text{ of } O + \text{impact rating})/$$
$$2 \times PRR \text{ (result rounded up to next whole number)}$$

where P of O = possibility of occurrence (rated 1–10; refer to Table 3.1 for more information).

The impact rating (rated 1–10) is calculated as follows:

$$\text{Impact rating} = [\text{financial} + \text{regulatory} + (0.5 \times \text{operational})$$
$$+ (2 \times \text{confidentiality}) + \text{integrity} + \text{availability}]/6.5$$

In this formula, the ratings utilized for the risks and the impact of the losses are weighted and averaged together. The 0.5 multiplied to operational means that the operational risk is half as important to us as the other risks, and the 2 multiplied to confidentiality means that confidentiality is twice as important to us as the other items. The 6.5 is the total possible value looked at when taking operational as half a unit and confidentiality as a double unit and giving one point each for financial, regulatory, integrity, and availability. These numbers can be adjusted for your organization; this is presented here only as an example of the concept:

PRR = Percentage of Residual Risk (calculated by the formula 100% − PRM)

where PRM = Percentage of Risk Mitigated.

See Table 3.7 for an example of how we determine risks using the backup power scenario discussed earlier:

$$\text{Impact rating} = [3 + 6 + (0.5 \times 10) + (2 \times 3) + (3 + 8)]/6.5 = 4.76, \text{ or } 5$$

$$\text{Adjusted impact rating} = (2 + 5)/2 \times 0.25 = 0.875, \text{ or } 1,$$
$$\text{or no real impact on the organization}$$

Table 3.7   Risk Determination for No Backup Power

Vulnerabilities	F	R	O	C	I	A	P of O	IR	PRM	PRR	AIR
No backup power	3	6	10	3	3	8	2	5	75	25	1

Notes: F= financial; R = regulatory; O= operational; C = confidentiality; I = integrity; A = availability; P of O = possibility of occurrence; IR = impact rating; PRM = percentage of risk mitigated; PRR = percentage of residual risk; AIR = adjusted impact rating.

3.1.7.2 Effort Matrix

We have completed the risk determination and now we must make a determination on how much effort (or cost) will be involved in the mitigation efforts to get the listed vulnerabilities down to an acceptable risk level. A subjective ranking of low, medium, or high can be utilized and defined prior to implementation. Another AIR calculation should be obtained after adjusting the PRR due to additional controls that may be in place to mitigate some of the risks. The benefit for such mitigation efforts should outweigh the effort. To take the example that we used earlier regarding the backup power supply, the effort may be considered low because the cost of an individual backup power supply for a workstation is rather inexpensive, and installation is fairly easy. The benefit, on the other hand, may be considered high because it should protect the system up to around 25% of residual risk remaining.

3.1.8 Step 8—Recommendations

Recommendations should be made for any vulnerability that is considered to be medium or high risk and that requires further mitigation efforts to get down to an acceptable level. Recommendations should come from industry best practices, from technical experts providing the assessment, or from multiple respected and reliable sources. Recommendations should be fully researched and documented prior to being made and should address the appropriate weaknesses identified.

3.2   Technical Evaluation Plan (TEP)

Another important aspect of the assessment is the testing or validation of controls. On the administrative side, this is done by conducting interviews and observing processes that prove compliance with company policies and procedures. On the technical side, it may be a little more complex. An advanced understanding of networks, operating systems, computers, routers, and other items is required to conduct a comprehensive technical evaluation. I use the term "evaluation" rather than "audit" because the word audit has a negative connotation. The assessments described in this book are utilized to strengthen the company's posture and should not be perceived as audits, although they may be considered as such. It is important that a good rapport is established between the independent auditor and the technical group and other key personnel.

3.2.1 Methodology Overview

The methodology used to conduct the following is the National Security Agency's INFOSEC Evaluation Methodology (IEM). The IEM is an internationally recognized methodology independent of any application or industry that incorporates companies' requirements and needs along with specific regulatory requirements. The IEM is technically focused and provides 10 IEM baseline activities that are required to be included as part of the evaluation. Ultimately, after completing the 10 baseline activities, the company is provided with an understandable and usable set of recommendations that, when implemented, will improve the overall security of the organization. The technical tools used to collect INFOSEC information will be a combination of commercial, freeware, and shareware tools. These tools will assist in gaining a larger cross section of the system/network status and provide a means to identify and eliminate false positives throughout the evaluation process. The following are the 10 baseline activities used to collect the information about the company's current technical security posture:

■ port scanning;
■ SNMP scanning;
■ enumeration and banner grabbing;
■ wireless enumeration;
■ vulnerability scanning;
■ host evaluation;
■ network device analysis;
■ password compliance testing;
■ application-specific scanning; and
■ network sniffing.

These areas are presented here as part of the risk assessment process; however, further details of each activity and the tools specific to conducting each will be described later.

3.2.1.1 Port Scanning

Port scanning is a low-level review of the open ports on the target systems being tested. Without going into great technical detail, the main goal is to determine what Transmission Control Protocol (TCP) or User Datagram Protocol (UDP) ports are operating on or "listening" to the systems being evaluated. The information gathered during this process can be used to investigate unauthorized or unknown services that have not been documented or do not provide a function of the organization.

3.2.1.2 SNMP Scanning

Simple Network Management Protocol (SNMP) scanning is the search for a specific management service, supported by most operating systems and network devices. SNMP is a basic protocol used to support the management of network resources. Most SNMP implementations use UDP and TCP over port 161 and 162 for communications. This will tie into port scanning as being an investigation into one of the most commonly used management services for gaining more information about the target systems.

3.2.1.3 Enumeration and Banner Grabbing

Enumeration and banner grabbing are the processes involved in gathering more information about the services running on the target system. This activity or task is often referred to as *fingerprinting* the system to discover what types of systems are running on the network.

3.2.1.4 Wireless Enumeration

Wireless enumeration is a little bit different from the other enumeration activities because it is trying to discover weakly controlled access points to the network and data exposure points. This activity will even be performed on a network that does not allow wireless access to verify and validate that no rogue or unknown access points have been installed contrary to policies.

3.2.1.5 Vulnerability Scanning

Vulnerability scanning tests the target systems for known vulnerabilities. Because different tools utilize different databases of known vulnerabilities, it is recommended to utilize at least two different tools during this activity. Not all weaknesses in every product have been identified; thus, it cannot be guaranteed that any system is 100% secure; however, this scan should assist in hardening the system against known vulnerabilities.

3.2.1.6 Host Evaluation

Host evaluation is the process of evaluating a specific host for weaknesses in configuration or patch level. A typical baseline is to evaluate all servers and a sample base of workstations. High-assurance devices must be evaluated.

3.2.1.7 Network Device Analysis

Network device analysis uses many of the other IEM baseline activities to focus on the high-assurance security components of a system. These devices are normally perimeter units that make up the boundary protection of the network.

3.2.1.8 Password Compliance Testing

Password compliance testing is the validation of the organization's password policy. Most systems include the ability to define password requirements for users based on policy. This testing is to ensure that technical controls support the policy and that they are not bypassed by system or individual accounts.

3.2.1.9 Application-Specific Scanning

Application-specific scanning takes vulnerability scanning from a generalized system review to a more detailed, service-specific testing level. Applications may include custom in-house systems, commercial databases, or clusters of single functioning resources such as Web sites and e-mail. Application-specific scanning can include limited testing that may be performed by general vulnerability scanners, custom application-specific vulnerability scanners, automated or manual configuration reviews, or any combination of these.

3.2.1.10 Network Sniffing

Network sniffing is a way to see what is really traveling across the network. A sample amount of data will be reviewed to ensure that firewall policies and other network devices are functioning within acceptable levels.

3.2.2 Role of Common Vulnerabilities and Exposures (CVE) in the Technical Evaluation Plan

The CVE project is meant to be a method for providing a standardized naming and information convention for discovered security vulnerabilities. Such a convention allows for cross-referencing vulnerabilities across multiple vendor products and security tools. The CVE list is meant to be a dictionary of weaknesses, not a vulnerability database. The CVE list takes into consideration that not all weaknesses are vulnerabilities and has set aside a classification for exposures.

3.2.3 Executive Summary

This summary should be placed at the beginning of the report and highlight the medium- to high-risk vulnerabilities discovered during the assessment. The executive summary may include the following sections.

3.2.3.1 Background

The background section of the risk assessment report provides a little information regarding when the assessment was done and possibly the reason why it was conducted. It will give the objectives of the assessment. It may state that the risk assessment is part of a legal requirement or regulation as part of the company's business activities.

3.2.3.2 Summary

The summary section of the risk assessment report provides the opinion of the assessor in regard to his or her professional belief as to the controls in place providing reasonable assurance against unauthorized access to the sensitive information held within the company's assets. A statement may be made that no medium- or high-risk vulnerabilities were found and that a top-down governance approach to information security was evident.

3.2.3.3 Identified Medium- and High-Risk Vulnerabilities

The identified medium- and high-risk vulnerabilities section lists the medium- and high-risk vulnerabilities based on the adjusted impact rating calculation. If no medium- or high-risk vulnerabilities are found, then it should be noted that the controls in place are providing adequate security. The following are specific areas that should be included in the risk assessment report and addressed accordingly.

3.2.3.4 Information Risk Management and Compliance

The information risk management and compliance section should include a statement that management sets clear policy direction and demonstrates support for and commitment to information security through the issuance and maintenance of an information security policy across the organization. An assessment may be made as to whether or not the policies that exist are being followed by all employees. In addition, an assessment should be made as to whether or not compliance efforts are adequately validating enforcement of existing policies.

3.2.3.5 Information Security Risk Assessment

The information security risk assessment section should include a statement regarding whether or not a risk assessment had been made on the system under review in the past. A comparison between the present assessment and the previous assessment may possibly be noted here. In the absence of a previous assessment, documentation should be made about some of the resources utilized to gather a list of components of the system under review, such as detailed inventory sheets, interviews, diagrams, etc.

3.2.3.6 Logical and Administrative Access Control

The logical and administrative access control section describes some of the policies or procedures that may or may not be in place specifically addressing how individuals are given access to the system under review. A determination will be made as to whether or not the policies and procedures are adequate and are being followed or whether they need improvement.

3.2.3.7 Physical Security

The physical security section describes the physical layout of the system under review. For instance, if we are looking at servers as part of the system components, then a description of where the servers are being housed would be appropriate here. An example of this would be that the servers are located in a secured and dedicated server room protected by badge access doors utilized only by authorized individuals. Visitor logs are maintained for authorized visitors and surveillance cameras cover both the entrance and terminals of the servers in the room. See Chapter 4 for a detailed look into conducting a physical security assessment.

3.2.3.8 Encryption

If encryption is a part of the system control, then a description of the algorithm, key space, and control over keys should be noted here.

3.2.3.9 Malicious Code

If the system under review contains any type of workstation or server that is susceptible to viruses or other malicious code, then a description of the control should be noted. For instance, statements such as "centralized antivirus software is deployed across all servers and workstations," "antivirus software is updated on a continuous basis," and "Internet access is restricted or filtered" are implemented on the systems reviewed in this assessment.

3.2.3.10 Systems Development, Acquisition, and Maintenance

The systems development, acquisition, and maintenance section contains a description of the types of software or components utilized in this system and whether they were developed in house or are proprietary. It should also include a statement regarding what steps were followed to determine the software or components used in the system, how the software or components were acquired, and what steps are being taken to maintain these systems.

3.2.3.11 Personnel Security

The personnel security section may make a note such as that all employees must undergo and successfully pass an extensive background check prior to being hired by the company. It can include any other important information regarding the steps or process involved in selecting the individuals to work with the system under review.

3.2.3.12 Electronic and Paper-Based Media Handling

This section includes statements on how electronic and paper-based media are handled, such as utilizing crosscut shredders on paper media that are no longer needed and destroying digital media physically or with an approved Department of Defense (DoD) software application.

3.2.3.13 Logging and Data Collection

The logging and data collection section makes a note regarding the logging, auditing, or data collection of the system and how this information is maintained.

3.2.3.14 Service Provider Oversight

The service provider oversight section will list any vendors that may be involved with any components of the system under review. Special service-level agreements or conditions may also be noted here.

3.2.3.15 Incident Detection and Response

The incident detection and response section contains a statement that a documented incident-response procedure is in place or indicating the lack of one. If the system is composed of an Intrusion Detection System (IDS) or an Intrusion Prevention System (IPS), then it should be noted here.

3.2.3.16 Business Continuity

Business continuity includes a statement regarding the adequacy of the documented business continuity or disaster recovery plan in place. In addition, a statement of how this plan is communicated to others should also be added.

3.3 Follow-Up

Once the risk assessment report has been completed and vulnerabilities have been identified, it is necessary to deal with them. The best course of action and probably the most important step is the follow-up or the follow-through. A meeting should be set with the business owners of the systems under review. The results should be discussed and any issues as to the severity of the noted items should be worked out. Once everyone is in agreement that certain actionable items need to be corrected, the report should note the actionable items that need to be corrected. The report should now include the vulnerability, the action to take to correct the problem, the department or person responsible to see that the issue is corrected, and possibly a date by which this item will be completed.

It is important to realize that not all findings or issues will be corrected or that it may not be feasible to implement all corrective actions. The risk assessment's goal is to determine and provide management the best information available to make the proper business decisions on the proper course of action to take. Five strategies can be utilized in handling risk:

Risks can be ignored. Some executives may feel that if the risks are not given attention, they do not exist. One should be warned against such thoughts because risks are usually inherent to business activities. Risks do not go away by themselves and most of the time they get worse as time passes.

Risks can be mitigated. This was touched upon earlier and it is important to note that costs and benefits need to be determined.

Risks can be transferred. This is usually done by purchasing insurance and transferring risks to this third party. Again, insurance can be expensive and you still may be required to maintain controls on the asset to the level of risk acceptance that the insurance company carries. This risk level may be more stringent than your company's risk level, so a cost/benefit analysis should be taken into consideration.

The activity that gives rise to the risk can be eliminated. If the activity is no longer being performed, then there is no longer a risk in that activity.

Risks can be accepted. It is common practice that any residual risk rated medium or high after mitigation efforts have been introduced should be formally accepted by the leaders of the organization (i.e., the president, board of directors, etc.). The rationale behind this decision should also be properly documented.

3.4 Tracking

After the follow-up meeting has been conducted and decisions have been made, a system should be designed to track these issues. A spreadsheet or database will assist in tracking these items. In addition, a mitigation tracking report should be established and given to the board of directors on a monthly basis. This tracking report will include summary details of issues found and the course of action being taken to correct these issues. As the issues are completed, it is important to note them so that the board of directors sees that improvements are being made. In lieu of a board of directors, the president of the company should want to see this report.

3.5 Conflict Resolution

It is important to note that individuals have different views and perspectives. There will most definitely be some issues when the risk assessment report comes out and findings or vulnerabilities are noted. Some executives may feel that the report is a personal affront to their departments or job responsibilities. This could not be further from the truth. Everyone working for the company is responsible for making the company stronger and this report should be treated as a means of making things better.

In some cases, an item on the risk assessment report may not be viewed as important or as a lower risk than what is calculated. The assessor should be able to document and justify why the finding or vulnerability was noted as such. The assessor may have to give an example or actually exploit the vulnerability to demonstrate the effect it would have on the system or the company as a whole. The methodology described previously is sound; if it is correctly followed, it will take a lot of the opinions and subjectivity out of the equation. Again, it is not a perfect system, but it is effective and can be a valuable tool if appropriately utilized.

It is strongly recommended that if an agreement is not reached and the finding is such that it can cause harm to the company, the issue should be taken before an executive committee, the president, or the board of directors. It is important to note that policies or procedures surrounding the risk management program should include steps regarding this conflict resolution. Remember that executives are ultimately responsible for the security of their organizations.

3.6 Test Plans

A schedule should be designed to test the controls of the system on a regular basis. This should take place at least yearly, but may occur more frequently depending on how often the system changes. At any time at which a major change to a system occurs, as defined by your organization, a risk assessment should be performed on the system. Because the initial risk assessment has already been done, it should be easier to make changes to the existing system. If tracking of mitigation efforts took place throughout the process and a proper change management process was done, the risk assessment should dovetail off this and should be fairly easy to produce.

It is important, however, that the assessor not assume that he or she will find the same things that were found before. Thorough testing should still be performed as it was initially done and a comparison should be made of any differences, as well as a comparison between the two results.

3.7 Summary

In this chapter, we discussed the eight steps in the risk management process. We went through system characterization and threat identification, identifying vulnerabilities, conducting a control analysis, and determining the likelihood of events' occurring. We determined the impact ratings using predefined formulas for pre- and postmitigation efforts. We determined the effect of that loss of confidentiality, integrity, and availability of an occurrence may have on our operations.

In addition, we discussed the methodology behind conducting a technical evaluation plan as part of our risk assessment. We looked at the 10 different areas that the TEP covers and the requirement of using at least two different types of tools to test or collect evidence of the sufficiency of the controls in place. We further discussed the different components that should be included in an executive summary of a risk assessment report and the follow-up requirements.

Documentation and tracking of efforts to mitigate risk are important to demonstrate your compliance efforts and information security governance activities. We discussed how to resolve conflicts between the findings and aligning information security goals with business objectives. Finally, we completed this chapter discussing certain test plans that should be in place for the continued effort of improving the information security program.

Reference

Stoneburner, G., Goguen, A., and Feringa, A. 2002. *Risk management guide for information technology systems.* Falls Church, VA: Booz Allen Hamilton Inc.

Chapter 4

Physical Security

Objectives

- Explain and understand access control systems and methods.
- Describe the difference between Discretionary Access Controls (DACs), Mandatory Access Controls (MACs), and nondiscretionary access controls.
- Describe the different classification of access controls: administrative access controls, physical access controls, technical access controls, and logical access controls.
- Understand the importance of auditing.
- Conduct a physical security assessment.
- Understand important elements of alarm systems and surveillance systems.
- Explain some special considerations for server and records rooms.
- Describe some preventive equipment maintenance activities that should be done to your systems.
- Explain the proper steps in destroying paper and electronic media.
- Describe the differences between passive and active information gathering and how to conduct each.

4.1 Access Control Systems and Methods

Throughout the next sections of this chapter, we will discuss what is involved in conducting a physical security assessment. One of the most important aspects of any information security program involves physically securing the company's assets. We will examine the access control systems and methods. This area examines the types of controls implemented around the physical access to the facility. We look at where the company's valuable information is physically stored and who has access to these areas. Is your company utilizing metal keys and locks on the door to protect restricted areas? Is your company a little more advanced and utilizing an electronic badge system to monitor this access? Think like a criminal and ask yourself how you would go about getting into a certain area where you were not allowed.

Whatever method your company chooses to restrict physical access, you should consider the following: First, you should consider the policies or procedures you have in place to authorize your employees to gain access to your facility. Do you train your employees on proper policies regarding access control? Do your employees allow "piggybacking"—holding the door open for others to access your facility? Do you require each individual person to utilize his or her badge or key to access your facility? If your company is using punch cipher codes (these types of locks require a known code to authenticate entry), is someone able to look over an employee's shoulder to get the code?

Do not assume that these types of access controls are impenetrable. For example, key locks have been around for a long time. It was assumed that a key was an authorization token; the mere fact that someone had possession of a key meant that the person had authorization to be in the area to which the key allowed access. One of the most common types of key locks is the tumbler lock. Without going into the technical aspects of locks, a tumbler lock works off the principle that a key is cut at different depths. These keys uniquely match their corresponding locks. A vulnerability to these types of locks is to utilize lock-picking techniques. These techniques attempt to exploit the mechanical makeup—a flaw inherent to locking mechanisms. Lock manufacturers employ different mechanisms to prevent lock picking in an attempt to make their locks better or more difficult to pick. As these new locks are developed, individuals craft their skills to overcome these prevention techniques. As new lock-picking techniques or devices are employed, the manufacturers must find ways to overcome these vulnerabilities. The cycle never ends.

For many years it has been assumed that physical access to a key is required to make a duplicate of that key. In fact, it has been recently proven that an individual can take a picture of a key from a distance and be able to recreate a duplicate of it. With the enhancement of technology—specifically, with cameras, sophisticated software, and cutting devices—a key can be created without having physical control of the key.

What can you do to protect your company? It is imperative that you make your employees aware of these types of threats and train them on the company's expectations pertaining to the proper procedures on gaining access to your facility. Another important point related to this awareness is that your employees should

Table 4.1 Access Control Matrix

Database Object	Read	Write	Execute	Change
Administrator	X	X	X	X
Power user	X	X	X	
User	X		X	

accept and take personal responsibility for the access your company allows them. Does your company make your employees sign an agreement or acknowledgment of acceptance of this responsibility?

Finally, your company should verify that any extra keys to your facility are kept in a secure location accessed only by authorized individuals. There should be an inventory key sheet along with a list of all extra keys being stored. All keys should be accounted for and a regular review should be conducted of this inventory sheet. Any discrepancies should be reported to management and investigated immediately.

Once physical access is reviewed, we move on to the technical side. In our access control systems and methods review, we also take a look at access levels that your employees may or may not have on their workstations. Although most software developers have made great improvements in their applications, some software does not work properly under restricted accounts. Some applications require users to have local administrative rights on their system. This creates a huge vulnerability, especially if the user also has access to the Internet. The user can download and install all types of malware programs such as key loggers or viruses. Unless some other controls are in place to restrict the types of software or programs allowed to be loaded on the system, attackers can use this as an avenue to gain access to your network. Does your IT department utilize any tools to monitor the software that is loaded on your systems? Is all software loaded on the systems properly licensed to the company?

4.1.1 Discretionary Access Controls (DACs)

There are a few access control models that can be used. One of these is the *Discretionary Access Control* (DAC). In this model, information owners give or assign rights to objects. Objects may be folders, files, directories, or other items that require access controls on them. The access is restricted based on the authorization granted to the user. Some operating systems such as Unix, Windows, Netware, Linux, and Vines use discretionary access controls through the implementation of Access Control Lists (ACLs). An access control matrix can be utilized to visualize the rights held by users to an object. Look at Table 4.1 for some examples. These rights are based upon classification and can be one or more of the following:

- *Read:* user may list the object's content, but cannot make any changes to the object.
- *Write:* user may add, delete, or make changes to an object's content.
- *Execute:* user may search, read, or execute the program of an object.
- *Change:* user may add, delete, read, write, or execute the program of an object, but cannot change the control permissions assigned to an object.

4.1.2 Mandatory Access Controls (MACs)

A *Mandatory Access Control (MAC)* assigns sensitivity labels or security labels to objects. Every object is given a label and only users that have rights to certain labels may access the object. In this form of access control, changes to object levels are based on predetermined rules and are made by administrators, rather than information owners, as in the DAC model. Generally, MAC is more secure than DAC and is used in highly sensitive environments. See Table 4.2 for some examples of the types of security labels utilized in the military and in commercial business.

4.1.3 Nondiscretionary Access Controls

Nondiscretionary access controls (or *role-based access controls*) are based on the user's role in the organization. This is best used in companies with a high turnover rate. It is a lattice-based structure determined by the sensitivity level assigned to a particular role.

4.1.4 Administrative Access Controls

There are several different categories of access control: administrative, physical, technical, and logical. Administrative access controls generally involve management and deal with the administration of personnel. Examples of administrative access controls include policies and procedures, separation of duties or rotation of duties, awareness training and knowledge testing, background investigations, and work habit audits, testing, and review of the supervisory structure.

Table 4.2   Security Labels Examples

Military Security Labels	Commercial Business Security Labels
Top secret	Confidential
Secret	Proprietary
Confidential	Corporate
Unclassified	Sensitive

4.1.5 Physical Access Controls

Physical access controls generally focus on controls that can be physically touched or have some physical device to provide the type of control under review. Examples of physical access controls include network segregation, physical and logical segregation, perimeter devices, guards, fences, lighting, alarms, computers, locks, removable CD-ROMs, work areas, data backup, and cabling.

4.1.6 Technical Access Controls

Technical access controls, as the name implies, deals with technical controls that are primarily implemented through software or programs. Some examples of technical access controls are antivirus software, encryption, transmission protocols, network architecture, passwords, intrusion detection systems, and network access.

4.1.7 Logical Access Controls

Logical access controls, unlike physical access controls, cannot be physically touched. These types of controls primarily focus on the logical structure or framework in place at the company. They look at the thought processes that went into the creation of the controls in place. Some examples of logical access controls include system access, network architecture, network access, encryption and protocols, and auditing and control zones.

4.1.8 Common Access Control Practices

Several control practices are available and can be found in the security framework utilized at the company or through industry best practices that we discussed earlier. Some common access control practices include denying anonymous access, limiting or otherwise monitoring administrator accounts, setting unsuccessful log-in attempts to a low number, removing old or unused accounts, enforcing least privilege access rights, changing default passwords, enforcing password changes, and sanitizing or otherwise destroying physical media.

4.1.9 Auditing

One of the most important access controls that a company can implement is auditing. To describe what auditing is, let us first define a few terms used by auditors. The first term to understand is an *event,* which is any activity that can be logged in some form. Some examples of events are system events, which occur to the operating system; application events that occur to specific applications; or user events such as unsuccessful log-ins or elevated privilege activities.

Another term to understand is *logs,* which are the records of events and usually include date, time, and user ID. These logs form an *audit trail,* which is an electronic record of access and operations performed on a computer system.

To conduct efficient auditing exercises, access controls are monitored. We can monitor these controls in several ways. One is to utilize an Intrusion Detection System (IDSs), which looks for unusual activity or events on the network. This system may use predefined signatures of known unusual activity or will get a baseline of the systems monitored and work off of differences or anomalies of those systems. An IDS can be set up network wide or on a specific host. An IDS can be passive, by just monitoring activity, or reactive. When an IDS becomes reactive, it turns into an Intrusion Prevention System (IPS). An IPS takes certain defined actions when certain events occur.

For example, to test some of the controls in the physical security realm, walk around your facility and verify that all restricted doors are locked. Observe employees entering and exiting the building and note whether they hold the door open for others. If you utilize an access badge system, do you have a policy that states all employees should utilize their own cards to enter and exit the facility? Sample some workstations by looking at the programs installed on these systems. Verify that this software is appropriately licensed to the company. Note whether the sampled user has the appropriate rights assigned to him or her or has administrative rights to do basically anything he or she wants to do on the systems. Do you allow your employees open access to the Internet?

4.2 Physical Security

Without reliable and properly secured facilities and personnel, your organization's ability to conduct business would be diminished. Likewise, the preservation and enhancement of your organization's reputation are directly linked to the manner in which your facilities and personnel are managed. Therefore, maintaining the safety and security of your organization's assets are of paramount concern.

A physical site assessment is one way in which you can determine the level of physical security implemented at your facilities. As always, we utilize a risk-based approach to this assessment. This methodology was adapted from information provided by Mary Lynn Garcia in her book, *The Design and Evaluation of Physical Protection Systems* (2001).

Specific to physical security assessments, we develop a *threat matrix.* For this matrix, we classify *threats* as *outsider threats and insider threats.* Outsiders may include terrorists, criminals, extremists, or hackers. Insiders are defined as anyone with knowledge of operations or security systems who may have unescorted access to your organization. We also determine the motivational level of each. Motivations that might prompt attackers to undertake criminal actions against the organization can be grouped into three broad categories:

- *Ideological* motivation is linked to a political or philosophical system. This group includes terrorists, anti-nuclear extremists, and certain groups of philosophical or religious fanatics.
- *Economic* motivation involves a desire for financial gain.
- *Personal* motivation is specific to specific individuals. Examples of this may be in a form of recreation, such as hacking attempts, or drugs and alcohol dependencies, which can be to blame for others.

Table 4.3 demonstrates the greatest areas of concern. It ranks the likelihood of the potential actions of specific threats from low likelihood of the event happening to high expected likelihood of the event happening. It ranks the motivation of the attacker from low or not being motivated to attack to being highly motivated to attack the organization. It also lists some possible capabilities of these attackers. This is just an example to describe the thought process involved in creating a threat matrix. Your organization is unique and may have many other different types of attackers with varied motivations and capabilities (Garcia 2001).

After we complete the threat matrix, we must develop a risk level and consequence matrix. We utilize the following equation to determine the risk level and consequences seen in Table 4.4:

$$R = P * [1 - (P_1)] * C$$

where

$R =$ risk to the facility of an adversary gaining access to or stealing critical assets. (Value ranges from 0 to 1.0, where 0 is no risk and 1 is maximum risk.) Risk is measured for a period of time, such as 1 year or 5 years.

P (default is 1; this assumes the attack will occur) = probability of an adversary attack during a period of time. (Value of 0 is no chance at all of an attack; 1.0 is certainty of attack.) P is sometimes considered a conditional risk, and it is assumed that an attack on a facility will occur.

$P_1 =$ probability of interruption (calculated from the estimate of adversary sequence interruption [EASI] detailed next.) This is the probability that the defined adversary will be interrupted by the response force in time to stop the attack. (Value of 0 means the adversary will definitely be successful; 1.0 means adversaries will definitely be interrupted in their path.)

$C =$ consequence value. This is a value from 0 to 1 that relates to the severity of the event. This is also known as the normalizing factor.

This physical security site assessment looks at the EASI method, which calculates the probability of an interruption to an adversary's sequence of actions aimed at a particular crime. These sequences are broken down into individual tasks with given times of completion. The EASI is the probability that the response force will be notified when sufficient time remains in the sequence for the response force

Table 4.3   Threat Matrix

Outsider Threat	Type of Attacker				
	Terrorist	*Criminal*	*Extremist*	*Hacker*	
Potential action (likelihood: H, M, L)					
Robbery	Low	High	Medium	Low	
Theft	Low	High	Medium	High	
Sabotage	High	Low	High	High	
Other (murder, vandalism)	High	High	Medium	High	
Motivation (H, M, L)					
Ideological	High	Low	High	Medium	
Economic	Low	High	Medium	Medium	
Personal	High	Medium	Medium	Medium	
Capabilities					
Number of people	1 or 2	1 or 2	<10	1 or 2	
Types of weapons	Explosives	Guns	Guns	None	
Equipment and tools	Minimal	Minimal	Minimal	Computer	
Transportation	1 or 2 Vehicles	1 or 2 Vehicles	Multiple	1 Vehicle	
Technical experience	Low	Medium	Medium	High	
Insider assistance	None	Possible	Possible	Likely	
Insider Threat	*Access to Asset*	*Access to PPS[a]*	*Theft Opportunity*	*Sabotage Opportunity (H, M, L)*	*Collusion Opportunity (H, M, L)*
Employees	Often	Often	Medium	High	High
Managers	Often	Often	High	High	High
Security guards	Seldom	Often	Medium	Medium	Medium
Vendors	Seldom	Seldom	Medium	Medium	Low

[a]   PPS = physical protection system.

Table 4.4 Consequence Matrix

High consequence	Murder	Sabotage	Robbery
Medium consequence		Theft	Collusion
Low consequence		Vandalism	
Probability of occurrence	**Low**	**Medium**	**High**

to respond. The response force can be on-site security guards or law enforcement response. The notification of the response force is called an *alarm*.

An adversary action sequence takes place along a path consisting of a starting point, a sequence of detection sensors, transit and barrier delays, and a terminal point. This is related to the same defense in depth concepts we discussed earlier in Section 2.10 in Chapter 2. The transits and barriers can be thought of as tasks the adversary must perform. Current versions of the EASI allow specification of where the detection sensors are located with respect to the task delays—before (B), after (E), or during (M) the task delay. Table 4.5 shows an example of an EASI for a robbery attack at a financial institution:

Table 4.5 Robbery EASI

Estimate of Adversary Sequence Interruption		Probability of Guard Communication	Response Force Time (Seconds) Mean	Standard Deviation
		0.95	300	90
				Delays (in Seconds)
Task	Description	P (Detection)	Location	Mean	Standard Deviation
1	Drive in front of building	0	M	10	3
2	Run to building	0	M	10	3.6
3	Open door	0.9	M	2	1
4	Run to teller line	0.9	M	2	1
5	Control-room demand $	0.9	M	30	2
6	Receive money	0.9	M	60	30
7	Run to vehicle	0.9	M	15	7
	Probability of interruption		0.020536116 or 2%		

Figure 4.1 models the facility by separating it into adjacent physical areas. Protection layers and path elements are defined between the adjacent areas. Detection and delay values are then recorded for each area to calculate the EASI. Table 4.6 provides the abbreviations used for each protection element along with a list of those elements per protection layer, as indicated from Figure 4.1.

Along with conducting a physical site assessment and going through the different exercises listed previously, you should also take some of the following into consideration: How many entry and exit points do you have in your facility? Are they all connected to the alarm system? Are all of your locks free of defects or do they need repair? Do you have floodlights on the exterior of your building and in your parking lot? Are they working properly? Do you have windows that can open and close? If so, are they also alarm contacted or are these windows equipped with glass-break sensors as part of your alarm system? Do you have access to your roof from the outside? Can someone use a nearby ladder to gain access to your roof? Is there access to the roof from the inside through a roof hatch? Is this roof hatch secured by a lock?

4.2.1 Alarm Systems

Alarm systems are essential and are one of the key detective controls. The objective of an alarm system is to detect unusual activity or security violations. The alarm system attempts to detect these at the earliest possible moment and with the best possible efficiency.

When selecting an alarm system, it is best to use a reputable company for the installation and monitoring of the system. You should conduct your reference checks on your alarm company and get recommendations from people you trust. Just like other pieces of equipment, your alarm system needs to be maintained properly and tested frequently to make sure it is working at its optimal level.

Of course, it should go without saying that the alarm system should be turned on and utilized. A formal procedure should be in place for the daily arming and disarming of the system. The system is worth nothing if it is not used as it was intended to be used.

In addition, the alarm system should be installed on all external doors and protect those interior doors that secure restricted or sensitive areas such as the server room and records room. The alarm system should also be equipped with glass-break sensors or motion detectors throughout the main hallways.

Remember that the system should be designed from the point of view of a criminal. The question that should be asked is how a determined criminal would access your facility. Are controls in place to protect these avenues of attack?

4.2.2 Surveillance Systems

Closely integrated with alarm systems are surveillance systems, which consist of cameras that capture real-time video footage of events that have taken place. Many

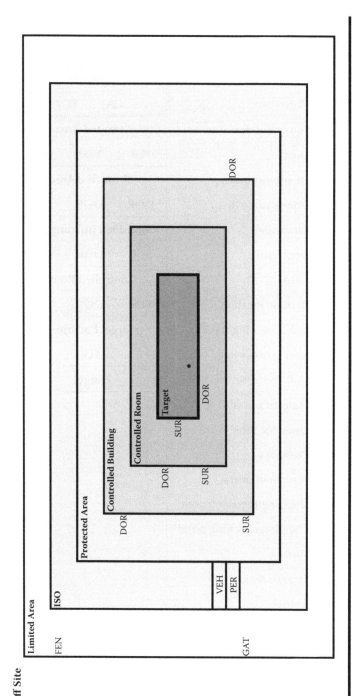

Figure 4.1 Adjacent physical areas model.

Table 4.6 Protection Elements

BPL	Bulk process line	**Off-Site**		
CGE	Cage	GAT	FEN	
DOR	Personnel doorway	**Limited Area**		
DUC	Duct	PER	VEH	ISO
EMP	Emergency portal	**Protected Area**		
EMX	Emergency exit	DOR	DOR	SUR
FEN	Fence line	**Controlled Building Area**		
FLV	Floor vault	SUR	DOR	SUR
GAT	Gateway	**Controlled Room**		
GNL	Generic location	SUR	DOR	
HEL	Helicopter flight path	**Target Enclosure**		
IPL	Item process line	FLV		
ISO	Isolation zone	**Target**		
MAT	Material portal			
OPN	Open location			
OVP	Overpass			
PER	Personnel portal			
SHD	Shipping/receiving door			
SHP	Shipping/receiving portal			
SUR	Surface			
TNK	Storage tank			
TUN	Tunnel			
VEH	Vehicle portal			
VHD	Vehicle doorway			
WND	Window			

different types of cameras can be used, but some of the major considerations should be the quality of the images and the sufficiency of the lighting in the areas covered by the cameras. Cameras should have a clear field of view: There should be no objects blocking the cameras or blind spots that could allow someone entry into the facility without being captured on film.

It is recommended that all entrances and exits be covered by surveillance that will allow you to view the faces of those that enter and exit the facility clearly. Cameras should also cover sensitive areas such as server rooms and records rooms. Cameras should also specifically view terminals in the server room and the cabinets that house the sensitive records in the records room. One of the main reasons for cameras covering the computers in the server room and the filing cabinets in the records room is to keep an eye on employees. Even though these employees are authorized to access these restricted areas, we want to make sure that they are using these areas in accordance with policies and not for their personal use.

Now that the cameras have been installed and cover all necessary areas, we need to make sure that the images are being recorded. Currently, the standard recording is in a digital format. This is done through dedicated computers with video cards installed that allow the direct storage and viewing of video images. Most of these Digital Video Recorders (DVRs) can be connected to the network to allow authorized remote viewing of images from anywhere within the organization. Due to the compression levels of some of the new video standards, large amounts of video imaging can be stored on relatively small amounts of disk space. This allows for more days of storage prior to the disk space being overwritten. You should always make sure that recorded video contains accurate date and time stamps and that the recording equipment is checked daily for proper operations. It is also important that recording equipment be kept in a secured location with proper ventilation.

4.2.3 Server Room and Records Room

Throughout our previous discussions, we have made a point to bring special attention to the server room and the records room. Some physical security requirements for both of these special rooms should be considered. Both the rooms should be in a restricted and secured area. They should have no other purposes than to store the servers and records. They should be locked at all times and the walls surrounding the rooms should go all the way up to the ceiling. You would be surprised to know in how many locked secured rooms someone using a small ladder can crawl over the wall and through the drop-down ceilings of these supposedly secure areas due to the walls not extending up to the ceiling like they should. Each room should maintain a visitor log and only authorized individuals should be allowed to access these areas.

Along with the access control of these rooms, we also need to be concerned with some environmental issues. We need to make sure that acceptable fire detection or suppression systems are in both the server room and the records room.

It is recommended that an inert gas system be used for the server room and a delay sprinkler system be utilized for the records room. There should also be adequate fire detection and suppression throughout the rest of the facility in the way of smoke detectors, fire detectors, heat detectors, and fire sprinkler systems. The servers should be located at least 3 inches off the floor and the room itself should not be susceptible to flooding. Battery backups or UPS systems should be installed to control power spikes and a tamper-resistant power-shutoff switch should be located in the proximity to turn off power to the server room in case of a fire.

4.2.4 Preventive Equipment Maintenance

In addition to the preceding environmental controls, a preventive equipment maintenance schedule should be in place. Let me assume that you own a vehicle and that, every so many months or so many miles, you take your vehicle in for an oil change or regular maintenance. Why do you do this?

One reason is because the vehicle may be under warranty and if this maintenance is not done and something goes wrong, your warranty may not cover the repair. Another reason is that you may be afraid that your vehicle may not operate like it is supposed to or break down over continued use. Either way, you want your vehicle to run in the most optimal way possible. The same is the case for servers (and even workstations). You must keep them in an environment that has low humidity and cooler temperatures and is free of dust—all defined by the equipment manufacturers. This will keep your warranty active, and your servers will be more likely to run efficiently and for a longer period of time.

The following is just a short list of suggestions to maintain a preventive equipment maintenance program (Cray 2002):

- *Physical server maintenance.* Conduct a physical examination of the systems, especially if they are in a separate physical location, on a routine basis. Make sure these systems are located in areas recommended by the manufacturer. You should check temperatures and relative humidity in these areas. Servers should also be checked for cleanliness such as dirt or dust getting into fans, power supplies, or other critical parts of the servers. You should use compressed air to blow the dust out of these components. Note: It is important that you never use a vacuum to suck dust or dirt out of the servers. A vacuum may accidentally suck "jumpers" off the servers. Jumpers are small connectors that sit on the motherboards of some servers. They are used to control some of the functionalities of the servers and, if lost, may cause damage to them.
- *Cables.* Check cables and neaten them up as appropriate. Cables can become loose and cause systems to drop off the network. They can also become pinched or crimped, causing issues with these systems communicating to

other systems on the network. Cables should fit tightly into their respective ports. Cable ties can be used to keep the cables in their proper raceways. The cables of proper length should be used to prevent stretching or excessive cable lengths. Different network infrastructures have different maximum length or run requirements and these cable lengths should be monitored to keep within these restrictions. This also allows for faster troubleshooting when cables can be easily traced.

■ *Tapes.* If you are utilizing tape drives, it is important that cleaning tapes are run on these drives on a regular basis. This is important for successful back-ups because tapes are susceptible to dust and dirt. They can also be damaged by overuse and stretching, which can cause issues with backups. For these reasons, it is important that tapes are kept in good condition.

■ *Diagnostic scans.* Many different types of diagnostic scanners that check components such as power supplies, hard drives, memory chips, etc. are available. Diagnostic scanners provided by the hardware manufacturers should be routinely utilized on these servers to determine any issues that need to be repaired or investigated further.

4.2.5 Destruction of Paper and Electronic Media

Another important aspect of physical security is the physical protection and destruction of paper and electronic media. Sensitive documents should be secured at all times and should not be left on desks unattended. These documents should be locked away in designated filing cabinets. If sensitive documents are no longer required and are not under retention restrictions, they should be shredded using cross-cut shredders or placed is secure shred/burn bins for later destruction. (See Section 6.6 in Chapter 6 for further information on the records retention schedule.) Electronic media should also be physically destroyed or securely formatted using a Department of Defense-approved wiping solution prior to being discarded or sold. Because it may be possible to recover data from electronic media that have only been formatted, the Department of Defense developed standards to wipe certain media clean of information and to make this information unrecoverable.

4.3 Social Engineering

Social engineering is a term used to describe a category of techniques used to trick people into performing some action or divulging some sort of sensitive information. It usually takes two forms. One is a passive form in which the attacker rarely sees or talks to the victim; the other is a more active approach to gathering or tricking individuals out of information. There are several forms of social engineering; the most common ones are listed next.

4.3.1 Phishing

Phishing is a term used to describe activities of criminals who utilize e-mail to masquerade as official entities to fool an individual into revealing user names, passwords, and possibly even credit card or bank card information. The activity usually employs e-mail or instant messaging that gets a person to go to a fake Web site and enter information. This fake Web site appears to be real and may include official logos, headers, or other related items that fool a person into divulging sensitive information.

4.3.2 Pharming

Pharming is similar to phishing, but without the lure. In pharming, the criminal may hijack resolving servers or plant certain files that, at a technical level, will direct the user to malicious Web sites. Without the use of e-mail or instant messaging, a pharming technique is more sophisticated and may require more technical aptitude to craft; however, it can be more serious because this type of attack does not require much in the way of user interaction. Again, this technique attempts to fool a user and get him or her to enter sensitive information into a fake Web site.

4.3.3 Vishing

Vishing is a new technique involving Voice over Internet Protocol (VoIP) in conjunction with social engineering to get sensitive information. Because it is believed that land line telephone services carry a level of trust, vishing attempts to exploit this trust by gaining control over VoIP servers. VoIP systems can now interconnect with landline servers, so they have become a target of attack. They can be manipulated through vishing attacks; this leads to caller ID spoofing to trick individuals into thinking that phone calls are coming from legitimate entities. Because these calls can be masked, it is difficult for law enforcement to trace or monitor the sources of these types of criminal activities.

4.3.4 Passive Information Gathering

A way to protect yourself from social engineering attacks is to conduct a Passive Information Gathering (PIG) exercise against your organization. A PIG attempts to identify well-known and common sources of information through the use of search engines and review of the organization's Web site, publicly available databases, and other related sources to obtain as much information about the organization and its operations as possible. The purpose of this exercise is to identify potential security vulnerabilities that can be exploited from information obtained from publicly available sources on the Internet. Vulnerabilities of this nature typically involve obtaining information that can lead an attacker to additional exploits such as social engineering, phishing, or other related attacks. The following four facets take place during passive information gathering exercises.

4.3.4.1 Facet One—Review Web Site

Using review of the organization's Web site, this facet identifies information that the organization provides to the public about its services, products, and operations. The information of interest includes, but is not limited to, job listings that list specific software, newsletters, and other information that provides an insight into the activities of the organization. Other areas to look at are press releases, white papers, design documents, sample deliverables, open positions, key personnel, contact information, etc.

4.3.4.2 Facet Two—Archived Information

In this facet, the publicly available Wayback Machine is utilized to review what type of information the organization may have posted on its site in the past. The same type of information in facet one is reviewed, but it is obtained from previous pages of the site that have been archived. The Wayback Machine is located at http://www.archive.org.

4.3.4.3 Facet Three—Information from Other Sources

This facet reviews other publicly available sources that somehow link back to the organization. These sources may consist of searching the EDGAR database of the Security and Exchange Commission (SEC), newsgroups, job sites, hacker sites, newspapers, magazines, and other related organizations. Google groups can also be searched by going to http://www.google.com/groups.

4.3.4.4 Facet Four—Google Searches

This facet reviews one of the largest search engines with specific search queries to obtain such information as site directives, link directives, related directives, info directives, cache directives, file types, and default Web materials. All of this information can potentially be utilized by an attacker for further attacks or exploits. Some Google searches can locate personal information of key personnel of your organization—for example, by using a general phonebook search: phonebook:<name>; business phonebook search: bphonebook:<name>; and residential phonebook search: rphonebook:<name>. Other Google search directives can be used, such as

- site directive: <phrase> site:<website>
- link directive: link:<website>
- related directive: related:<website>

- info directive: info:<website> (includes results from both link and related directives)
- cache directive: cache:<website>

File type searches on Google can be conducted by using the following command in the search field: site:<website> .<file type>, where <website> is the name of the site www.mysite.com and <file type> is the file extension, such as the following: .asp, .jsp, .php, .cgi, .xls, .ppt, .doc, and .pdf.

Many other Web sites can also provide information, such as

- www.anywho.com
- www.whitepages.com
- www.switchboard.com
- www.reversephonedirectory.com
- www.phonenumber.com
- www.smartpages.com
- www.samspade.org
- http://www.highprogrammer.com/cgi-bin/uniqueid

One of the best and most useful tools that I have found to conduct passive information gathering exercises is Maltego.

4.3.4.5 Maltego

The following is an excerpt from Maltego's Web site:

What is it?

- Maltego is a program that can be used to determine the relationships and real-world links between:
  - people
  - groups of people (social networks)
  - companies
  - organizations
  - Web sites
  - Internet infrastructure such as:
    - domains
    - DNS names
    - netblocks
    - IP addresses
  - phrases
  - affiliations
  - documents and files
- These entities are linked using open source intelligence.

■ Maltego is easy and quick to install. It uses Java, so it runs on Windows, Mac, and Linux.

■ Maltego provides you with a graphical interface that makes seeing these relationships instant and accurate—making it possible to see hidden connections.

■ Using the Graphical User Interface (GUI) you can see relationships easily—even if they are three or four degrees of separation away.

■ Maltego is unique because it uses a powerful, flexible framework that makes customizing possible. As such, Maltego can be adapted to your own unique requirements.

What can Maltego do for me?

■ Maltego can be used for the information-gathering phase of penetration testing, making it possible for less experienced testers to work faster and more accurately.

■ Maltego has fantastic applications in:
  – forensic investigations
  – law enforcement
  – intelligence operations
  – identity fraud investigation
  – identity verification processes

■ In fact, Maltego can be used by anyone who manages interrelated information.

Maltego is accurate, fast, and reliable. If access to "hidden" information determines your success, your company needs Maltego. (Paterva 2007)

4.3.4.6 Metagoofil

Metagoofil is another recent tool developed to conduct other types of passive information gathering exercises. This tool is a metadata analyzer. Metadata are the data stored about a file, but not the content of the file. They consist of dates and times when the file was created, the author of the file, the program used to make the file, and other information related to the file. This tool utilizes the Google file type searches discussed in Section 4.3.4.4 and runs an extractor program on the files it obtains. It presents the findings in an html report. Metagoofil can extract information from the following public documents: .pdf, .doc, .xls, .ppt, .odp, and .ods. More information about this tool can be found at http://www.edge-security.com/metagoofil.php.

4.3.5 Active Information Gathering

Active information gathering comprises techniques that go out and test systems or actively obtain information. This can be by active port scanning of a network to see what ports are open, conducting active tests to see what operating systems are running, or even contacting an employee and attempting to trick him or her into revealing some sensitive information.

4.3.6 Covert Testing

When a test or review of the effectiveness of your information security program is conducted, physical attempts should be made to try to obtain unauthorized access into sensitive areas. This covert testing exercise should be performed by trained and trusted security professionals. In the course of this testing, the professional will attempt to social engineer his or her way into the facility by tricking employees into letting him or her in. This can be done by having the professionals pretend to be authorized persons or even by just "piggybacking" into the facility by way of the generosity of an employee.

Through my experiences, I have had about a 90% success rate of conducting these types of exercises for my clients. I have found the most success by getting into the mind set that I belong at the organization. I dress the part and act as a fellow employee. I have had much success in using techniques such as talking on the phone when walking up to the employees' entrance, carrying multiple items in my hand, or waiting for individuals that may be carrying multiple items and offering to help them. I have also played the roles of new employees or vendors. Pretending to be a telephone repair person has allowed me to gain access into the telecommunications/wire rooms. It is surprising to see how little it takes and how trusting individuals are when it comes to letting unknown persons into a facility.

4.3.7 Clean Desk Policy

Every company should have a "clean desk" policy. In short, this policy states that when documents containing sensitive information are not in use, they should be locked up. At the end of the day, desks should be cleaned and no information should be readily available to unauthorized individuals. Although most areas of a facility are restricted to some extent, the company may still hire outside cleaning crews to clean after hours. Similarly to covert testing, the clean desk policy should be tested. This is a random check of desks and work areas conducted routinely to make sure that employees are securing sensitive information or destroying this information as required. You will probably be surprised how much information is available when not in use; I have found this to be one of the most eye-opening exercises for executives.

4.3.8 Dumpster Diving

I know you may be asking, "Why are we talking about digging through trash in this book?" The answer is that "dumpster diving," as it is technically called, is an important exercise to determine whether certain controls are being followed. This activity helps to determine that staff members are separating documents containing sensitive information from documents containing public information. It helps to determine whether shred bins are being emptied into the shredder or instead are just being thrown out as regular trash. It is important to determine what type of footprint the company is leaving about itself in terms of the information that can be compiled from sources such as trash bins. I realize that this may be a dirty job (no pun intended), but someone has to do it or the criminal elements will do it for you. It would be considered bad business if a news organization came across word that your company was just tossing away sensitive information in the garbage. This could have untold effects on your reputation and could lead to other legal actions.

In dumpsters, I have discovered sensitive information that the company thought was being shredded. The information that I found could have had some significant impact on my clients. As a good rule of thumb, dumpsters should be secured. Shred bins should be emptied every night and shredded in accordance to company policy. Employees need to be well trained and versed in distinguishing the type of information that needs to be shredded and the type that can be tossed in the regular trash. If there is any doubt, the best course of action is to shred it.

4.4 Summary

In this chapter we discussed one of the most important aspects of information security: physical security. As we have learned in other chapters, if an attacker gains physical access to any of your business assets, you no longer own those assets. We discussed different types of access control systems and methods such as discretionary access, mandatory access, and nondiscretionary access. In addition, we discussed different types of physical, technical, and logical access controls that can be implemented to secure your organization along with some common access control practices. No discussion about controls would be complete without an audit. An audit demonstrates the compliance or effectiveness of a control.

We further discussed specific details about physical security and some best industry practices regarding alarm systems, surveillance systems, server and record rooms, preventive maintenance, and destruction of paper and electronic media.

No matter how much is spent or how many technical controls are in place, nothing substitutes for the proper education and training of your personnel. Social engineering is a strong attack technique that utilizes the flaws inherent in trusting individuals. We discussed different types of social engineering techniques and some ways to prevent these attacks.

In addition, we discussed four different facets of passive information gathering and the importance of controlling the type of information that may be publicly available on your company. We also discussed active information gathering and covert testing scenarios. We never claimed that implementing information security was going to be easy or clean, and thus we discussed some dumpster diving activities that should be performed to verify that sensitive information is not going out with the trash.

References

Cray, A. July 17, 2002. Scheduled preventative maintenance, part 1. Retrieved February 20, 2008, from System Toolbox: http://www.systemtoolbox.com/article.php?articles_id=118

Garcia, M. L. 2001. *The design and evaluation of physical protection systems.* Woburn, MA: Butterworth–Heinemann.

Paterva. November 21, 2007. Maltego–Paterva: A new train of thought. Retrieved February 22, 2008, from Paterva with permission: http://www.paterva.com/web2/maltego/maltego.html

Chapter 5

Business Continuity Plans and Disaster Recovery

Objectives

- Understand the different phases involved in preparing a Business Continuity Plan (BCP).
- Understand the steps involved in conducting a business impact analysis.
- Conduct a business impact analysis on your company.
- Explain the differences in a hot site, warm site, and cold site.
- Explain the different types of backup processing.
- Describe the different types of tests that can be performed to test the business continuity plan.
- Understand complications involved in the business continuity plan.
- Understand the steps involved in preparing a disaster recovery plan.
- Explain the difference between Business Continuity (BC) and Disaster Recovery (DR).
- Understand the elements and areas of concern in a disaster recovery plan.
- Understand the important elements of both the BC and DR plans as they relate to providing training to your employees.

5.1 Business Continuity

A key component of a business is its survivability. This means that a business can survive and maintain a competitive advantage during rough financial or economic times. It also means that a business can survive accidental events that may cause detrimental effects to the business. To lay out the framework or structure for survivability, a company must have a Business Continuity Plan (BCP) in place.

A BCP is a formal, documented, and approved plan belonging to an organization describing its approach to responding to emergency events (both internal and external). A key component of a BCP includes a framework for executing critical business functions within an acceptable time frame and with minimal damage or delay.

Although many individuals think that business continuity is the same as Disaster Recovery (DR), there are some major differences between the two. Business continuity primarily deals with the maintenance of or continuation of revenue-producing activities, while disaster recovery usually focuses on the amount of time it takes for individual information systems to come back online after a significant event. Business continuity focuses on long-term disruptive events that can lead to major issues to the ongoing viability of an organization, while disaster recovery focuses on short-term events primarily related to the recovery of systems back to the most current state that they were in prior to an event happening.

Numerous books have been written just on these sections of business continuity and disaster recovery. We will attempt to summarize some of the important points and steps that should be taken when you design and implement your organization's business continuity/disaster recovery plan.

We spoke of some of the focus that business continuity planning takes into consideration, but what are some of the reasons why BCP is important to your organization? For starters, it is important to establish a BCP in an effort to be proactive and prepared for certain unexpected events. It allows the organization to take corrective actions when they are needed, even if managing personnel are not available. It saves time, stress, and money, and there is less chance that mistakes will be made during already stressful situations. A good BCP keeps the money coming in and minimizes the losses that may occur to the business. It also minimizes the effect on the organization's public image and loss of life. The BCP identifies necessary resources that are available when needed and can also cover legal requirements.

An essential part of the business continuity plan is to conduct a Business Impact Analysis (BIA) or assessment. We have already gone through a detailed methodology on risk assessments and a BIA is not much different. A BIA focuses on the "bottom line" of risks. If a risk will not have an appreciable impact on the organization, it is not important under a BIA. An impact analysis proves some of the information needed to develop an effective information security strategy.

A few standardized methods of performing a BIA have been designed through Control Objectives for Information and related Technology (COBIT), National

Institute of Standards and Technology (NIST), and the Software Engineering Institute's OCTAVE. All of these methods have one primary goal in mind: to determine the criticality of resources and the impact of events.

When you design your business continuity plan, it is important that you understand the Recovery Time Objectives (RTOs). An RTO is the amount of time a resource can be unavailable before severe damage is caused to the organization. To define the RTO, you must be able to identify the critical resources, the priority that these resources need to be recovered, and the interdependencies between these resources. The RTO is a critical factor in determining contingency process costs, and you will find that there is a breakeven point at which the impact of the disruption begins to be greater than the cost of recovery.

It is important that security always stays on the forefront in the minds of personnel, even when disaster strikes. You should always be aware of what is going on and even maintain least privileges as much as possible. In addition, you should have redundant systems in place, such as data backups, equipment, communications, facilities, personnel, and procedures. You should also consider purchasing a redundant power supply such as a generator that can last for at least 72 hours and that covers some of the critical areas of the facility, such as the server room, the alarm systems, and other surveillance or security systems.

We will now go into a detailed process that can be followed in designing your business continuity plan. Figure 5.1 outlines the process involved in completing a business continuity plan.

5.1.1 Phase 1—Project Management and Initiation

As stated previously, many of the same methodologies that went into conducting our risk assessment will go into developing our business continuity plan. Let us review just a few terms here as they relate to the BCP. As we already know, a threat is some event and a vulnerability is some form of weakness in our security. The risk, as the word will be used in our BCP, is the potential of a threat happening. We used a combination of quantitative and qualitative methods to determine the level of risks in our risk assessment. As a review, quantitative analysis attempts to place a value on assets. In terms of our BCP, we can analyze the loss of revenue, liability, other expenses related to a disruptive event, failure to comply with contracts, or violating regulations. We are estimating if we are using a qualitative analysis. In our BCP, this may be in terms of competitive advantage, market share, or public confidence. These are harder to place actual value on, but nevertheless are still important to consider when conducting business.

In the project management and initiation phase, we need to make sure that we have support or, as executives, provide this support to individuals assigned the tasks of completing the BCP. Again, this book was written to make the business case for support of the information security program. It is also important to maintain the awareness of the BCP and ongoing evaluation of the adequacy of this plan.

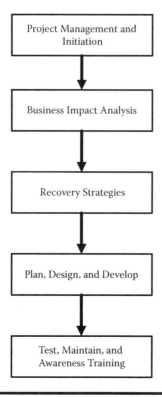

Figure 5.1 The business continuity plan process.

Just as we did in our risk assessment, we need to assess the threats that our organization faces. In relation to our BCP, these threats can be unauthorized access, hardware failures, facility events, natural disasters, loss of key personnel, communication systems failures, utility failures, etc. We need to be able to identify our critical business functions and determine what impact each of these threats poses and the probability that the event will occur. As an executive, you will be presented with an analysis and summary of these threats along with possible recommendations as to the remedial measures that can be utilized to lessen the event's impact on the organization.

5.1.2 Phase 2—Business Impact Analysis

To conduct an effective BIA, we will review a few topics that we have touched on earlier as they relate to the BIA. First, a BIA is a risk analysis with some additional calculations. A risk analysis looks at possible negative scenarios, looks at the possibility that these scenarios will occur, and then looks at the cost associated with the failures of systems caused by the scenario. BIA primarily focuses on the Maximum Tolerable Downtime (MTD) that a company can handle for each associated critical business function. By default, the MTD is considered to be around 30 days. Few, if any, businesses could sustain the loss of any critical business function for longer than 30 days. Maximum downtimes can be defined in the following ways:

Normal: under normal operations, resources such as water pipes or water lines should be down no longer than 7 days.

Important: resources considered to be important to the operations of the business, such as a server, should be down no longer than 72 hours.

Urgent: urgent operational resources, such as network cards, your authentication server, or maybe even your Web server for e-commerce activities, should be down no longer than 24 hours.

Critical: resources considered critical, such as the data center, should be down only minutes or less than an hour.

In this phase, we conduct a BIA by identifying the risks and their maximum tolerable downtime. We identify the minimum functional requirements that our organization requires to remain operable. We also attempt to put a quantitative value on our assets. All of these figures should be placed into a document that shows all of the possible outages (or threats) and the impact value they would have on your company. In addition, you will want to associate business functions with information systems and determine their criticality to the revenue stream. This will assist in identifying the operational and financial issues if these processes cannot operate at their optimal levels.

The impact of customer confidence, additional operating expenses, competitive advantage losses, and loss of revenue must also be placed in the calculations if a disaster occurs. Again, the primary focus is on determining the acceptable recovery time of processes considered critical to the business.

The following sections are a summary of how to perform a business impact analysis.

5.1.2.1 Step 1

Gather impact information related to economics and operations by utilizing a questionnaire and interviewing business owners that can identify critical business functions based on their potential losses. A critical business function is a vital function that the organization needs to operate or remain viable.

The best way I have found to perform step 1 is to identify each department or business unit of the organization. Once this is determined, have each department head fill out a questionnaire. I found the one provided by the FFIEC Business Continuity Planning Booklet of March 2008 to be pretty good, but your organization should modify the questionnaire accordingly. I have included a paraphrased copy of the questionnaire here:

1. How do business systems, business processes, business units, and software programs work together? Which ones are dependent on each other and could not function if this dependency did not exist?
2. What type of equipment is required to perform your business functions?
3. What type of backup do you have in place if the servers go down? How would you continue to function?
4. Are your systems redundant in nature or do you have single points of failure? What are the risks to these systems?
5. What vendors do you rely on to conduct your business functions? What would happen if your vendor is not able to perform?
6. Do you have service-level agreements in place with these vendors? What are their responsibilities? What are the company's responsibilities related to these service-level agreements?
7. What are some of the security controls that may be required to implement recovery procedures (e.g., different types of physical access to employees, different access levels to the network, access to certain systems that employees may not normally have access to, etc.)?
8. What are the minimum staff levels and what type of space is required for your business function at the recovery site?
9. What special forms or supplies does your business unit require at the recovery site?
10. What communication equipment does your business unit require?
11. If your business unit is sharing a common recovery site, how would this impact you?
12. Are all your employees cross trained for different business functions in your department?
13. Are defined backup procedures in place? Do members of your staff know their roles and how to perform these functions?
14. What are some of the personal needs of your staff? Have these adequately been taken into consideration?
15. During a disaster, will your department require some cash on hand to conduct its business functions? What would be some of the issues regarding cash management or liquidity?

Once the questionnaires have been completed, develop a list of all service providers or vendors. This list should include contact information, emergency contact information, minimum response times, service-level agreement information, systems with which the providers work, etc. This list should be dated and kept current when providers change.

Next, complete a list of all key personnel. Key personnel are defined as individuals that have a substantial role in the recovery or operations of the company. They are usually executive-level personnel; however, do not forget employees with special skill sets, roles, or functions in the company that are required for continuing operations of the company. The list should contain the department for which they work, home numbers, cell numbers, other emergency contact information, etc. Again, this list should be dated and kept current.

Through the interview process, you should be able to determine the different applications that are considered essential. A list of all software products should be compiled to include the systems on which they are installed, versions, vendors that maintain these applications, platform dependencies, costs, different features, users of the application, etc. This list should be dated and kept current accordingly. This list may be compiled from data obtained from your change management process, which we will discuss further in Section 5.3.

The company's critical data or information should be noted. These data should be classified according to your data classification scheme. A list should be developed to include the data, the classification, vendors responsible for the data (if applicable), departments responsible for the data, personnel responsible for the data (to include the business owner of the data), the criticality rating of this information, etc. The criticality rating of the data is set by the data classification. For example, your company may have data classified as public information, which would be valued at a criticality rating of 0; internal use valued at 1; confidential information valued at 2; and restricted information valued at 3.

In addition to the critical data, the hardware should be noted. A list of all hardware should be completed to include systems, types, asset numbers, value, processor, vendors involved with the system, the operating system, memory allocations, disk space, description, type of software and data stored on this hardware, etc. The business criticality rating of these systems should be performed. This will list the system from low (value of 0) to critical (value of 3). An adjusted criticality rating will be calculated based upon the criticality of the information or data stored on the system, as well as the system itself. For example, if a server contains a crucial database of the business, the adjusted criticality rating can be expressed as follows:

$$\text{Adjusted criticality of the hardware} = \text{the business criticality of the hardware} \times \text{the information criticality}$$

In our example, the business criticality of the hardware can be considered critical with a value of 3. The information criticality can be considered confidential information with a value of 2. The adjusted criticality of the hardware would be 6 (3 × 2). The adjusted criticality is used to determine the relative importance of a piece of equipment.

It is important that communications be available during an emergency situation. For this reason, you should list emergency communications. This should answer what type of communication is required to continue operations to include vendor information, department, and personnel responsible.

Every business has certain records considered to be vital for the continuing operations of the business. These vital records should be listed, such as loan documents, signature cards, policies, procedures, etc. Include vendor information, department, and personnel responsible.

As we will discuss in Section 5.1.4, several types of recovery scenarios are related to recovery sites or facilities. These facilities should be listed along with any vendor information if a recovery contract is set up with a third-party provider.

5.1.2.2 Step 2

You should now be ready to conduct a vulnerability assessment on the critical business functions. This assessment should define loss criteria using qualitative methods such as low, medium, or high or may use quantitative methods such as actual dollar amount of losses. The vulnerability assessment should assist in defining the critical support areas of the company.

During this step, you should be able to identify events, such as natural events, technical events, malicious activity, pandemics, and regulatory events, that may lead to exploitation of vulnerabilities of your business functions. From there, identify threat sources and link the threat events to these sources. Each threat should contain a specific threat description—whether it is internal, external, or both—and the possibility of occurrence. We have already given some definitions of this in Section 3.1.5 in Chapter 3. Now, identify threat actions and link the threat sources to these actions. You should also list any mitigating factors or controls that may be in place for each of the threat sources.

5.1.2.3 Step 3

An analysis of the preceding information should be conducted. You should now be able to document the relationship between business processes and their related information systems. You should be able to identify processes that are required to maintain the business's revenue stream and the financial impact to the business of the loss of these processes. The last part of this step is to meet with business owners to discuss and validate the documented analysis. You may need to make corrections accordingly in order to make these calculations as accurate as possible.

5.1.2.4 Step 4

At this point, you have reviewed all of the information gathered, analyzed this information, and validated the accuracy. You are now ready to identify the time-critical business processes that require restoration within a certain amount of time. This time is called the maximum tolerable downtime. You should also be able to document any other processes that may affect these time-critical business processes. Resources needed to support these processes should be identified.

5.1.2.5 Step 5

In this step, you will take the maximum tolerable downtime determined from step 4 and prioritize the processes. The business processes that require the least amount of MTD should be listed first. For example, a server that needs to be recovered with an MTD of 4–8 hours would be listed before a workstation that could be down for 24 hours.

5.1.2.6 Step 6

This is the final step of this phase; all information has been documented and should be presented to executive management, emphasizing key points. Executive management should review all information and approve these documents as necessary.

At the completion of this phase, you should have an idea of exactly how much it will cost the company if an unwelcome event occurs. You should be able to come up with recovery time frames and maximum allowable downtime for critical business functions. Some of these may include telecommunications, transaction processing, information technology, and other critical business areas. You will have an idea of exactly what functions need to be given priority and know what resources need to be operational first in order to maintain business functionality. Hopefully, upon successfully completing this phase, goals will be developed and ideas will be generated as to what steps need to be followed after an event and their order of occurrence.

5.1.3 Phase 3—Recovery Strategies

In the recovery strategy phase, we will look at specific strategies or plans that can be implemented to remediate some specific events. These events can include fire, water, electrical interruptions, environmental issues, backups, and emergency response plans. These remedial measures should take a team-based implementation approach and should be tested to make sure that the plan designed will work as expected.

To develop recovery strategies, the significant events that have already been determined throughout the previous phases should be utilized. Brainstorming activities can take place between the key business owners to assist in developing a consensus of what remedial measures need to take place. Because a business impact analysis has already been developed, the information gathered and the priority levels assigned should be the basis for developing recovery strategies. We will discuss recovery strategies in more detail in Section 5.2.

5.1.4 Phase 4—Plan, Design, and Develop

Although many of the specific steps and much of the information have already been gathered throughout the other phases, we should now put this information into a logical plan. As a review and to emphasize the important factors behind the entire business continuity project development process, you must provide management support. You must also develop a quality team that can come up with cost-effective solutions for recovery or mitigation efforts. The plan should be tailored toward mitigating exposures to threats and should be integrated into your risk management program. Understand that the BCP takes a lot of resources, time, and effort to be effective; however, as already explained, it is an essential part of your business. It may also be a regulatory requirement depending on the type of business you are in.

Some elements that need to be considered in the design and development of your BCP should be off-site storage facilities, fire protection, climate controls, security access controls, backup power, redundant equipment, communications, workspace, and office equipment. Utilizing the information gathered up to this point, the BCP should obviously include the critical business processes identified, the MDT of each, lists of vendors, incident response teams and team members, testing requirements, and exit plans.

Another element that should be noted in the BCP is alternate site locations. Essentially, a BCP will cover five types of sites: hot sites, warm sites, cold sites, reciprocal agreement sites, and mobile facilities.

5.1.4.1 Hot Site

A hot site is a fully operational site with identical equipment to carry on the critical services of the organization. Hot sites are usually fairly expensive due to the amount of resources required to maintain these facilities.

5.1.4.2 Warm Site

A warm site can usually be functional within 24–48 hours. Some equipment and communications systems may be in place. This type of site is used when an operation cannot be down for more than a week. It is less expensive to maintain than a hot site; however, it may take a little more time to get it prepped for operations.

5.1.4.3 Cold Site

A cold site is basically just a "shell" with no equipment installed. This site is usually the least expensive option and is used for operations that can be down for a week or longer.

5.1.4.4 Reciprocal Agreements

A reciprocal agreement is a way to partner with other businesses to provide reciprocal space in case of an emergency. Reciprocal agreements are not binding and they can be a little one sided when an emergency does occur. Your business may not be able to function fully by sharing the resources or space of another company. It is recommended to proceed with caution when entering into a reciprocal agreement.

5.1.4.5 Mobile Facilities

The use of mobile facilities is a recovery strategy that takes into consideration a "rolling" or mobile office scenario. These offices can be outfitted with emergency equipment and work area to keep some of the critical business functions going. Because they are mobile, they can be quickly set up and taken down anywhere that a disaster may strike. The cost of such facilities will vary, depending upon the resources and nature of these units. It is recommended that a cost-benefit analysis be utilized to determine if these mobile facilities are viable options.

5.1.4.6 Backup Processing

Backup processing should also be included in the BCP. Backup processing enhances an organization's ability to recover quickly. The three main types of backup processing are electronic vaulting, remote journaling, and database shadowing.

5.1.4.6.1 Electronic Vaulting

In electronic vaulting, bulk electronic data are transferred to an alternate location such as one of the recovery sites discussed previously. An advantage in this method is that the data can be sent to the recovery sites at specific times to manage resources better. For instance, the data can be transferred at night when other daily business processes are low.

5.1.4.6.2 Remote Journaling

In remote journaling, journals or data logs, rather than entire files, are transmitted to an alternate location. This process is usually done live and in parallel to other transactions when they occur. This method has a high level of fault tolerance and is usually the fastest way to recover because the databases utilized are synchronized with the most current data at both the primary and secondary sites.

5.1.4.6.3 Database Shadowing

Database shadowing creates duplicates of databases across multiple servers. This method may be more resource intensive because both databases and journals are transferred to alternate sites. This is normally done in real time as opposed to electronic vaulting done in batches at off-hours.

5.1.5 Phase 5—Testing, Maintenance, and Awareness Training

The final and probably one of the most important of all the phases is the testing, maintenance, and awareness training phase. In this phase, you will need to test the BCP to make sure it will work as expected. You need to keep the BCP current or updated if problems are discovered during the tests. You need to make sure that everyone is aware of what their responsibilities are during an activation of the plan, and you need to provide your employees with training on the BCP.

Testing the BCP proves the feasibility of the recovery processes. It ensures that the procedures developed are adequate, that they have been appropriately communicated to the entire organization, and that upper management is showing its support of the plan by directing the execution of these exercises. It is important that, once the test has been completed, an after-action review takes place and notes are kept so that the plan can be updated accordingly.

In the following sections, we will discuss some ways that a BCP can be tested.

5.1.5.1 Creating Checklists and Conducting Desk Checks

In this test, the plan contains easy-to-follow checklists for each role for each individual if the plan is activated. The test goes through each checkpoint in the order provided to verify that the instructions are correct and will accomplish the expected goal. This type of test is a preliminary test and is not sufficient by itself to validate the adequacy of the BCP. This is the most inexpensive and least resource-intensive test.

5.1.5.2 Walk-Through Test

In a walk-through test, representatives from each functional area meet to examine different scenarios and to test all phases of the plan. This test attempts to validate whether everyone knows what is expected of him or her in the event of a disaster and that the plan accurately reflects the organization's ability to recover successfully from an event. This test is less resource intensive than the live test.

5.1.5.3 Live Exercise and Simulation

Live exercises and simulations should be performed at least once a year and should include a mock event that will be played out and steps that will actually be performed by each employee. This test may also include unforeseen issues that will need to be overcome by the participants to carry out the BCP effectively. This test will continue up to the point of actual relocation to an alternate site; it gives a really good look at the effectiveness of the BCP.

5.1.5.4 Parallel Testing

Parallel testing is considered an operational test of the BCP and determines whether or not recovery can be performed at an alternate location. Systems that are restored at the alternate facility are compared against those that continue to run in parallel at the primary location to verify the validity of the process. The operations are not suspended at the primary location.

5.1.5.5 Full Interruption

This is a full-blown test of the BCP in which normal operations are shut down and the alternate site becomes the primary operating site. This test is by far the most effective to determine the quality of the BCP; however, business operations may be affected and this type of test is usually the most expensive and resource intensive.

5.1.6 Complications to Consider in BCP

Many unforeseen issues can arise, even when the best BCP is put together. Some of these complications, which should be included or taken into consideration when designing your BCP, follow.

5.1.6.1 Media, Public Officials, General Public, Police, etc.

When an event occurs, there should be a well-trained and well-spoken representative to coordinate the release of information to the public. All requests for information should be directed to this individual, who should be given the proper authority to speak on the organization's behalf. It is important that the right information is given to the media or public. It may be the case that the type of event will require police involvement and an active investigation may occur. If this happens, it is important that as little information be given to the public as possible and that law enforcement be consulted prior to releasing statements. It is also important not to be too protective of information, which might give the public a sense that the company is holding back or not telling the truth about the events. Effective media relations must include a quick response to an event that is delivered truthfully, openly, and with integrity. You may even want to have certain scripts developed ahead of time or take other preemptive measures so that responses do not have to be created on the fly.

5.1.6.2 Employee Relations and Family Relations

It is important that the organization properly manage its relationship with employees and their families. Of primary concern in any BCP should be the safety of the organization's employees. Not only should employees be protected physically, but maintaining salaries and benefits during serious situations should also be considered.

5.1.6.3 Protection against Criminals

Consideration should be made to include protective measures against looting, vandalism, and fraud. This may include hiring security to protect the primary and secondary locations from these criminal elements.

5.1.6.4 Legal Issues

The BCP should include measures to protect the organization from lawsuits. Legal counsel should be notified and proper steps should be taken to protect the organization and key personnel from civil suits depending on the type of event that occurred.

5.1.6.5 Financial Issues

In a disaster situation, how funds will be disbursed and the procedures that may change during emergency responses must be determined. Some items to consider may be where checks are stored, who has authority to sign these checks, how these types of expenses will be paid, and where receipts will go, as well as other accounting methods that need to be considered during an event. You should consider having backup authorizers in the case of primary or executive personnel being unavailable.

5.1.6.6 External Groups

As already touched on, it is important that the BCP contain notification procedures and escalation paths that have already been laid out and determined prior to an event. These notifications should include emergency responders, police, fire, utilities, customers, shareholders, and other related organizations.

5.2 Disaster Recovery

Disaster recovery is an important feature of any BCP. Disaster recovery strategies focus on five primary areas: business, facilities and supplies, users, technology, and data.

5.2.1 Business

The first area is business. Under DR as it relates to the business as a whole, we look at the MTD and the critical business processes such as IT security, administration, accounting, human resources, and legal. We also look at the relationship between the critical business functions and associated IT systems along with the system resource requirements such as equipment and network connectivity.

5.2.2 Facilities and Supplies

The second area that the DR strategy looks at is the facility and supplies. Under DR, primary focus is on the alternate sites, space requirements, physical security, fire protection, and the overall infrastructure. You must determine the minimum space requirements to recover critical as well as nonessential business processes. You must also focus your attention on utility and environmental needs such as power, heat, ventilation, air conditioning, and water supplies.

5.2.3 Users

The third area of DR focuses on users. You must take into consideration manual processes, records, and other employee needs. If electronic methods are not available, can your employees still work with manual forms? Are these forms available at the recovery sites? Can they still access necessary paper records until the digital records are restored in a disaster scenario? Can your employees get to work? Will they still have houses? How will they be fed? If key personnel are not able to get to work, are there sufficient backup documentation and other trained personnel that can cover and get the required systems operational? These are just some of the questions that must be answered as part of the disaster recovery strategy.

5.2.4 Technology

The fourth area focuses on technology. This area addresses telecommunications, network and data communications, subscription services, mutual aid agreements, and service bureaus.

5.2.5 Data

Last, but not least, are data. This area focuses on recovery of data back to a point in time as close as possible to the moment that disaster struck. Strategies in this area address critical data and software backups, off-site storage, and retrieval methods.

There are many types of disruptive events and most of them can be classified as discussed earlier under Section 3.1.2 in Chapter 3. As a reminder, we will list some of the common categories of disruptive events and some examples of each:

■ *Natural disruptive events* are not man-made. These events can occur suddenly and can completely incapacitate critical business functions. Examples include floods, tornadoes, earthquakes, blizzards, and volcanic eruptions.

- *Terrorism disruptive events* occur with man-made intentions. Few of us can forget the tragic events of September 11, 2001, and how they raised the terrorism threat to an all-time high. Terrorism is defined as actions that, through the use of force, are meant to influence government or to put the public in fear and are rationalized for political, religious, or ideological purposes. Examples of terrorist events include sabotage, espionage, bombing, kidnapping, germ warfare, or even cyberwarfare.

- *Technical disruptive events* may be malicious or unintentional. They can be part of terrorist activities or criminal activities. Examples of technical events include data corruption, device failure, power failure, telecommunication failure, hacking, defacement of Web sites, and remote exploitation of the network or network devices for some ill gain.

- *Accidental disruptive events* may be natural or man-made. They are usually sudden, unexpected, and unintentional events that can cause personal harm or property damage. Examples include fires, explosions, utility outages, vehicle collisions, and hazardous material spills.

- *Miscellaneous disruptive events* may be malicious or accidental. These types of events include human error, vandalism, hardware or software failure, and employee strikes.

5.2.6 Event Stages

There are five stages of an event that need to be addressed under our Disaster Recovery Plan (DRP). Some of these have already been discussed when we designed our business continuity plan, but they are listed here again for simplicity:

Stage 1—the disaster. In this stage, what actually happened is determined and analyzed.

Stage 2—initializing the emergency response. In this stage, the emergency response plan is activated; this may include notifying first responders, law enforcement, or other internal and/or external groups, depending on the event. The emergency declaration or heightened notification based on the notification levels of the event usually rests with the highest ranking executive involved in the event. As part of the disaster recovery plan, this should be decided ahead of time as part of the operation's chain of succession.

Stage 3—impact assessment. This stage is used to assess the real damage of a given situation, rather than the perceived or reported damage. As an executive, you may be asked to make some tough decisions and having an effective disaster recovery plan already laid out will assist you in making these decisions.

Stage 4—initial recovery phase. This stage gets secondary facilities up and running if applicable and gets the critical business functions back on line. Incident response team members should know what they should do to get the recovery process completed.

Stage 5—returning to normal business. This stage gets other nonessential business functions running and attempts to get business back to normal operations. This may include an extended stay at the alternate site or may call for the recovery of the primary site. The declaration to call an emergency clear should rest with the chief executive officer.

5.2.7 Disaster Recovery Testing

In comparison to the business continuity plan testing procedures, disaster recovery plans are more detailed and specific to certain critical business functions. The steps involved in testing the disaster recovery plan include determining test objectives, selecting appropriate tests, and making sure that all components of the plan are tested. These components may include software, hardware, data and voice communication, personnel, procedures, and utilities.

To conduct these tests you should read through the disaster recovery plan and think of ways this plan should be utilized. The plan should be reviewed when new business processes, technologies, or interruptions are discovered. Similarly to BCP testing, parallel system tests should be conducted on the DRP and objectives of these tests should be validated. To test responsiveness of contractors, vendors, or emergency response teams, random checks should be made to ensure 24-hour availability.

It may go without saying, but with the current availability of high bandwidth to almost all areas, remote operations should be considered a requirement. If events cause such disruption that employees are not able to get to the primary or secondary site, an alternative would be for them to work from home utilizing Virtual Private Network (VPN) technology. We will touch on this technology later in this book.

When disaster recovery plans are tested, consideration should be made for data backups. Here are some standard industry best practices:

■ Perform daily or incremental backups on all critical data and perform full backups of all systems at least weekly.
■ Make sure that backups are kept secure at another facility and, if tapes are used, make sure that these tapes are encrypted and properly inventoried.
■ Make sure that you are using systems that are redundant in nature—especially in the network—to prevent a single point of failure.

A DRP is considered effective and valid if the following criteria are successfully met:

■ Response to the DRP occurs within the allowable time frame.
■ Data backups are successfully restored to their previous levels just prior to an event occurring.
■ Alternate sites are operational and adequate to sustain critical business functions.

■ Incident response team members can perform all assigned duties and responsibilities during the emergency and they, along with other service providers, are accessible 24 hours a day.

5.3 Business Continuity Planning and Disaster Recovery Training

It is important that employees and key personnel be trained in business continuity and disaster recovery. These are the individuals that will most likely be involved in the preparation of the plan or carrying out the plan when it is put into place. In the next paragraphs, I lay out a training outline that you can use and modify for your organization. It also summarizes the goals of business continuity that we have been discussing.

As an overview of the BCP, it is important for the business to remain operational and viable following serious and unexpected disruptive events. Most businesses depend heavily upon technology to process information and to serve their customers. This technology needs to be recovered in the minimum possible time following a disruptive event. Backup and recovery of critical functions require a significant level of preparation and advanced planning. This is one of the reasons why a BCP has been developed. The BCP is designed to assist the business to manage a crisis in a controlled and structured manner. The BCP contains emergency contact details, mitigation strategies, emergency procedures, and a process to keep communications open during an event. The major elements of a BCP consist of succession plans or management backup procedures, damage assessments, and a BIA.

The BIA described earlier in Section 5.1.2 can be summarized into three parts. The first part of the BIA looks at specific items, such as departments, operating environments, key personnel, software applications and hardware, emergency communications, vital records, and facility requirements. The second part considers threats by identifying specific events, threat sources, threat actions, and mitigating factors. The third part of the BIA identifies critical functions. It determines the MTD, recovery point objectives (RPOs), RTOs, acceptable losses, criticality rankings, risk assessment, recommendations, and secondary functions or interrelated processes. Once a BIA is complete, a gap analysis should be performed to determine any deficiencies that exist between any existing BCP and the company's current policies and procedures.

Employees should be made aware of the critical business functions specifically identified by the company and that this was determined by the BIA. They should also be aware that the BCP is supported by senior management or the board of directors. They should understand that the enterprise-wide BCP contains multiple elements. The BCP is tested on a regular basis and changes are made to improve the process.

The process involved completing the business continuity plan, including conducting a BIA, risk assessment, risk management, and risk monitoring and testing. Certain individuals in the company will be responsible for the development, implementation, maintenance, and testing of the program. This can be assigned to one individual or, most likely, to a group of individuals. Completing a BCP may involve business line managers, risk managers, IT managers, facility managers, the Audit Department, etc. In addition, employees have responsibilities defined under the BCP that may be outside their normal scope of work.

Some of the responsibilities assigned to employees may include keeping procedure manuals up to date, assisting in testing, cross-training duties, safety training responsibilities, or maybe even personal hygiene training related to a pandemic. In any event, current emergency procedures should be posted in prominent locations throughout the facility.

In addition to these responsibilities, employees may be assigned to specific disaster recovery teams. Figure 5.2 shows an example of possible teams that may be involved in your company's disaster recovery procedures.

The company should have a business continuity policy in place. This policy establishes the framework to identify critical processes, assess risks, develop the plans, document thresholds, provide for testing and for training, and identify responsibilities and assignments of duties. The policy should include a scope. The BCP is an enterprise-wide scope that covers all business functions. It develops action plans for the reactivation of all vital services and components along with providing provisions for these services. For example, if a crucial third-party service provider is unable to provide the agreed upon services, the BCP should indicate other alternatives that the company has to continue operations without this provider. The policy should include when the BCP is updated. This should be done at least annually or within 30 days of a major change, as defined by your company. The policy should also include a statement detailing how it is to be reviewed and tested formally, as well as how the results of these tests are documented.

One of the areas of most concern in the BCP is for information services. The BCP should outline where data backups, recovery, restoration, and vital records are stored. Security of any off-site locations should be addressed concerning the storage of critical data files, software, documentation, forms, and supplies. Alternate procedures should be maintained reflecting any processing work that may require a manual process or alternative electronic processes. Procedures should be in place to back up or repair equipment along with getting power back online at the primary and secondary sites.

Another area that is often overlooked is the likelihood that the company could be significantly affected by a pandemic event. Pandemic planning should be considered as part of the BCP. This will include monitoring of potential outbreaks, educating employees, communication and coordination of critical providers, and providing hygiene training and tools to employees.

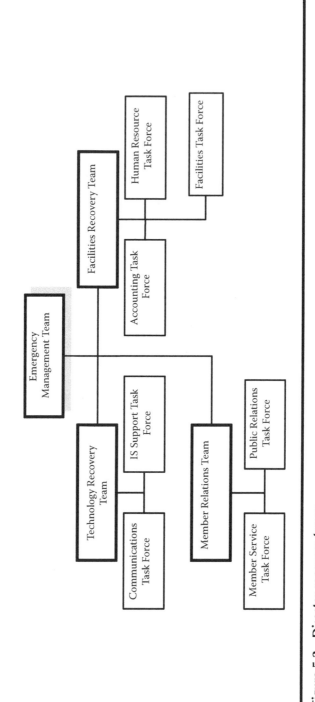

Figure 5.2   Disaster recovery teams.

In regard to risk monitoring and testing, testing policies should be drafted to state the expectations for testing, continuity functions, departments, support functions, and crisis management. A good testing strategy will consist of documenting test plans, developing scenarios, providing different methods of testing, setting up schedules, and defining expectations. Management assumptions should be confirmed and a cost-benefit analysis should be conducted prior to testing. Recovery and resumption objectives are important for testing and testing should be conducted throughout the enterprise. This testing should demonstrate employee readiness. Test results should be compared against stated objectives and deficiencies should be assigned to someone to rectify; these problems should be tracked until they are resolved. Recommendations should be made for future testing. In addition, tests should be observed by independent parties and any retesting should be conducted in a timely fashion.

5.4 Summary

In this chapter, we discussed the different phases and steps in developing business continuity and disaster recovery plans. An important part of any company is the sustainability of the company. A business continuity plan assists in providing documented, formulated, and tested processes to continue business operations during the occurrence of adverse events. A disaster recovery plan assists in detailing specific steps that need to be taken to restore critical systems to full service levels.

Throughout this chapter, we provided detailed instructions on producing a comprehensive business continuity plan that takes all important elements into consideration. We also emphasized the importance of testing and running through exercises to validate the effectiveness of these plans. Furthermore, we discussed one of the most important parts of a business continuity plan: specifically, conducting a business impact analysis. We discussed the importance of following a standard process to determine the importance of critical business functions and defined multiple elements for the efficient recovery of these systems and processes.

Reference

FFIEC Business Continuity Planning Booklet. March 2008.

Chapter 6

Administrative Controls

Objectives

- Understand the importance of change management.
- Explain the different phases and steps involved in change management.
- Explain the importance and the need for special skills involved in computer forensics.
- Understand the computer investigation model.
- Understand the steps and components involved in managing an incident.
- Explain some of the laws involved with computers and privacy.
- Understand the importance of the chain of custody.
- Explain why having ethics is so important in today's economy.
- Understand operational security controls—specifically, separation of duties, job rotation, and least privilege concepts.
- Understand records retention policies.
- Describe how to conduct effective security awareness training.
- Develop real-world examples of security breaches.
- Explain security management practices and some security countermeasures.
- Understand the complexities of vendor relationships as they relate to information security.
- Explain a Service-Level Agreement (SLA) and its importance.
- Describe how to conduct a vendor review.
- Explain the elements involved in conducting vendor assurances.
- Explain the elements involved in conducting due diligence.

- Develop a comprehensive service provider survey.
- Understand how to manage security risks in vendor relationships.
- Explain and understand the three tools in vendor relationships: due diligence, key contractual protections, and information security requirements.

6.1 Change Management

In this chapter, we will be discussing several different administrative controls utilized in your information security program. One of these controls is known as change management, or configuration management as it may sometimes be called. It is a mechanism by which the entire life cycle of a particular system is monitored. Change management addresses change controls and ensures that accountability is maintained with the responsible parties involved in the system. Change management involves a commitment to the continuous improvement of the system and requires that an audit be conducted after changes are made to the system.

Change management consists of a change control process that maintains the quality of the system by controlling the different versions of the system. When a change occurs on the system, the version is sequentially upgraded. These upgrades are required to be documented along with the changes that occurred to improve the system. If something occurs with the system or it is not functioning as expected after the change, there must be a way to revert the system back to an older version that was properly functioning.

The change control process normally involves three phases (discussed in the following sections): request phase, process phase, and release phase.

6.1.1 Request Phase

In the request phase of change management, requests are made for changes to an existing system. This is normally initiated by the users of the system because they work with the system all the time. In this phase, a review of the resources involved in the change will be conducted. A cost estimate will be produced and the request may be prioritized against other requests to determine which of them will be completed first. There should also be discussions involving the business need for the change and the return on the resource investment or difficulty of the change.

6.1.2 Process Phase

In the process phase of change management, we evaluate the change, develop coding or other programming to affect the change, test the change, and verify that the change is acceptable to proper operations of the system. These changes are normally conducted on test systems that are exact replicas of the original systems so as to maintain a good working baseline in comparing the changes that have taken place to the system.

6.1.3 Release Phase

The final phase of change management is the release phase. In this phase, the change is "pushed out" into production. This phase involves documenting the change in a sequential version of the system and concludes with the new version going "live" into a working environment.

When a sequential version of the system is documented, the version numbering usually keeps to a standard syntax. For changes that are tested internally, the version number scheme often uses an alpha designator. For changes that are tested externally, the version number scheme often uses a beta designator. You may have often heard of a software product being in beta testing. This means that the software has gone through most of the internal testing and is released to a select group in the public to be externally tested. Some issues with a beta product may need to be corrected prior to the final release to the public. The release version often uses whole numbers with decimals for interval releases. For instance, you may see a software version called version 1.01. A minor change to the programming may upgrade the version to 1.02. A major change or overhaul of the coding may upgrade the software version to 2.00 or 3.00 depending on the magnitude of the change.

6.1.4 Change Management Steps

The following are steps in performing change management:

1. Decide what the functional attributes of the changes should be and the business reason for these changes.
2. Decide what the physical attributes of the changes should be and the resources required (including cost) of the changes.
3. Make sure that information security is taken into consideration and a risk assessment is conducted on the changes, if necessary.
4. Assign a version number to the system (or software) if programming is conducted internally.
5. Assign the change control phases based on the functional attributes defined in step 1. These phases will be utilized to determine when testing should be conducted on the changes.
6. Audit the system on a continuous schedule to verify that any changes implemented have not created any unexpected results. Again, these changes should never be conducted on production systems.
7. If necessary, implement a version tracking system to track the changes, testing, and results of audits.

8. Once all key personnel and business owners agree that the changes are appropriate, deploy these changes to the production system.

9. Continue auditing the system on a scheduled basis and document results of these tests.

In summary, change management is a systematic process that should have a well-documented procedure for all changes to software upgrades, hardware replacements or additions, and/or any other system or business processes in place. Requests for changes should be approved by management. Documentation for changes should include procedures to recover to a previous version of the system if unexpected results occur. It is very important that these changes are properly tested prior to deploying them into the production environment.

6.2 Computer Forensics

Another important administrative control is the right to monitor or investigate the activities of your employees who utilize the network and systems your company owns. A great way to communicate this right is through the use of a log-on warning banner. You can review an example of one in Appendix C.

In brief, an effective log-on warning banner has four essential elements. First, it is imperative that you notify any users of your system that it is a restricted system utilized for the benefit of your company. It is important that potential users understand that they are required to have authorization to use company-owned systems. It is imperative that you notify these individuals that it is a violation of law to utilize the system in an unauthorized way and they can face criminal and civil penalties.

Second, you should notify your users that they should have no expectation of privacy when utilizing the system. As already stated, the system is supposed to be used for business purposes and the system is the property of the company. Third, along with no expectation of privacy, you should notify your users that the system is subject to monitoring and logging of activity. The system administrators can set up special programs to track user behaviors along with logging systems to determine specific user activities. System administrators may also be required to furnish these logs to law enforcement and cooperate with law enforcement in investigations of certain activities.

Finally, the system should provide the users the opportunity to make a decision of whether or not they want to abide by these rules or exit without logging in to the system. There should be an implicit consent that if the user continues to log in to the system, he or she agrees to comply with the terms of use, monitoring, and possible search of the system used.

In the case of investigating or monitoring user activities, computer forensics plays an important role. Computer forensics is "the preservation, identification, extraction, documentation, and interpretation of computer media for evidentiary and/or root cause analysis" according to Warren G. Kruse, II, and Jay G. Heiser, authors of *Computer Forensics: Incident Response Essentials* (2001). Computer forensics may also be known as IT forensics or digital forensics, and individuals that conduct this type of forensic work should have the proper training, certifications, and knowledge to handle such investigations.

> IT forensics is an investigation process that is rapidly becoming a field in its own[;] it is the process of identifying, preserving, and analyzing electronic data in a forensically sound manner, conducting examinations within the constraints of local law, in a reproducible manner, and compiling the results in such a way as to withstand courtroom scrutiny....Investigations are the sytematic and thorough gathering, examining, and studying of factual information that results in the factual explanation of what transpired. (Kleiman 2008a)

Digital forensics may be more technical than other types of investigations; however, the same forensic management processes apply. These processes ensure that any investigation is done within the scope of established procedures with the ultimate goal a report that will stand up to cross examination and be admissable in court.

Currently, there is a controversy in several states requiring Digital Forensic Experts (DFEs) to obtain a Private Investigator's (PI) license. Several other states have specific exemptions to PI licensing requirements. A recent resolution on computer forensics, dated August 11–12, 2008, was adopted by the House of Delegates of the American Bar Association. This resolution, number 301, urges

> state, local and territorial legislatures, state regulatory agencies, and other relevant government agencies or entities to refrain from requiring private investigator licenses for persons engaged in: computer or digital forensic services or in the acquisition, review, or analysis of digital or computer-based information, whether for purposes of obtaining or furnishing information for evidentiary or other purposes, or for providing expert testimony before a court; or network or system vulnerability testing, including network scans and risk assessment and analysis of computers connected to a network....the American Bar Association supports efforts to establish professional certification or competency requirements for such activities based upon the current state of technology and science. (American Bar Association 2008)

This is not a legal opinion, but it appears that the controversy over requiring a digital forensic expert to be licensed as a private investigator stems from two major facts. The first is that digital forensics is an accepted scientific discipline. This is proven through the formation of the Digital Forensic Certification Board (DFCB) by the National Center for Forensic Science, a program of the U.S. Department of Justice, Office of Justice Programs National Institute of Justice, hosted by the University of Central Florida (visit http://www.ncfs.org/dfcb/ for further information on professional certification for digital evidence practitioners). There is also the formation of the Digital and Multimedia Sciences (DMS) section of the American Academy of Forensic Sciences (AAFS) on February 20, 2008. It had been 28 years since the last AAFS section was formed.

The second part of the controversy appears to stem from the possibility that it may contradict federal rules of evidence. In *U.S. v. Ganier* 6th Circuit Nov. 15, 2006, an IRS special agent who was a qualified computer forensic specialist was offered by the government prosecutor as a fact (lay) witness. In her opinion, Judge Moore recognized that, although many computer applications are common knowledge, the ability to interpret the output of forensic software required qualification as an expert witness under FRE 702. It is therefore the responsibility of the court to determine if the witness is qualified, if appropriate scientific principles were utilized and applied to the matter at bar. (Kleiman 2008b)

There are a number of other reasons that digital forensic experts seek to be exempt from the PI statutes, but the overriding one is that a DFE and a PI have different roles, responsibilities, education, and training:

1. A DFE is a forensic scientist who, by his/her knowledge, skill, experience, training, and/or education, assists courts in understanding digital evidence and/or in determining facts based on digital evidence. If a DFE is required to obtain a private investigator license, then all forensic scientists should be licensed.

2. A DFE also serves in other capacities such as litigation support, electronic-discovery services, information security, computer network security, and video data analysis. These professionals are also monitored by courts (as expert witnesses) or by businesses (as owners of the data) and their attorneys.

3. Requiring a DFE to be licensed as a private investigator may:
   - Provide false assurance to consumers that a PI is qualified to offer digital forensics services.
   - Provide false assurance to consumers that a DFE is qualified to conduct private investigations.
   - Reduce the effectiveness of law enforcement investigators who might seek and rely on assistance from a private sector DFE, especially one that may be located [out of state].
   - Create conflict and confusion with respect to the roles and responsibilities of a DFE versus a PI.
   - Diminish citizens' access to justice through the diminishment of the available pool of qualified DFE persons who are not licensed PIs and have no desire to obtain a PI license and/or conduct the typical work of a PI.

4. Unequal regulation by states requiring a DFE to obtain a private investigator license will be costly and burdensome to litigants and may conflict with the Federal Rules of Evidence [as discussed earlier].

5. The cross-border nature of computing and telecommunications demands flexibility in digital evidence collection. State PI licensing statutes, on the whole, do not address problems with jurisdiction and reciprocity, and may impede the collection of digital evidence. (Kleiman 2008b)

As a special note of reference, the preceding information was composed from letters sent to legislative bodies of state written by Doug White, a professor at Roger Williams University, and Gary Kessler, a professor at Champlain College. Professor White was able to obtain the first PI exemption for DFEs in Rhode Island.

In the end, a digital forensic expert must be able to provide expert witness testimony:

> An expert witness is a witness having "special knowledge" about which they [*sic*] are to testify[;] that knowledge must generally be such as it is not normally possessed by the average person. This expertise may derive from either study and education, or from experience and observation. In the U.S. court system, an expert witness must be qualified to testify as such. To qualify they [*sic*] need not have formal training, but the court must be satisfied that the testimony presented is of a kind which in fact requires special knowledge. *Note: Qualifying as an expert witness is a grueling process! If budget allows, the forensic specialist should be able to devote, in some cases, large blocks of time on an investigation, and needs to be dedicated to the task and not responsible for other non-case-related duties.* (Kleiman 2008a)

> More often than not, the involvement of the Computer Forensics [CF] expert [or digital forensic expert] only occurs as the result of an ongoing investigation carried on by a third party—not by the CF expert [DFE]. In other words, the CFE [DFE] does not set out to investigate an individual. That decision is taken by someone else, who then proceeds with their [*sic*] investigation. During said investigation, this third party may decide that a hard drive, a computer, or any other digital media may contain information that would pertain to the investigation, and require the services of a CF expert [DFE]. A CFE [DFE] provides technical expertise in a supporting role to an ongoing investigation. (Jacquet 2007)

> Computer-related evidence is like any other evidence you might find with one exception: It tends to be very volatile and can easily be damaged or destroyed. Handle all computer equipment with extra care and

follow documented procedures for preserving computer and electronic evidence. Following documented procedures gives you some ammunition in court if a defense attorney wants to get your evidence thrown out of court because of potential mishandling. It is advisable that only officers with sufficient knowledge and hands-on computer experience deal with computers, peripherals, diskettes, programs, etc., as well as with other technical or specialized equipment, during the execution of a search warrant and subsequent examination of the seized property. (Diliberto 1996)

Policies regarding Computer or Digital Forensics must be in place to support your team. Digital Forensic policies should include the limitations and scope of authority for each role of your forensic team members. These roles should be well defined and indicate who has authority over what areas of the case. There should be a requirement for a communication plan, chain of command, chain of custody, basic IT controls, and guidelines for forensics recovery. The policy should specify the type of training that team members should have and the type of testing that may be conducted during an investigation. The policy should also cover reporting structure, jurisdiction, data and media control, privacy, and audit trails. The policy needs to be well documented and contain version control as it is updated on [a routine] basis and when new technology in the Digital Forensic field is developed. Finally, the policy should address how to handle variations to policy, framework, and established procedures. (Kleiman 2008a)

6.2.1 Computer Investigation Model

Some of the same processes used in disaster recovery are also followed in the computer investigation model. You will probably find it beneficial to include the computer investigation model and forensics process in your disaster recovery plan. This model creates a logical flow of the elements involved in computer forensics as seen in Figure 6.1, including

- *Assess the situation* to determine the scope or magnitude of the incident and the proper course of actions that should be taken: first, to prevent further damage or access to the system; second, to capture evidence or protect logs of the event; and, third, to restore the system back to its original state just prior to the event's taking place.
- *Acquire the data* to protect and preserve the evidence in its original form.
- *Analyze the data* to relate evidence to the event in an effort to prosecute the attacker.

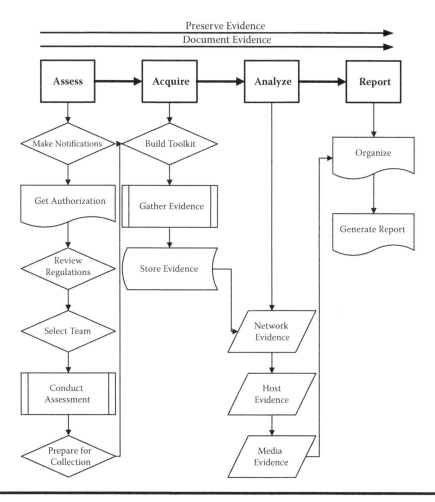

Figure 6.1   Computer investigation model.

■ *Report the investigation;* this may have occurred earlier in the process per your organization's policies and procedures. However, it is listed here in this order to make a note that throughout the process, important facts need to be documented and the final report should be written to tie all the evidence together to prove certain activities of the event.

One of the most well-respected organizations for computer forensic experts is the International Society of Forensic Computer Examiners (ISFCE). The ISFCE is responsible for the Certified Computer Examiner (CCE) credential that is recognized as a prerequisite for those individuals conducting computer forensics in certain states. As stated before, computer forensics is a highly advanced topic beyond the scope of this book; however, if you are interested in additional information, you can go to the ISFCE Web site: http://www.certified-computer-examiner.com/.

6.3 Incident Management

A study conducted by Verizon Business covering four years and more than 500 investigations involving 230 million records contends that nearly nine in ten breaches could have been prevented with reasonable security measures.

"Your Data Breach Was Probably Avoidable," *eWeek,*
June 16, 2008

Along with the right to monitor and log employees, you must also be prepared to handle any type of incident that may occur to your systems. Incident management consists of policies and procedures that provide actionable steps on how to deal with certain events, such as intrusions, cybertheft, denial of service, and other security-related acts. Incident management should tie into your business continuity and disaster recovery plans. In addition, the policies and procedures implemented to handle incidents should also comply with regulations that govern your industry.

Incident management is important because it is not a matter of "if" a security-related event is going to happen to your company, but rather "when" this event will occur. When it occurs, will your company be prepared to handle it appropriately?

An "incident," in context, is any action that will result in harm or a significant threat of harm to a company's security. An "event," on the other hand, is the actual or observable occurrence of such an act. Incident management will cover both incidents and events, and handling of an incident is similar to what law enforcement and medical personnel do as first responders.

Two resources that I have found to be very valuable when implementing an information security incident management program are the National Institute of Science and Technology (NIST) Special Publication (SP) 800-61, "Computer Security Incident Handling Guide and the SANS Institute—Incident Handling Step by Step," and "Computer Crime Investigation Guide."

The predesigned forms at http://www.sans.org/incidentforms/ include some of the following to assist in your incident handling procedures: incident contact list, identification checklist, survey, containment checklist, eradication checklist, and communications log. These forms follow the six stages of incident handling: preparation, identification, containment, eradication, recovery, and lessons learned. If these steps look familiar, they should; they are similar to some of the steps that we touched on under our business continuity, disaster recovery, and computer forensics areas.

To discuss incident management, we must introduce you to the emergency action plan. These steps were designed by over 90 experienced incident handlers. They have been tested in many different types of situations and have held true. Figure 6.2 reviews the steps of the emergency action plan.

The first step is to remain calm. Even in the most stressful situations, your calm will reflect on others and they will also calm down. The next step is to take your time and not hurry. If you assess the situation and think for a second before you act, it could save you costly mistakes in the end. The third step is to become a good record keeper and take good notes. When an incident occurs, you want to answer who, what, when, where, why, and how. These questions are very important in allowing you to assess the situation accurately.

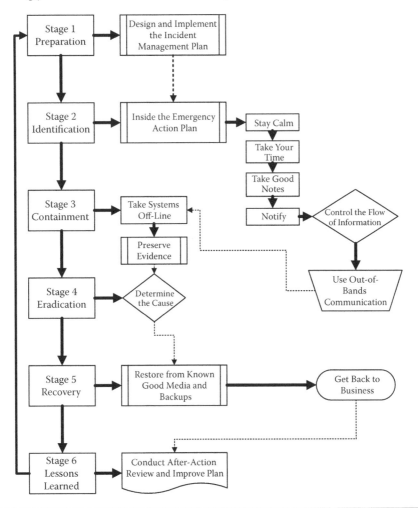

Figure 6.2   Six stages of incident handling and the emergency action summary.

The next step is to notify and go into "incident mode." Notification can be sent to the emergency medical system in case of a medical emergency or to law enforcement in case of a criminal act. The incident should also be reported to management, which should at this point act in a supporting role to assist the primary person in handling the incident. It is important that members of management not be so hands on at this point, especially if they are not on site of the incident. Unless the individual handling the incident is ill equipped to handle it appropriately, management should be hands off. However, management may still need to take a leadership role in directing the action per set policies and procedures.

As the event escalates, it will be very important to control the flow of information and enforce a "need to know" policy. Details of the incident should be told to the minimum number of individuals with the caveat that the information is private and should be handled as such. Find alternative communication channels. For instance, if the computer network was compromised, you do not want to utilize e-mail or chat; instead, you may need to communicate by phone or fax.

One of the next major steps is to contain the situation. You do not want any more damage to be caused than has already occurred. This may mean that systems will be taken down so as not to cause problems to other systems. These decisions should be made at the highest level after assessing all of the details.

Once the event is contained, you will want to preserve the evidence. This may mean that an exact backup is made of an affected system. When we talk about a backup of a system, we are talking about a bit-by-bit, low-level backup of the hard drives and/or memory of the system. This should be done by experienced individuals. (See Section 6.2 for further information.)

Once a complete backup has been done, the problem should be eradicated. At this step, you want to try to figure out what happened and take steps to correct the deficiencies. This may mean closing holes or patching vulnerable systems so that the same event does not occur again.

Recovery is the next step. An affected system will need to be restored to its original form by utilizing original media and known good backup tapes. You need to get back to business.

After everything is said and done, you need an after-action review or "lessons learned." You need to learn from your experience in dealing with this event and determine whether or not the incident management plan that was in place worked as expected. If any areas need improvement, they should be reviewed and the plan updated accordingly.

One of the key points to address in a formal incident management policy is the establishment of an incident response team, which should include the following:

■ security personnel (those that deal with computer security issues and physical security issues);
■ operational personnel (such as system administrators);
■ network personnel (such as network administrators);

■ legal personnel (may include internal and external counsel);
■ human resources personnel;
■ public relations personnel;
■ audit personnel; and
■ union representatives (if your organization has unions).

The incident management policy should address specific responsibilities and authority assigned to staff members, officials, and to individuals on the incident response team when it comes to dealing with a security incident. The policy should include specific actions and time frames based on a multitude of possible scenarios. In addition, the policy should contain escalation and notification procedures along with making sure employees and contractors report any observed or suspected security weaknesses. There should be a mechanism in place to track, quantify, and monitor the types, amounts, and costs of incidents. Finally, the incident response team members should have a good understanding of the proper steps to take in collecting evidence, especially digital evidence, as discussed earlier in Section 6.2.

Although there are many different types of incidents, some incident types that you may want to cover specifically in your incident management policy and procedures are espionage and insider threats, unauthorized access and use, and malicious codes and viruses.

A practical way in which you can utilize the information discussed on incident management is to choose the NIST SP800-61 framework. Use this framework to establish a monitoring or tracking database to keep record of the information detailed in the following seven subsections.

6.3.1 Reporting Information

The ISC^2 has the "9 Cs" method for documenting or reporting information. This includes chronological, clear, complete, comprehensive, concise, confidential, correct, creditable, and candid (or free from bias, prejudice, or malice). All reporting information should include the organization name, date, case or incident number, general information, and names and signatures of those involved. Documentation should also include inventories of equipment and the maintenance on this equipment along with the person responsible for performing this maintenance. Records should also include methods and other processes used for investigation, quality control, and presentation. They should contain all movement of documents for chain-of-evidence purposes, communications with team members and external parties, and a detailed report of the results of the investigation (Kleiman 2008).

Incident number: I assign incident numbers based on the year, month, and date the incident was reported along with the initials of the primary point of contact for the incident. For example, if the incident was reported on February 9, 2008, and I am the point of contact, the incident number would be 20080209JJT. (Of course, you can utilize any method you want, but I would definitely recommend that you assign a number to the incident for ease of tracking.)

Incident reporter: This is the name of the individual who initially made the report of the security incident.

Organizational unit: This is the name of the department in which the incident reporter works.

Reporter's phone number and e-mail address (self-explanatory).

Location of the incident: If your company has multiple offices, this would be the name of the office in which the incident occurred.

Severity: This may be low, medium, or high, depending on a predefined rating scale.

Address of the incident: This includes the city, state, and zip code.

Cost of the incident: This is a running total of the costs that your company has realized in handling the incident and the actual damages the incident has caused.

My database also contains information on each of the steps involved in managing an incident.

6.3.2 Steps

Step 1: *Confirmation.* List the steps that were taken to confirm the incident. Here you want to prioritize handling the incident based on its business impact along with identifying the resources that have been affected. You will also want to attempt to predict the resources that may be affected due to this incident.

Step 1a: *Analysis.* Detail the type of analysis that went into the incident and estimate the current and potential technical impact of the incident. Again, we are looking at the technical side here, so prioritize these items based on your analysis along with the resources affected by the incident.

Step 2: *Notification.* List all of the individuals notified both internally and externally. I also include a specific area where I can check off each required notification item based on the company's notification procedures.

Step 3: *Containment*

Step 4: *Evidence collection*

I combine these two steps into one in regard to containing the incident and then acquiring, preserving, securing, and documenting the evidence. Detail the actions taken as part of this combined step.

Step 5: *Eradication.* List the actions taken to eradicate or mitigate the damage caused by the incident. You want to identify and mitigate the vulnerabilities that caused the incident and remove any malicious code, inappropriate materials, or other components as part of your steps to eradicate the damage.

Step 6: *Recovery.* List the steps that were taken to recover from the incident and return the affected systems back to an operational state. You will also want to confirm that the systems are functioning as expected. You may want to include additional monitoring to look for any future related activities.

Step 7: *Report.* As part of my tracking database, I utilize all of the notes taken to complete an incident report.

Step 8: *After-action review.* Remember to hold your lessons-learned meeting after the incident has been taken care of. In this area, you will want to note what actions have been taken as a result of the incident.

6.3.3 Notification

Following our company's notification procedures, my database contains check boxes to indicate that certain individuals or groups were notified accordingly. For instance, all security incidents are required to be reported to the information security officer. The information security officer, in turn, assigns an incident handler to be the point of contact on the incident. The company has a security committee that also needs to be notified for all security incidents. The security committee reports the incident to the chief executive officer. If the incident is rated as medium or high severity, the board of directors is notified. I leave a field in the database to describe how the board of directors was notified (e.g., during board meeting and the date of the meeting). The company has a supervisory committee that also needs to be notified if the incident rating is medium or high severity. Again, I leave a field open in the database to describe how the supervisory committee was notified.

In addition to the internal notifications, some external groups also need to be notified, depending on the severity level of the incident. This may include customers, industry regulators, insurance company, legal counsel, or others as defined by your incident management policy.

I make a special area for law enforcement notification that includes not only whether law enforcement has been notified, but also the date and time of notification. I also include the information on the agency notified, the contact person, the direct phone number of the contact, and any additional remarks relevant to the notification.

6.3.4 Incident Details

This area is completed by the information security officer or other executive originally notified of the incident. As part of the report, I not only include the reporter's information as described earlier, but also note the following items:

Date and *time:* this includes date and time at which the incident occurred and date and time at which the incident was discovered.

Type of incident: this can include, but is not limited to, inappropriate use, denial of service, unauthorized use, unauthorized access, espionage, probe/scan, fraud/hoax, malicious code (worm/virus/other), misuse of system (internally), misuse of system (externally), theft of data, or other.

Technical impact: this can include, but is not limited to loss/compromise of data, system downtime, damage to systems, other organizations systems affected, financial loss, or other.

Current status: this can be an ongoing investigation, a pending investigation, or a completed incident investigation.

Type of data: this can reference your data classification structure and note what type of data was affected by the incident. This should help determine the severity of the incident.

Sensitivity of the data: this can be low, medium, high, critical, or unknown based upon predefined levels.

Actions: this is a summary of current actions being taken on the incident.

Source of the incident: the source of the incident is described, including host names and IP addresses of the identified source.

Description of the incident: this includes a description of the incident and how it was detected. You also want to describe what happened as part of the incident. The details in this section can assist you in the eradication process.

Resources affected: the resources affected by the incident are listed, including the host name and IP address of the company assets affected. This area should tie into your business continuity and disaster recovery plan to determine the proper recovery time and maximum tolerable downtime of the systems affected, especially if business-critical systems are involved.

Other organizations contacted: the dates, times, contact name, and contact number of outside organizations that have been notified of the incident are listed. This can include your software vendors, regulators, law enforcement, etc.

Comments: this area is for any additional items worth mentioning that were not included in the previous areas.

Once this information is completed, the database assists in producing a formatted report entitled "Security Incident Report."

6.3.5 Incident Handler

The next area in the database consists of information that the assigned incident handler is responsible for completing. This information includes the following:

Current status of incident response (self-explanatory)
Summary of the incident (self-explanatory)
Logs of actions: this consists of a list of all documentations or logs that have been used to keep notes or to track actions of individuals involved in the incident. (See "actions to date" for further information.)

Contact information for all involved parties: this lists all individuals involved in the incident, such as other incident response team members.

Evidence gathered: a complete inventory of all evidence gathered or involved in this incident is listed.

> There are three questions traditionally asked when a document is tendered as evidence:
> 1. *Authentication:* What is the document [evidence]? Where did it come from? Who or what created it?
> 2. *Best evidence:* Is this document [evidence] the original? If not, is it a copy that is admissible under an exception to the original document rule?
> 3. *Hearsay:* Is the document offered for the truth of the assertions it contains? If so, is it admissible for its truth under an exception to the rule against hearsay?
>
> It is best practices to treat all cases as [though] they may end up in litigation[;] therefore, we should ensure our evidence follows the rules of evidence. Rules of evidence [are] defined as rules meant to assist in the search for truth by guarding against unreliable evidence which could be prejudicial, misleading, inaccurate, or distracting. Further, they require the evidence be relevant, material, and competent. (Kleiman 2008)

Comments: any other comments that the handler may have regarding the incident are noted.

Cause of the incident: the handler should be able, upon his or her investigation, to give an expert opinion on the key factors that allowed the incident to occur. This area will be important in determining the steps to take in eradicating the problem.

Business impact of incident: this can be a description of the incident's effect or impact on the business, possibly based on the cost of the incident.

After this section is completed, the database generates a formatted report entitled "Incident Handler Report." This report is used in notifying the committees, board of directors, CEO, and others, as necessary.

6.3.6 Actions to Date

In my database, I keep a running log of actions taken on the incident. I list the date and the details of those actions, which can include the person causing the action, the type of action, and maybe the results of those actions as they relate to the incident. As part of the documentation process and tracking process, I feel that this area is important for later review or examination.

6.3.7 Recommended Actions

Recommendations have been made from several sources as they relate to recovering from the incident or making sure the incident does not occur again. This area keeps track of the date the recommendation was made and the details behind the recommendation, including who made it and the disposition of the recommendation—whether it was acted upon or the details behind not acting upon it.

My database also includes sections for additional instructions on specific industry-reporting requirements. For instance, the financial industry is required to report suspicious activity by completing a Suspicious Activity Report (SAR). I list the detailed instructions of this report and the requirements behind filling it out. It is nice to have these instructions in one area for reference when an incident occurs. A lot of the information gathered already is required to fill out this SAR report.

6.4 Laws, Investigations, and Ethics

As we discussed in Section 2.2 in Chapter 2, multiple laws require us to have an information security program in several different industries. These laws can be considered some of the primary administrative controls that we implement and the reason we implement them in our organization. For the purposes of this book, I want to discuss a few specific laws related to information security and how they relate to our current discussion around administrative controls.

6.4.1 Laws

Criminal acts against persons or property can be divided into two broad categories: criminal and civil. Generally, law enforcement will be involved in criminal cases, which violate public law, while internal incident handlers may be involved in civil cases that deal with compensation for monetary damages or losses. Damages may come in the form of compensatory, punitive, or statutory sanctions being brought against the violator. Violators may be required to pay compensation for damages to their victims, they may be imprisoned, or they may be fined under certain laws.

6.4.1.1 Computer Laws

Some laws that you may want to become familiar with as they relate to computers and computer systems include

> *U.S. Code Title 18 Section 1030: the Computer Fraud and Abuse Act.* This law makes it illegal to access a computer without authorization and commit fraud. It also makes it illegal to cause damage to a computer and traffic in passwords that may allow unauthorized access.

Comprehensive Crime Control Act of 1984. This law overhauled federal sentencing guidelines and revised the bail and forfeiture procedures.

Computer Security Act (CSA) of 1987. This law made the National Institute of Science and Technology (NIST) responsible for the security of unclassified, nonmilitary government computers, with the National Security Agency (NSA) providing technical assistance. Some parts of this law were superseded by the Federal Information Security Management Act (FISMA).

6.4.1.2 Infrastructure Protection Laws

Other laws deal with terrorism, infrastructure protection, and espionage, such as the following:

Economic Espionage Act of 1996. This law modified Title 18 and extended it to foreign governments and business. It also classified the theft of trade secrets as a criminal offense.

National Infrastructure Protection Act of 1996. This law extended federal protection beyond government computers to pipelines, utilities, communications, and other related assets considered part of the national infrastructure.

USA Patriot Act of 2001. This law changed the authorities the government can rely on to conduct real-time network surveillance. It allowed the government to assist the service providers in monitoring the activity of hackers with the permission of the providers, owners, and operators.

6.4.1.3 Privacy Laws

The following laws deal with privacy:

Privacy Act of 1974. This law controls the collection and use of personal data by government agencies.

Electronic Communications Privacy Act (ECPA) of 1986. This law prohibits access to electronic communications and establishes the procedures that law enforcement are required to follow when accessing such information.

Health Insurance Portability and Accountability Act (HIPAA) of 1996. This law specifically deals with the health care industry and relates to the privacy and security of "personally identifiable information."

Gramm–Leach–Bliley Act (GLBA). This law is similar to HIPAA, but deals with the protection of sensitive customer information in the financial industry.

6.4.1.4 Intellectual Property Rights

It is also important to understand intellectual property rights. The following are some terms and clarifications related to intellectual property rights:

Patents protect inventions. They are only valid in the United States for 20 years from date of application. A patent owner has the right to exclude others from making, selling, or importing the invention.

Copyrights protect works and contents. Intellectual works include literature, drama, music, art, and other types of works, both published and unpublished. The protection lasts for the author's life plus 70 years.

Trademarks protect brands.

Service marks protect services.

Trade secrets protect business-sensitive information.

6.4.2 Investigations

Some of what we are going to talk about has already been covered in Section 6.2; however, let us take a second to summarize the steps involved in an investigation. More specifically, these steps will be geared toward computer crime investigations.

Before any investigation can begin, an incident has to occur and be detected. After damages that the incident may have or would have caused are minimized, the incident needs to be reported to management. The objective is to eliminate some of the potential for liability with which the company may be faced when an incident occurs. After a damage assessment has been performed, witnesses are collected and a determination has to be made on whether or not the incident constitutes a criminal act. Other decisions will need to be made regarding the next proper course of action. These choices may include hardening security, maintaining surveillance on the attack, or consulting with legal counsel regarding possible prosecution. Thus far, these steps are similar to those previously discussed in Section 6.3 and Section 5.2 (Chapter 5).

The next step involves conducting the investigation. When conducting an investigation, you need to consider a few items. First, you need to consider the cost of the investigation. Always consider the amount of time, effort, and resources that will be involved in conducting an investigation as compared to the incident that has occurred. You want to make sure that there is some rationale behind how much will be spent and how much damage was caused by the incident. Second, you want to consider the controls around the investigation. Who will be conducting the investigation and how will information be disseminated that comes out of the investigation? Finally, you want to know your legal obligations in regard to the investigation. You definitely want to seek legal counsel on this matter prior to engaging in any type of investigation to make sure that you are not overstepping your rights and violating someone else's rights.

When conducting an investigation, you may want to consider using a private investigator or seeking assistance from law enforcement. Both options have pros and cons. For instance, if you seek law enforcement assistance, the investigation may take a little more time due to requirements around obtaining search warrants and building up enough probable cause to ensure that an incident reaches the threshold of a criminal act. On the other hand, a private investigator can be hired to work on behalf of the company to conduct internal investigations. Once evidence is obtained, the investigator can later turn this over to law enforcement to carry on the criminal part of an investigation. In either circumstance, you should seek the advice of counsel to help determine the company's best course of action.

Potential suspects, witnesses, and interviewers will need to be identified. You may also need to hire experts to assist in collecting certain types of digital evidence if necessary. Proper documentation of all actions taken, interviews, evidence collected, and other related items should be done. A report should ultimately be written providing a synopsis of the incident to management.

> It is ill-advised to be caught up in the middle of something that should be turned over to law enforcement agencies. Confer with LEGAL COUNSEL before making any policies pertaining to certain types of incidents, such as those dealing with child pornography (Kleiman 2008).

> Companies and their lawyers who fail to keep up with child pornography law do so at their peril. The bipartisan resolve of state and federal legislators to combat child pornography has led to laws that put the fate of those who innocently possess child porn—such as counsel and their forensic experts—largely at the mercy of prosecutorial discretion. Dealing administratively with employees who use company computers to view or download child pornography no longer suffices. In fact, company lawyers or managers risk serious criminal penalties if they merely terminate an offending employee and delete only visibly illicit images from his desktop computer. The law generally treats child porn like heroin: Merely knowing about possession of it is a crime. Possession on behalf of a client to assist in an investigation or defense is no exception. As one court put it: "Child pornography is illegal contraband." Notably, this statutory affirmative defense is not available if three or more images are found—and usually where there is one such image, there are dozens or hundreds more. Thus, if a company finds multiple child porn images on an employee's computer, the affirmative defense evaporates, and handling or even destroying the images may expose the company to criminal liability. (Howell and Luehr 2004)

6.4.2.1 Chain of Custody

Other detailed steps to the investigation can be found in Sections 6.2 and 6.3. We will not talk about them again here except for one minor point in regard to the "chain of custody." You may have heard this term before, but what is the chain of custody?

Before we explain this, let us get a little background on evidence. Any evidence submitted to the court must be the best type of evidence available. There are many different types of evidence—for example, real evidence or tangible objects that prove or disprove a fact, best evidence that provides the most reliable testimony of facts, and secondary evidence that may not be viewed as reliable, such as oral contracts. Some other types of evidence include

- *Direct evidence* is "testimony of a person who has firsthand knowledge of what happened" and evidence that can prove a fact by itself—for instance, a witness testifying to facts obtained by any of the witness's five senses. "Hearsay evidence [pertains to] a rule that declares not admissible as evidence any statement other than that by a witness while testifying at the hearing and offered into evidence to prove the truth of the matter stated. An example of hearsay would be secondhand testimony from someone who was told something by another person who witnessed it firsthand" (Kleiman 2008). There are two exceptions to the hearsay rule: "official written statements, such as those given to law enforcement personnel, and dying declarations in which the person with the firsthand knowledge told the witness the information before dying" (Kleiman 2008).
- *Demonstrative evidence* can prove or disprove a fact by providing examples or experiments to "demonstrate" how something could have occurred.
- *Documentary evidence* is documented evidence of fact. This is common in computer-related crime and can include business records, manuals, financial statements, printouts, etc.
- *Conclusive evidence* is irrefutable and cannot be contradicted.
- *Circumstantial evidence* can prove an intermediate fact.
- *Corroborative evidence* is supportive in nature.

No matter what type it is, evidence needs to be secured from tampering to be admissible in court. For this reason, the chain of custody was developed. This is a formal record of who obtained the evidence, where and when the evidence was obtained, who secured the evidence, and who controlled the evidence at all times. The chain of custody accounts for everyone who accessed or handled the evidence and provides assurance against tampering.

Along with the chain of custody, evidence has a life cycle. The life cycle of evidence includes the collection of evidence, the storage of evidence, the preservation of the evidence, the transportation of this evidence to court, and the final destruction or return of the evidence. A good reference for searching and seizing computers and obtaining electronic evidence in criminal investigations can be found here at http://www.cybercrime.gov/s&smanual2002.htm.

6.4.3 Ethics

Ethics can be defined as knowing the difference between what is the right thing to do, and what you have the right to do. (Yeschke 2003)

> Every society has moral codes and rules of conduct that are derived from the society's goals, and generally learned through implication. From this, we derive what we believe in and what we stand for. Every organization should have policies that define their ethics[;] although these can be implied, they are best if expressed. (Kleiman 2008)

> Ethics denotes the theory of right action and the greater good. Ethics is not limited to specific acts and defined moral codes, but encompasses the whole of moral ideals and behaviors, a person's philosophy of life. (Wikipedia 2008)

Laws are usually based on ethics. Laws are meant to force individuals to act in certain ways, but they do not cover all situations. Most professional organizations today require their members to follow some code of ethics. These are developed to shape the behaviors of the membership. For instance, the International Information Systems Security Certification Consortium (ISC²) requires that all Certified Information Systems Security Professionals (CISSPs) commit to a specific code of ethics. This code of ethics requires the professional to protect society, the commonwealth, and the infrastructure; act honestly, responsibly, and legally; provide diligent and competent services to principles; and advance and protect the profession at large. Other organizations, such as the Information Systems Security Association (ISSA), require their members to ensure that the Confidentiality, Integrity, and Availability (CIA) of an organization's resources are maintained.

In contrast, some individuals do not follow a code of ethics. Instead, they have "MOM": Motivations, Opportunities, and the Means to commit a crime. Motivations are the "who" and the "why" of the crime. Opportunities are the "where" and "when" and usually occur when weaknesses are present. Means is the skill level or capabilities of the criminals.

On this same line of discussion, I thought I would throw in here a little talk about hackers and crackers. A lot of individuals believe these two terms to be synonymous; however, hackers and crackers are totally different individuals. Crackers conduct serious crimes. They usually work in small groups and are sent out to steal or destroy information. They are usually more organized, more driven, and a lot more dangerous than hackers. They will usually have the motivation, the opportunity, and the means to commit a crime.

Hackers, on the other hand, have been given a bad rap for quite a while. Hackers are most interested in honing their skills and enhancing their knowledge. They are not interested in destroying or stealing anything, but rather see hacking as a game. The hacker's attitude is one that finds the world full of fascinating problems just waiting to be solved. He or she feels that no problem should have to be solved twice and therefore will usually share the information obtained from solving a problem with other hackers. Hackers feel that boredom and drudgery are evil and freedom is good. Hackers also feel that attitude is no substitute for competence. Hackers believe that nobody who can think should ever be forced into a situation that bores him or her. For this reason, hackers will usually work for themselves, or by themselves, because they feel that anyone who can give orders can stop someone from solving whatever problem might be interesting. If you are interested in learning more about the hacker culture, go to http://www.catb.org/~esr/faqs/hacker-howto.html.

6.5 Operations Security

A study conducted by Verizon Business that covered four years and more than 500 investigations involving 230 million records reported that in 59% of data breaches, the company had security policies and procedures in place, but not implemented.

"Your Data Breach Was Probably Avoidable," *eWeek*,
June 16, 2008

Another administrative control is operations security, or OPSEC. OPSEC is defined as denying certain individuals information regarding the organization's capabilities and other plans by protecting business functions. OPSEC protects business functions by identifying, controlling, and safeguarding indicators associated with these functions. The OPSEC process identifies critical information and then analyzes threats to this information. It analyzes vulnerabilities to these threats, assesses the risks, and applies countermeasures to mitigate these risks.

OPSEC protects resources by reducing the potential compromise of the confidentiality, integrity, and availability of the information system. It is concerned with protecting data and processing resources along with ensuring compliance. OPSEC attempts to balance security with business needs by controlling access to the network and functions along with specific hardware assets.

6.5.1 OPSEC Controls

We have already touched on a few of these controls in Section 4.1 in Chapter 4, but there are more as they relate to OPSEC controls. OPSEC controls are divided into five categories:

- *Preventive controls* are used to prevent damage to or destruction of property and information. Examples of these types of controls may include antivirus software, file encryption, and user registration processes.
- *Detective controls* identify and react to security incidents. These types of controls can activate other controls such as preventive controls or corrective controls. Examples of these types of controls include firewalls, IDS software, and audit logs.

- *Corrective controls* are used to restore systems to their original states. A couple of examples of this would be backup tapes or original software CDs.
- *Deterrent controls* are used to discourage security breaches and minimize the possibility of these occurrences. An example would be floodlights installed in darkened areas around the building.
- *Application controls* include enhancements to applications that monitor installation processes and software application updates.
- *Transaction controls* are used to verify input and output data along with protecting processes by accepting or rejecting data at certain points through the process.

6.5.2 Separation of Duties

Operational security elements consist of ensuring that separation of duties is implemented into each high-risk business function or transaction. There should not be one person that can compromise the security of your organization. Separation of duties can be seen in different job functions. For instance, a person that modifies a change to a system should not be the same person to approve this change. Likewise, programmers should not test their own code.

6.5.3 Job Rotation

In addition, job rotation should be implemented to fulfill particular tasks in a company. There should be some overlaps of job functions because this will assist in the continuity of business functions. Rotating jobs will also assist in identifying fraudulent activities more easily. Along with job rotation, vacations should be mandatory, especially for those in high-risk areas. Again, this will allow for easier identification of fraudulent activities.

6.5.4 Least Privileges

The principle of least privileges should always be used and individuals should be given the least number of privileges to do their jobs adequately. This "need-to-know" access can be accomplished through clearance levels, sensitivity levels, or modes of operations. Security administrators should modify these security levels or profiles as opposed to modifying individual user accesses. Users should be accessing only the resources they need to do their jobs and should not be granted elevated privileges.

To confirm that your organization is running an effective information security program, everyone needs to be accountable for his or her actions. Systems, software, and resources should be monitored and audited on a regular basis. Logs should be maintained and reviewed on a continuous basis for unusual activity.

6.6 Records Retention

Over 10,000 records-retention regulations are in effect in the United States. Many of these are state mandated. Legal counsel should assist in making records-retention decisions. The following are some of the regulations and their requirements:

- The *Sarbanes–Oxley Act (SOX)* calls out specific record types that need to be retained for 7 years.
- The *Health Insurance Portability and Accountability Act (HIPAA)* requires that patient records and related data (including e-mail) must be archived in a secure manner for at least 2 years after the death of the patient.
- *Title 21 CFR Part 11—U.S. Food and Drug Administration (FDA)* calls for the following records-retention period for manufacturing, processing, and packing of the following:
  - food: 2 years after release;
  - drugs: 3 years after distribution; and
  - bio products: 5 years after end of manufacturing.
- *Federal Acquisition Regulations (FAR) Subpart 4.7—Contractors Records Retention* requires all individuals and companies that contract to supply goods or services to the federal government to retain all related hard copy or electronic records. (Note: The retention of records is based on the class of records and can range from 2 to 4 years.)
- *Title 17 CFR Part 1—U.S. Commodity Futures Trading Commission (CFTC)* requires record keepers to store required records for the full 5-year maintenance period.
- *Federal Energy Regulatory Commission (FERC)* says that records for public utilities industries must have a life expectancy equal to or greater than the specified retention periods.
- The *National Archives and Records Administration (NARA) Part 123* specifies what government agency records are kept and for how long.
- *Federal employment-related regulations* require that all companies with employees be regulated by one or more of these regulations, which also include some sort of records retention. Some of the better known regulations include:
  - Title VII of the Civil Rights Act of 1964;
  - Age Discrimination in Employment Act;
  - Americans with Disabilities Act;
  - Family and Medical Leave Act;
  - Equal Pay Act of 1963;
  - Vocational Rehabilitation Act;
  - Employee Retirement Income Security Act of 1974;
  - National Labor Relations Act; and
  - Fair Labor Standards Act.

Again, you should seek legal counsel's advice to assist in determining the proper records retention policies that your company or specific industry is required to follow.

6.6.1 Federal Rules of Civil Procedure*

In light of the vast volume of computer and other electronic files and communications, as well as the Federal Rules of Civil Procedure pertaining to e-discovery, companies now realize the need for a comprehensive records retention policy. Current business standards dictate that it is not only a best practice to have a policy, but it is also a part of meeting minimum standards of legal compliance and prudent business operations. Commentators and courts have routinely indicated that every company should develop its own written policies, given the substantial risks of not having an effective policy, as well as the numerous benefits from a policy.

Keeping everything is not the answer. Companies that say they keep everything do not. Employees will always discard paper records, electronic files, and e-mails. In light of this inevitable destruction of records, it is imperative for an organization to adopt a policy governing destruction in order to avoid liability for selective destruction of records or spoliation.

Failure to retain records in compliance with applicable law and in connection with pending or threatened claims can result in regulatory and court sanctions, fines, unnecessary expense, and other adverse consequences. Inadequate and ineffective records storage and retention practices can result in (a) the loss of valuable trade secrets, confidential information and other important business and proprietary information; and (b) the breach of privacy laws and regulations. The cost (time, money, and resources) of complying with litigation discovery requests can be significantly reduced through implementation of cost-effective records retention and e-discovery policies and practices.

The benefits of an effective records management program include easier and timely access to necessary records, complying with statutory and regulatory retention obligations, reducing storage costs, protection of confidential and proprietary information, and meeting e-discovery obligations. An effective records retention policy can mitigate the risks of not actively managing electronically stored information (ESI), such as the inability to locate and use important business information efficiently; sanctions due to the failure to comply with statutory and regulatory retention and destruction laws; increased costs due to inefficiencies from inaccessible information; and the inability to comply with e-discovery requirements, court orders, and other litigation-related requirements.

Companies are spending more resources than ever to meet their legal obligations to preserve records. This results in higher costs of storing, locating, and producing ESI. The courts have just started to provide guidance in this area, so judgments

---

* Section 6.6.1 was provided, with permission, by Chanley Howell, Esq., a partner at Foley & Lardner, LLP.

and sanctions that have been imposed on Fortune 500 companies for their failure to preserve ESI properly have forced management to focus carefully on its records retention policies—for example, *United States v. Philip Morris USA, Inc.,* 327 F. Supp. 2d 21, 26 (D.D.C. 2004) ($2.75 million sanction for failure of 11 employees to follow litigation hold requirements for e-mails); *SEC v. Lucent Technologies Inc.,* SEC Accounting and Auditing Enforcement Release No. 2016, 82 SEC Docket 3224 (May 17, 2004) ($25 million); *In the Matter of Banc of Am. Sec. LLC,* SEC Admin. Proc. File No. 3 11425, Exchange Act Release No. 34 49386, 82 SEC Docket 1264 (Mar. 10, 2004) ($10 million); *In re Prudential Ins. Co. of Am. Sales Practices Litig.,* 169 F.R.D. 598, 617 (D.N.J. 1997) ($1 million).

Companies that invested the time and resources to prepare a comprehensive records retention policy have learned that they can comply with their discovery obligations efficiently. In contrast, companies that have not prepared in advance have found themselves unable to make required disclosures and to comply timely with discovery obligations without incurring tremendous costs. Most significantly, companies that have not prepared for e-discovery have suffered evidentiary and monetary sanctions.

As noted by Judge Shira Scheindlin of the Southern District of New York in the first of the seminal *Zubulake* decisions, "the more information there is to discover, the more expensive it is to discover all the relevant information until, in the end, 'discovery is not just about uncovering the truth, but also about how much of the truth the parties can afford to disinter'" (*Zubulake v. UBS Warburg,* 217 F.R.D. 309 (S.D.N.Y. 2003); quoting *Rose Entm't, Inc. v. William Morris Agency, Inc.,* 205 F.R.D. 421 423 (S.D.N.Y. 2002). An effective records retention policy can assist companies in dealing with the tremendous volume of electronic records and in reducing the costs of complying with electronic discovery requests.

In developing a records retention policy, the company should first analyze the records environment to assess areas and levels of risk to the organization that may result from existing records retention policies and practices. Based on identified risk areas, the company can then evaluate existing written and/or de facto policies, processes, and technologies to identify weaknesses, categorize risks, and recommend improvements. With the results of the risk and needs assessment in hand, the organization can then modify the existing policy or develop a new, practical, and cost-effective records management and retention policy that addresses and resolves any potential issues revealed during the risk and needs assessments.

To avoid court sanctions, costly e-discovery compliance, and missing court deadlines, companies should prepare in advance to respond properly to e-discovery requests and mandatory disclosures. The company should provide training to its personnel with respect to the policy to assist compliance with paper and e-discovery obligations. A critical aspect of litigation preparedness is knowing what electronic records the company maintains and where they are stored. The company should develop legally compliant data maps that categorize the company's electronic records and identify where the records are stored, as well as the appropriate records custodians who can provide electronic records as needed.

The records retention policy should address obligations under the Federal Rules of Civil Procedures relating to electronically stored information. These rules were amended effective December 2006, when numerous rules and regulations relating to electronic records—or as referred to in the rules, ESI—were added. Among other things, the rules require early treatment of e-discovery issues, as well as full and accurate disclosure of the existence of relevant ESI. If not properly planned, managed, and coordinated, locating and producing ESI can become very time consuming and expensive. Failure to comply with the discovery rules can result in court-imposed sanctions, fines, and adverse rulings. Accordingly, it is critical for companies to develop accurate documentation describing their ESI practices and policies on the "front end," rather than dealing with these issues on an ad hoc, case-by-case basis after litigation has commenced.

An essential component of every records retention policy is the retention schedule that identifies all different types and categories of records and the required retention periods. The retention periods may be based on a statute, regulation, or other law mandating that the record be retained for at least a specified period of time or, in the absence thereof, operational requirements dictating that records be available for at least a certain length of time. Failure to utilize an accurate retention schedule can lead to premature destruction of records, resulting in legal fines and sanctions, and loss of information needed for the ongoing operations of the business. The company's records retention policy should have a retention schedule that accurately and concisely identifies all different categories and types of paper and electronic records retained by the company, as well as legally compliant retention periods for each category or type of record.

e-Mail proliferation is a problem faced by every company. Confronted with growing storage costs and system performance issues, companies are limiting the amount of e-mail that employees can keep. Tape backups typically do not keep a complete record of all e-mails. Although limiting e-mail volume is legally appropriate and in many cases advisable, the company must also ensure that employees or an automated system does not delete e-mails required for ongoing business operations or legal compliance. Companies should implement polices and practices for ensuring that required e-mails are not prematurely destroyed—for example, by migrating or archiving required e-mail records to a document management system or secure networked data servers.

Improper destruction of records, or spoliation, can result in fines, sanctions, adverse legal rulings, and other undesirable consequences. Even inadvertent destruction of records can lead to adverse results, particularly when the company's records retention policy does not adequately deal with "litigation holds." The obligation to preserve records can arise before a lawsuit is initiated or a demand letter received. The records retention policy should properly address the retention of relevant records, including timely notice to employees, compilation and production of records, and suspension of normal records destruction with respect to relevant records.

Electronic records can be stored in a variety of locations—network servers, local hard drives, home computers, laptops, handheld devices, CD-ROMs, flash storage devices, Web-based e-mail applications, online backup sites, etc. Multiple locations add to the difficulty and cost of locating and producing records, and they increase the likelihood that records will be lost, not produced when they should be, and/or improperly disclosed to third parties not entitled to access the records. When a company is required to locate and produce electronic records in litigation (as a party or a third-party witness), it must search *all* locations for potentially relevant records and produce those records. Companies should require storage or records in locations and in manners that facilitate prompt and cost-effective location and production, and they should consider limiting the locations where electronic records may be stored by employees.

As noted earlier, electronic records should be stored only in company-approved and -controlled locations. The next step is to create a data map or inventory of where all electronic records and other ESI are stored (e.g., file servers, e-mail servers, identified drives, storage networks, removable media, etc.). This is important to facilitate the company in locating electronic records when they are needed for litigation or other legal proceedings. The data map is also critical to complying with the e-discovery rules that require early and proactive disclosure of electronic records and information regarding their location and accessibility.

Electronic records often contain sensitive information valuable to the company, such as trade secrets, financial data, business plans, and other confidential business information. Similarly, with the increase of legislation regulating privacy of personal information, companies are under increasing obligation to maintain the privacy of such data. Accordingly, the company should implement and enforce policies and practices that protect the confidentiality, integrity, and security of important business information and adequately protect the privacy of personal information.

Many companies use independent contractors and outsource functions and operations of the business, resulting in third parties having primary responsibility for storing, retaining, and disposing of company records. Outsourced functions include areas such as information technology, accounting, human resources, or other business processes. In such instances, the company should require the outsourcer to comply with the company's records management policies through appropriate contract language, monitoring, reporting by the outsourcer, and periodic auditing of the outsourcer.

The flip side of retention is destruction. In order to obtain the benefits of having a policy and avoiding liability for improper destruction of records, it is necessary to destroy records in accordance with the policy. The records destroyed by Arthur Andersen in the Enron matter were subject to destruction and could have been destroyed earlier. However, the records were not timely destroyed, but instead destroyed after notice of the investigation. A company should regularly destroy records in accordance with its policy, subject to suspension of destruction pursuant to a litigation hold.

The following is a sample checklist for assessing the completeness of a company's records-retention and e-discovery policies and procedures. A "no" answer indicates an area for further inquiry and investigation to confirm the deficiency is intended and appropriate under the circumstances.

1. Does the company have a written records retention policy?
2. Is there a single person with overall responsibility and accountability for the company's records-retention policy and practices and compliance with the policy?
3. Have the company's senior management and board of directors approved the policy?
4. Does the policy apply to all types and formats of documents and records (e.g., paper and electronic)?
5. Does the policy apply to all records of the organization, and not just certain companies, subsidiaries, departments, business units, locations, etc.?
6. Does the policy apply to third-party contractors and outsource service providers that have primary control of company records?
7. Does the policy contain a legally compliant retention schedule identifying categories and types of records and the retention period for each category or type?
8. Is the retention schedule reviewed and updated at least annually to confirm that record categories and retention periods are accurate?
9. Does the policy distinguish between active records (still needed for active operations) and inactive records (which are no longer needed for active operations and can be archived)?
10. Does the policy address litigation holds—suspension of destruction of records relevant to pending or threatened legal claim, action, or investigation?
11. Is a sample litigation hold notice provided?
12. Does the policy specify who determines when a litigation hold should be issued, who should receive the litigation hold, and scope of the litigation hold?
13. Do both the policy and the litigation hold notice require employees to locate and preserve records subject to the litigation hold?
14. Does the policy designate a member of the company's IT Department responsible for compliance with litigation hold notices and other e-discovery obligations?
15. Does the policy address notifying the IT Department and action to be taken by the IT Department for locating and preserving records subject to litigation hold?
16. Does the policy address procedures for notifying outside vendors and counsel with primary responsibility for retaining company records of a litigation hold?

17. Do both the policy and the litigation hold notice require employees to notify management of claims or potential claims triggering a litigation hold?

18. Does the policy address procedures for releasing or terminating litigation hold?

19. Does the policy address voice mail?

20. Does the policy address the company's backup practices and procedures (e.g., backup storage procedures, rotation of backup tapes, etc.)?

21. Does the policy address the company's procedures for off-site storage of inactive paper records?

22. Does the policy address confidentiality and security of company records, including data classification of confidential and sensitive records?

23. Does the policy address procedures to avoid unauthorized access to classified, confidential, or sensitive records?

24. Does the policy address use, security, and encryption of laptops for storage of electronic records, handling of confidential, financial, and personally identifiable information, encryption, etc.?

25. Does the policy address use, security, and encryption of removable media, such as flash drives, USB pen drives, external hard drives, memory cards, CD-ROMs, DVDs, and other removable media?

26. Does the policy address handling, storage, and confidentiality of employee personnel records, including medical records and personally identifiable information?

27. Does the policy address approved methods for destroying paper and electronic records, including confidential records?

28. Does the policy provide for purging, at least annually, of records ready for destruction?

29. Is the policy distributed to employees and new employees and made readily available, such as on the company's intranet or other policy repository?

30. Does the policy provide contact information in the event an employee has questions regarding the policy?

31. Does the policy provide for employee training regarding the policy?

32. Does the policy state who is responsible for auditing compliance with the policy?

33. Does the policy provide for periodic review and updates of the policy and retention schedules?

34. Does the policy contain audit requirements and/or procedures?

35. Does the company have an e-mail or electronic communications policy?

36. Does the policy prohibit, limit, or otherwise address authorized uses and personal uses of the company's e-mail system?

37. Does the policy expressly apply to all types of electronic communications, including text messages and instant messages?

38. Does the policy provide for company ownership of the e-mail system and e-mails?

39. Does the policy give the company the right to monitor e-mail usage and state there is no employee expectation of privacy?
40. Does the policy prohibit sending, requesting, and knowingly receiving e-mails that are slanderous, harassing, sexually explicit, unlawful, etc.?
41. Does the policy address transmission of confidential information?
42. Does the policy address transmission of attorney–client communications?
43. Does the policy limit or prohibit use of personal e-mail accounts for business e-mails through home computers or third-party e-mail providers?
44. Does the policy address limits on retention of e-mail (e.g., length of time, size of mailbox, or both)?
45. If the policy contains user or automatic deletion requirements, does the policy address proper archiving of e-mails so that e-mails required for retention are not inadvertently deleted?
46. Does the company have an e-discovery policy?
47. Does the policy designate a member of the IT Department to be responsible for dealing with e-discovery issues?
48. Does the policy contain a data map that inventories where electronic records are stored (e.g., network drives, local drives, backup storage, archive systems, etc.)?
49. Does the data map describe different software applications used by the company?
50. Does the policy address procedures for ensuring effective implementation of litigation hold notices?
51. Does the policy address procedures for ensuring complete and accurate searching and compiling of relevant and requested ESI, including appropriate use of keyword searching?
52. Does the policy address procedures for avoiding or minimizing the risk of inadvertent disclosure of ESI protected by the attorney–client privilege or work product doctrine?
53. Does the policy address procedures for effective communication among and between in-house counsel, the company's IT Department, and outside counsel?
54. Does the policy identify who should participate in development of the case management plan and discovery plan for specific litigation matters?
55. Does the policy address procedures for resolving conflicts and disputes between the company and outside counsel with respect to discovery obligations and adequacy of discovery searches?

6.7 Security Awareness Training

Providing security awareness training to your employees not only may be a requirement for your specific industry, but also is one of the most important administrative controls that you can implement in your organization. The weakest link to most information security systems or programs is made up of the users of the system. Security is inconvenient and humans are normally creatures of convenience.

I usually show individuals by example why security is important so that they can get the support that they need to implement effective security awareness training. It is not enough to tell individuals what to do and read the organization's security policies and procedures to them in an hour-long training class. I have found it to be more effective to base this type of training scenario on real-world examples to which the employees can relate. Through these example scenarios, it is the goal that employees' bad behavior will be modified and "buy-in" will be obtained so that they will want to follow and understand the reasons behind these policies and procedures.

It is also important that awareness be an ongoing effort. Once a year is not effective, and lessons learned will soon be forgotten. Spot checks and frequent reminders of security practices will go a long way in making an effective security awareness program.

6.7.1 A Cracker's Story

As I have stated earlier, I like to use scenarios to get my point across. The following is a short, fictional story that can be modified to express specific policies and procedures that your organization wants to convey through its information security awareness program.

It is a rainy Friday morning and Jan is running late due to the congestion on the road and making plans for the upcoming weekend. Luckily, she remembers to bring her umbrella. As Jan is walking up to the employee entrance of her office, she notices a young man talking on his cell phone. The young man is clean-cut and well dressed. Jan hears him say, "OK, honey. I have to go to work now and I'll talk to you later; love you," as he hangs up his phone.

Jan is having trouble folding up her older umbrella; it is stuck. The young man kindly offers to assist her. Jan does not know him and has not seen him before, so she asks him, "Are you a new employee?" The young man says, "Yes, ma'am, I'm a new IT employee." Jan has heard that they are hiring for some new positions. The young man is able to fold the umbrella up and as they walk into the building together, Jan thanks him and says, "I look forward to seeing you around; maybe later you can help me with a formatting issue I'm having with a Word document." The young man says, "That should not be a problem. I'll see you later."

The young man is J. Cracker. He is a seasoned professional in the arts of social engineering and computer penetration. J. Cracker has just gained physical access to the office and starts to wander around the building. Other employees cross his path and they wish him a good morning as they pass. J. Cracker finds an empty office nearby. The office has a computer, but no one is around. J. Cracker looks under the keyboard and finds a user name and password written on a sticky note.

J. Cracker takes out a little wireless router from his backpack and hooks it to the network cable that he finds under the desk. He then heads for the nearest exit. As he is about to reach the exit door, he notices an unoccupied office with a large file lying on the desk. The file contains summary reports combined with several other documents containing sensitive information. J. Cracker helps himself to the file and places it in his backpack. He exits the office and makes his way to his vehicle parked in the adjoining parking lot.

When J. Cracker reaches his car, he immediately takes out his laptop and connects to the wireless router that he just installed in the empty office. From there, he tries the user name and password he discovered under the keyboard to gain access to the computer that was sitting on the desk. They provide local administrator access to this system. J. Cracker starts searching the system and discovers other administrator accounts. He starts cracking these accounts, hoping that one of them will provide access to other systems that he can find on the network. In a matter of a few minutes, J. Cracker discovers other accounts that allow him access into several other systems and a router on the network.

J. Cracker is not satisfied just yet. He discovers that the user name and password he found under the keyboard allow him to access shared files that contain other sensitive documents. He begins to run different types of scans on the network and discovers a system running an SQL database with a default account and password on it. J. Cracker compromises this system and plants his own account. He continues to look through the system and comes across some instructions on remotely accessing one of the servers. He opens up this file to find a user name and password for a domain administrator account.

J. Cracker cannot believe his eyes: What he has found is the "Holy Grail" of the network. It is now "game over" for the organization because J. Cracker has full access to the entire network. As he is driving off, J. Cracker thinks that he has had a great day "at the office."

I know I stated that this was a fictional story, but the examples provided were from real experiences. They were modified slightly and combined together to form this story. After letting trainees read and take in all the elements of this story, I usually pose two questions:

1. Do you think that this cannot happen to your organization?
2. Do you feel that your organization is secure and that you would act accordingly in the same situation?

Sadly, I'm here to say that you would be surprised at what you will find if you are looking for it.

Make sure that the scenario reflects a couple of highlighted points that you want to make in your training. For this example, the two main concepts that were meant to be highlighted were defense in depth and least privileges. The training should define all concepts. For instance, the term "defense in depth" is used to refer to a layering tactic. This idea is not so much to prevent an attack totally because this is never or rarely ever the case, but rather to weaken an attacker over time by deploying defensive mechanisms into an attacker's way. These mechanisms are objects that an attacker has to overcome to get to his target. I'll explain this in a little bit. "Least privileges" are the minimal amount of access rights that allow a user to perform his or her duties efficiently and effectively. If both of these concepts had been deployed in our story, J. Cracker would be leaving his office empty handed.

The scenario should be broken down to cover the main points and detail examples of how easily certain policies and procedures can be put into real-world actions. For this example, I will show you how easy it would be to prevent J. Cracker from achieving his goals.

First and foremost, J. Cracker should never have gained physical access to the building. Jan should have questioned J. Cracker further and not let him in without proper authorization. In most industries, employees are trained to be helpful and service oriented. This is not the case when it comes to security. Each employee should be utilizing his or her own form of authentication (badge, key, cipher code, etc.) to enter any nonpublic area of the facility. "Piggybacking" or holding the door open for others should be discouraged. Although it may be a little more inconvenient for each person entering the building, this one easy rule could have prevented all other damaging subsequent events in the preceding story.

One person "dropped the ball" on this, but the other individuals should have questioned J. Cracker as he was passing them in the hallway. J. Cracker was not wearing an ID badge or visitor tag and he was not escorted by any known employee. He should not have been allowed to wander the halls of the office alone. It is important to express the fact that employees are given certain rights and that it is proper for them to exercise their rights, especially when it comes to protecting the organization's assets. In some situations, employees may feel that they spend more time at work than they do at home. Pose a question to them in regard to letting strangers into their homes; would they let that happen? The answer would probably be "no," so why would they let strangers in their building without question?

Throughout the rest of this scenario, you can tie your organization's policies and procedures back to real-world actions. To continue with our scenario, unattended offices should be locked, especially if they contain electronic assets or sensitive information. This would have prevented J. Cracker from gaining access to the keyboard, network port, and mortgage application file. Along with this, user names and passwords should never be taped to the bottom of keyboards or posted anywhere around the desks where they could be easily obtained. A "clean-desk" policy that states sensitive information should be secured at all times should be enforced.

Wireless access has become a major concern and most organizations prohibit it. I am not opposed to wireless; if it is properly implemented, it can be an effective and efficient business solution. Monitoring of rogue wireless devices is critical. This should be done on a regular and routine basis. The rogue device planted by J. Cracker would have been discovered and disabled.

Users should not be given administrative rights on their local systems. Although many software applications require such access to run properly, these vendors should be pushed to have their applications run correctly with limited user access rights. If this type of access is required, utilize certain accounts that provide this access only under certain time limitations and other functional limitations. J. Cracker would have been limited to this one system and not have been able to go further through this attack vector.

Users should not be allowed to install programs on their systems without IT's knowledge. These applications should be security tested and default passwords should be changed immediately upon installation. J. Cracker would not have been able to plant his local admin account through the SQL database, which would have prevented him from finding the Microsoft Word document.

User names and passwords should never be kept in Word documents or any other documents that can be easily accessible on the network. If password lists must be kept, then make sure that access is limited to authorized individuals only and keep these files encrypted. Even if J. Cracker had had control of a local system, he would not have found or been able to utilize any interesting information to further his attack.

A limited number of individuals should be authorized as domain administrators. These accounts should have stricter password requirements and each user should have a unique and complex password. Accounts should not be shared and any compromise to these accounts should be reset immediately. This falls under the "least privilege" rules that limit the number of people having full control of the systems.

In addition, a network monitoring or intrusion detection system should be installed. If J. Cracker was running these scans, alerts should have been set off and system administrators been notified that something was going on. At this point, an incident security management policy or procedures should have been in place and an incident response team would then be activated accordingly. Finally, a video surveillance system should be installed that would assist in the prosecution of J. Cracker.

To conclude the training, there should be a summary of the important topics covered and some time for questions and answers; your organization may require some proficiency exam to determine the level of comprehension on certain policies and procedures addressed throughout the training. Documenting training is important. This can be done in many ways, but, at a minimum, documentation should include the names of attendees, number of hours trained, topic of training, when and how training was conducted, and retention of testing material. This may be required by certain industries for audit purposes.

6.8 Security Management Practices

The fundamental principle, however, is quite simple—if you don't know where data is, you certainly can't protect it.

Peter Tippett, VP of Research and Intelligence for Verizon Business Security Solutions

I cannot reiterate enough how important it is to have good policies, procedures, and processes in place in your organization and for all of your employees to understand their responsibilities related to these policies and procedures. Your organization should maintain an organizational chart that is kept updated and contains the title or role of each individual. These individuals should report to one person or boss above them on the chart and everyone should understand where he or she falls within your organization. Specific to information security, the duties of those involved in information technology administration and support and those involved in security-related activities should be separated. A checks-and–balances system must be maintained and no one individual should have ultimate power or control.

Information systems security violations are driven by user accountability. Users are responsible for their behaviors and are expected to follow security policies. The significance of a security violation depends on the intent of the individual rather than the actual compromise. This security violation is any breach of a security regulation or policy that may result in a compromise. Whether it is intentional or unintentional, it should always be reported to the appropriate authorities. A security violation may result in criminal prosecution—no matter the severity of the incident.

6.8.1 Security Countermeasures

Different categories of security countermeasures can reduce the risks associated with threats and security violations:

- *Employee-related security countermeasures* include separation of duties, staff rotations, security training, clear definition of authority, and maintenance of policies and procedures manuals that everyone is aware of.
- *Human resource-related security countermeasures* include employee background checks that consist of reference checks, employer checks, criminal history checks, credit checks, and even drug testing. Another countermeasure would be the disclosure of any conflict of interest that may be present with employee and employer relationships.
- *Internet-related security countermeasures* include items already discussed related to penetration tests. These tests include operating system identification and enumeration, port scanning, and obscuring sensitive information such as domain name registration information.
- *Facility-related security countermeasures* include proper storage of information, proper handling of information, proper location of secured areas, subdividing rooms with fire-resistant walls, and even use of man traps (double doors allowing one to open when the other is closed, thus "trapping" an individual in the entryway).

6.9 Service Providers, Service-Level Agreements, and Vendor Reviews

A service provider can be defined as any person or entity that maintains, processes, or otherwise is permitted access to certain sensitive information based upon the services provided to the organization. In recent years, a lot of emphasis has been placed upon these service providers and regulations requiring them to maintain the same level of security as required by the organization that they are servicing. Ultimately, the organization could be held liable and responsible for the security or lack of security provided by its service providers. Excellent sources of information can be obtained from the *FFIEC Outsourcing Technology Services* and *FFIEC Information Security IT Examination Handbook—Service Provider Oversight—Security*.

To assist you in conducting vendor reviews of your service providers, I have developed the following procedures. The purpose of establishing this process is to ensure that all service providers pass a due-diligence review prior to being used, that agreements and contracts with service providers meet all the requirements set forth by the organization, and that service provider relationships are monitored for continued adherence to contract terms.

6.9.1 Vendor Relationship Policy

The first thing a company must do in regard to managing vendor relations is to develop a vendor relationship policy. This policy should apply to service provider relationships that present material financial, operational, or reputational risk to the organization if the service provider should fail to perform. All procedures indicated in your vendor relationship policy should be followed prior to entering into any contract.

As an example, your vendor relationship policy should

set the right internal expectations of the service provider;
establish strategies and risk tolerance;
perform background checks and interview vendor's other clients;
review the financial stability of vendor;
review the contract prior to signing;
reconcile to required insurance;
identify the deliverables;
review status and performance of vendor (business owners, in coordination with the business continuity director); and
maintain up-to-date versions of the contract.

6.9.2 Service-Level Agreements

Service-Level Agreements (SLAs) are important to understand and should be a required element of any vendor relationship. These SLAs are a written understanding of the responsibilities and duties that are expected of each of the vendor and of the client. The organization should very carefully review these SLAs, which should contain, at a minimum, the following:

The SLAs should specify that a vendor will not use or further disclose the information it may obtain from the client for any purpose other than as permitted by contract or required by law. It is important that your organization's information be kept confidential; because some service providers may have access to this information, it is essential that they understand that they must not disclose such information.

The SLAs should indicate that a vendor will use appropriate safeguards to prevent the use or disclosure of the information. These safeguards will be specified by the client as requirements to the SLA or the vendor will document the controls it utilizes. In either case, it is important that appropriate controls or safeguards be in place for the protection of the organization's information.

The SLAs should state that the vendor will report to the organization any use or disclosure of information that may not be provided for in the contract. This, in essence, is the information disclosure policy of the vendor. The client should be provided with a copy of this policy and have the right to review it. If this policy does not meet the organization's requirements, the vendor should be put on notice of the deficiency. The vendor may need to change its policy if it wants to continue to serve the organization. Along with this information disclosure, any subcontractors or agents of the service provider to whom the service provider provides sensitive or proprietary information should also agree to the same restrictions and conditions regarding disclosure of information.

At termination of the contract, the SLA should specify the return or destruction of all sensitive or proprietary information—in any form, including hard copy or electronic version—received from or created by or on behalf of the organization that the service provider maintains. The SLA should specify that the service provider may not keep copies or if it is not feasible to return or destroy all sensitive or proprietary information, the service provider must continue to protect the sensitive or proprietary information. The service provider should limit use and disclose the reasons that make returning or destroying the information infeasible.

The SLAs should authorize the organization to terminate the contract if the service provider materially violates the terms of the contract. This is the fail-safe clause of the contract that enforces the preceding requirements.

6.9.3 Vendor Reviews

Certain responsibilities need to be specified in the organization as they relate to service provider management and vendor reviews. For example, the Risk Management Department of your organization may be responsible for conducting the financial and business review of a proposed vendor. The department may also be required to verify that the proposed vendor has sufficient business continuity processes in place to ensure continued delivery of services for the duration of the contract. The Risk Management Department may be required to complete a risk assessment review of the business processes affected by the proposed contract to include an information security review. The department may also be required to assist the business owner in the periodic performance evaluation of the vendor.

As part of the service provider management, the organization should review audits, summaries of test results, or other equivalent evaluations of its service providers. To meet this requirement, the Information Security Department, for example, may be responsible for assisting the business owner in determining whether or not the vendor has access to sensitive information. As a point of reference, some service providers may not be required to have a review conducted on an annual basis based on their roles and the services they provide to the organization. The Information Security Department may be called upon to assist the business owner in making these types of decisions about the service provider along with determining a classification of the service providers. The department may also assist the business owner in determining the criticality level of the service provider based upon the services it provides.

In addition, the Information Security Department may be required to conduct at least an annual review of all service providers by conducting a review of the service provider contracts, the responses of the service provider to a predefined questionnaire, and the testing of service provider controls. The latter is generally conducted within accepted industry standards.

To conduct a review and to rate certain areas as appropriate related to vendor review, I look at eight distinct areas. Assurance, nondisclosure, audits, notifications, due diligence, personnel, remote access, and information sharing and analysis center. I give a weighted average to each based on the service provider's criticality level and classification, which have already been determined. The first area I look at is in the service provider's controls. This is the largest and probably most important area of the review. I look at four elements under these controls. They are contractual assurances regarding security responsibilities, controls, and reporting; nondisclosure agreements regarding the companies' systems and data; indepedent review of security by indepedent auditors; and coordination of incident response policies and contractual notification requirements.

6.9.3.1 Assurance

I determine whether or not the contractual assurances regarding security responsibilities, controls, and reporting are adequate. I verify that the contract adequately covers the service provider's responsibilities to secure my organization's information. I look for specific controls that are documented in the contract and the reporting procedures that the service provider follows if security is breached. Next I evaluate the adequacy of contractual assurances regarding security responsibilities, controls, and reporting against my organization's requirements. I then determine whether contracts contain security requirements that at least meet the objectives of my organization's industry guidelines and contain nondisclosure language regarding specific requirements. Finally, I determine whether any service provider access to my organization's system is controlled according to authentication, access controls, and/or network security procedures.

6.9.3.2 Nondisclosure

I already took a high-level look at the nondisclosure language in the first area, but now I am going to dig a little deeper into it. I am going to look at three elements of nondisclosure: the agreement itself, the appropriateness, and the security requirements.

First, I look to make sure that the SLA or service provider contract contains a nondisclosure agreement. This agreement should reflect my organization's systems, data, or any other information to which the service provider may be privy. I will then evaluate the appropriateness of the nondisclosure agreement. I will note whether or not the nondisclosure agreement meets my company's requirements. Finally, I will determine whether the contracts contain security requirements that at least meet the objectives of my organization's industry guidelines and contain nondisclosure language regarding these specific requirements.

6.9.3.3 Audits

Again, I look for three elements: independent review, scope, and testing. First, I verify that the service provider conducts independent reviews of its security through appropriate audits and tests. This can be accomplished by the service provider hiring an independent firm to conduct an audit or control test of its environment, or it may be done by internal staff that have independent roles within their organization. Second, I determine that the scope, completeness, frequency, and timeliness of third-party audits and tests of the service provider's security meet my organization's risk assessment requirements. Finally, I determine whether appropriate security testing is required and performed on any code, system, or service delivered under the service provider's contract.

6.9.3.4 Notifications

I look at three elements: coordination, adequacy, and appropriateness. I first look at the service provider's coordination of incident response policies and contractual notification requirements. Next, I evaluate the adequacy of incident response policies and contractual notification requirements in regard to the risks involved in the services provided by the service provider. Finally, I determine whether appropriate reporting of security incidents is required under the contract.

6.9.3.5 Due Diligence

I look at three elements under due diligence: sufficiency, ability, and oversight. First, I evaluate the sufficiency of security-related due diligence performed by my organization on the service provider. I look at the research and the selection process that my organization went through to determine what service provider would be chosen for the specific service offered. Next, I determine whether or not my organization assessed the service provider's ability to meet contractual security requirements. I look for independent audits, recommendations from other service provider customers, any reports of security breaches, or any other documentation that can substantiate that the service provider is performing in a security-conscious manner. Finally, I make a determination on whether my organization has proper oversight in place to evaluate the service provider's security controls adequately. Is my organization conducting its own testing on the service provider's controls?

6.9.3.6 Personnel

I look at two elements: personnel controls and assessment. I determine whether appropriate controls exist over the substitution of personnel from the service provider on my organization's projects and services. Depending on the project, it may take several months to complete. The service provider may go through multiple employees assigned to a specific project prior to its completion. I want to make sure that the service provider has appropriate controls in place before new personnel take over certain sensitive projects. I also want to determine whether my organization appropriately assessed the service provider's procedures for hiring and monitoring personnel who have access to my organization's systems and data. Does the service provider conduct a full background check on all employees assigned to my project?

6.9.3.7 Remote Access

Along with making sure that the service provider is conducting appropriate background checks, I will determine the extent to which the service provider has remote access to my organization's systems and data as appropriate. If remote access is required, I will determine to what extent and how this access is provided and if it falls within my company's requirements or not.

6.9.3.8 Information Sharing and Analysis Center

The last area that I review is to determine whether the service provider participates in an appropriate industry Information Sharing and Analysis Center (ISAC). This is important to judge whether or not the service provider stays current on vulnerabilities and disclosures of exploits, especially if the service provider provides software as a service.

6.9.3.9 Service Provider Survey

To conduct the preceding review, I designed a service provider survey. As an example, this survey consists of the following questions:

Where (if at all) is information stored within your computing resources or by your subcontractors, including any backups and print copies of information?
If this information is transported or transmitted by your organization between or among various sites (including off-site storage), in what format are the data and under what protections?
What electronic and physical security protections are in place to ensure that only authorized individuals have access to information? How can you affirmatively ensure on an ongoing basis that no confidentiality breach has occurred? How often are these safeguards tested and are tests documented in a manner that we can review?
What are your formal policies for notifying us should there be any breach, or even a possible breach, of confidentiality within your organization? At what point is communication initiated, how quickly, in what format, how detailed, etc.?
Are your employees who have access to our information bonded in any manner? What reference checking or other investigation is conducted prior to employment of these people by your organization? Is there any ongoing update of this reference information?
What process do you suggest whereby we can independently verify the preceding information if we should wish to do so?

Administrative Controls ■ 157

Does your company participate in an appropriate industry Information Sharing and Analysis Center (ISAC)?

In summary, the review will utilize a combination of contract review, responses to survey questions, and testing of service provider security controls to evaluate the preceding areas. The review should involve a review of the service provider's contracts—specifically, the parts of the contract that deal with responsibilities, controls, notification, nondisclosure, and third-party auditing. The review should also review the responses of the survey and may follow up with the service provider for additional information or clarification on a specific item under review.

6.10 Managing Security Risks in Vendor Relationships*

Newspapers and trade journals feature a growing number of stories detailing instances in which businesses have entrusted their most sensitive information and data to a business partner only to see that information compromised because the vendor failed to implement appropriate information security safeguards. Worse yet, those same businesses are frequently found to have performed little or no due diligence regarding their vendors and have failed to address information security adequately in their vendor contracts—in many instances, leaving the business with no remedy for the substantial harm it has suffered as a result of a compromise. In today's business environment, businesses must be far more rigorous in entering into vendor relationships in which sensitive information will be placed at risk.

In this section, we discuss three tools businesses can immediately put to use to reduce the information security threats posed by their vendors and business partners substantially, ensure proper due diligence is conducted and documented, and provide remedies in the event of a compromise. These tools are: (1) the vendor due diligence questionnaire, (2) key contractual protections, and (3) the use in appropriate circumstances of an information security requirements exhibit. Whenever a vendor or business partner will have access to a business's network, facilities, or data, one or more of these tools should be used.

Use of these tools will enable a business to achieve a number of important goals:

■ Protect valuable assets of the business. In many instances, a business's proprietary and confidential information is *the* most important asset of the company (e.g., new product plans, future marketing activities, prospective business transactions, trade secret information, source code, etc.).

---

* Section 6.10 was provided, with permission, by Michael R. Overly, Esq., a partner at Foley & Lardner, LLP.

- Establish that the business has used due diligence in protecting its information and systems. In the event of a compromise, the tools will assist the business in documenting its efforts to minimize risk.
- Protect the business's reputation and avoid the public embarrassment associated with a security compromise.
- Minimize potential liability. A compromise of corporate data may result in shareholder suits against the officers of the corporation for failure to exercise reasonable business judgment in protecting that information. If the information relates to consumers, the individual consumers or a class action representing all affected individuals may seek damages against the company. Finally, businesses frequently are entrusted with sensitive, confidential information of their business partners. For example, one partner might share certain trade secrets with another partner in connection with the joint development of a product. A security breach compromising the information may expose a business to claims by its partners for negligence or breach of contract for failing to protect the information.
- Fulfill regulatory compliance obligations. For example, businesses handling personally identifiable consumer information will likely be subject to state and federal laws and regulations (e.g., GLBA and HIPAA) requiring the business to secure the information adequately from unauthorized access and use.

6.10.1 Due Diligence: The First Tool

Although most businesses conduct some form of due diligence before entrusting vendors and other third parties with their sensitive information or access to their systems, the due diligence is often done informally, in a nonuniform manner, and not clearly documented. In very few instances is the outcome of that due diligence actually incorporated into the parties' contract. This ad hoc approach to due diligence is no longer appropriate or reasonable in the context of today's business and regulatory environment. To ensure proper documentation and uniformity of the due diligence process, businesses should develop a standard "due diligence questionnaire" that each prospective vendor or business partner must complete. Areas covered by the questionnaire include corporate responsibility, insurance coverage, financial condition, personnel practices, information security policies, physical security, logical security, disaster recovery and business continuity, and other relevant areas.

Use of a standardized questionnaire has a number of significant benefits:

- It provides a uniform, ready-made framework for due diligence.
- It ensures an "apples-to-apples" comparison of vendor responses.
- It ensures that all key areas of diligence are addressed and none are overlooked.
- It provides an easy means of incorporating the due diligence information directly into the parties' contract. That is, the completed questionnaire is generally attached as an exhibit to the final contract.

From the outset, vendors must be on notice that the information they provide as part of the due diligence process and, in particular, in response to the vendor due diligence questionnaire will be (1) relied upon in making a vendor selection, and (2) incorporated into and made a part of the final contract. To be most effective, the questionnaire should be presented to potential vendors at the earliest possible stage in the relationship. It should be included as part of all relevant RFPs or, if no RFP is issued, as a stand-alone document during preliminary discussions with the vendor.

Key areas for the vendor due diligence questionnaire include the following:

- The vendor's financial condition. Is the vendor a private or public company? Can we obtain copies of the most recent financial statements? Financial condition may not appear to be a critical factor for information security purposes, but the possibility that a vendor may file bankruptcy or simply cease to do business while in possession of a business's most sensitive information presents a substantial risk. In such instances, it may be difficult, if not impossible, to retrieve the data and ensure that they have been properly scrubbed from the vendor's systems.
- Insurance coverage. What types of coverage does the vendor have? What are the coverage limits and other terms? Is the coverage dependent on the number of claims made or based on occurrences?
- Corporate responsibility. Are there any criminal convictions, recent material litigation, instances in which the vendor has had a substantial compromise of security, privacy violations, adverse audit results, etc.?
- Will the vendor require the use of any subcontractors or affiliates in the performance of its services? Will the vendor use subcontractors or affiliates outside the United States? Where are the subcontractors and affiliates located? What types of services will they provide? What information, if any, of the business will be sent to these entities?
- Organizational security procedures. What are the vendor's information-handling policies? Do they have a dedicated information security team? Is there an incident response team? What are the vendor's information security practices with contractors and agents (e.g., due diligence, requiring nondisclosure agreements, specific contractual obligations relating to information security, etc.)?
- What physical security measures and procedures does the vendor employ?
- Does the vendor use system access control on its systems to limit information access only to personnel who are specifically authorized?
- If the vendor is a software developer, what are its development and maintenance procedures? What security controls are used during the development life cycle? Does the vendor conduct security testing of its software? Does the vendor maintain separate environments for testing and production? Does the vendor license code from third parties for incorporation into its products? If so, what types of code?

- If personally identifiable consumer information is at risk, does the vendor have a privacy policy? What is the revision history of the policy? Are there any instances where the vendor has had to contact consumers regarding a breach of security?
- What are the vendor's business continuity/disaster recovery plans? When was its last test? When was its last audit? Were there any adverse findings in the audit? Have deficiencies been corrected? What is the revision history of its plan? What security procedures are followed at the recovery site?

6.10.2 Key Contractual Protections: The Second Tool

In the overwhelming majority of engagements, the contract entered into between a business and its vendors has little or no specific language relating to information security. At most, passing reference is made to undefined security requirements and a basic confidentiality clause. Today's best practices in vendor contracting suggest that far more specific language is required. The following protections should be considered for inclusion in relevant vendor contracts:

Confidentiality. A fully fleshed out confidentiality clause should be the cornerstone for information security protections in every agreement. The confidentiality clause should be broadly drafted to include all information the business desires to be held in confidence. Specific examples of protected information should be included (e.g., source code, marketing plans, new product information, trade secrets, financial information, personally identifiable information, etc.). Although the term of confidentiality protection may be fixed—for, say, 5 years—ongoing, perpetual protection should be expressly provided for consumer information and trade secrets of the business. Requirements that the business mark relevant information as "confidential" or "proprietary" should be avoided. These types of requirements are unrealistic in the context of most vendor relationships. The parties frequently neglect to comply with these requirements, resulting in proprietary, confidential information being placed at risk.

Warranties. In addition to any standard warranties relating to how the services are to be performed and authority to enter into the agreement, the following specific warranties relating to information security should be considered:
  - a warranty requiring the vendor to comply with "best industry practices relating to information security";
  - compliance with applicable consumer protection laws, such as GLBA, HIPAA, and relevant state statutes;
  - compliance with the business's privacy policy in handling and using consumer information;
  - a warranty against sending the business's confidential information to offshore subcontractors or affiliates, unless specifically authorized to do so by the business; and

  – a warranty stating that the vendor's responses to the vendor due diligence questionnaire, which should be attached as an exhibit to the contract, are true and correct.

General security obligations. Consider including generalized language in the contract relating to the vendor's obligations to take all reasonable measures to secure and defend its systems and facilities from unauthorized access or intrusion, to test its systems and facilities periodically for vulnerabilities, to report all breaches or potential breaches of security immediately to the business, to participate in joint security audits, to cooperate with the business's regulators in reviewing the vendor's information security practices, etc.

Indemnity. In situations in which a breach of the vendor's security may expose the business to potential claims by third parties (e.g., a breach of consumer information may result in claims by the business's customers), the agreement should include an indemnity provision requiring the vendor to hold the business harmless from claims, damages, and expenses incurred by the business resulting from a breach of the vendor's security. That is, the vendor should protect the business from lawsuits and other claims that result from the vendor's failure to secure its systems adequately.

Limitation of liability. Most agreements have some form of "limitation of liability"—a provision designed to limit the type and extent of damages to which the contracting parties may be exposed. It is not uncommon to see these provisions disclaim the vendor's liability for all consequential damages (e.g., lost profits, harm to the business's reputation, etc.) and limit all other liability to some fraction of the fees paid. These types of provisions are almost impossible to remove from most agreements, but it is possible to require the vendor to exclude from the limitations damages flowing from the vendor's breach of confidentiality and its indemnity obligation for claims the vendor itself causes because of its failure to secure its systems adequately. Without these exclusions, the contractual protections described previously would be essentially illusory. If the vendor has no real liability for breach of confidentiality because the limitation of liability limits the damages the vendor must pay to a negligible amount, the confidentiality provision is rendered meaningless.

6.10.3 Information Security Requirements Exhibit: The Third Tool

The final tool in minimizing vendor information security risks is the use of an exhibit or statement of work to define specifically the security requirements relevant for a particular transaction. For example, engagements in which highly sensitive information will be entrusted to a vendor may require the vendor to observe strict practices in its handling of the information. The information security requirements exhibit may prohibit the vendor from transmitting the business's information over internal wireless networks (e.g., 802.11a/b/g) or from transferring that information to removable media that could be easily misplaced or lost. The exhibit may also contain specific requirements for use of encryption and decommissioning hardware and storage media on which the business's information was stored to ensure that information is properly scrubbed from the hardware and media. Other specific physical and logical security measures should be identified as relevant to the particular transaction.

Businesses are presented with unique risks when they entrust their proprietary and confidential information to their vendors, business partners, and other third parties. Those risks can be minimized by employing the tools discussed in this article: appropriate and uniform due diligence, use of specific contractual protections relating to information security, and use—where relevant—of exhibits or other attachments to the agreement detailing unique security requirements to be imposed on the vendor.

6.11 Summary

In this chapter, we discussed the different phases of effective change management processes, including requesting changes, processing changes, releasing changes, testing changes, and the different steps in change management. In addition, we discussed the components of managing incidents and, more specifically, computer forensics. Thanks to Dave Kleiman for providing a lot of information covering computer forensics from his extensive experience in this field.

We went on to discuss some laws, investigations, and ethics related to electronic evidence and chain of custody procedures. In addition, we discussed operational security controls to include separation of duties and the concept of least privileges. Records retention has become a big issue, and we discussed the proper control over and storage of electronic information that may need to be presented in court.

I cannot emphasize enough how important it is to train your employees and make them aware of security. I provided a story to demonstrate how easy it is, in most cases, to gain access to a facility using trusted employees. We discussed some security management practices and countermeasures that can be easily deployed to mitigate the risk of a security breach. We also heard from Michael Overly in regard to handling providers. He discussed managing security risks in vendor relationships and the different tools that can be used to manage these relationships.

References

American Bar Association. August 11–12, 2008. Resolution 301. Retrieved December 7, 2008, from Abanet: http://www.abanet.org/leadership/2008/annual/adopted/ThreeHundredOne.doc

Diliberto, F. C. 1996. *Investigating computer crime.* Boca Raton, FL: CRC Press, Inc.

Howell, B. A., and Luehr, P. H. October 14, 2004. Child porn poses risks to companies that discover it in the workplace. *Tech Trends/Litigation.*

Jacquet, D. 2007. *Computer forensics expert vs. private investigator.* Certified CSI, LLC.

Kleiman, D. 2008a. *Forensics for information managers.* (Self-published paper.)

Kleiman, D. 2008b. *Introduction to digital forensics and the PI issue.* Palm Beach Gardens, FL: D. Kleiman. (Self-published paper.)

Kruse, W. G., II, and Heiser, J. G. 2001. *Computer forensics: Incident response essentials.* Reading, MA: Addison–Wesley Professional.

Microsoft. 2007. *Fundamental computer investigation guide for Windows.* San Francisco: Solution Accelerators.

Wikipedia. 2008, February 16, 2008. Ethics. Wikipedia.org.

Yeschke, C. L. 2003. *The art of investigative interviewing,* 2nd ed. Burlington, MA: Butterworth–Heinemann.

Chapter 7

Technical Controls

Objectives

- Develop a system hardening checklist for workstations and servers.
- Recognize some of the common ports that may not be required on local workstations.
- Understand some other host security controls that should be implemented in your organization.
- Understand the differences among viruses, worms, and backdoor "Trojan horses."
- Understand the importance of implementing controls around multimedia devices.
- Understand the seven layers of the OSI model and how it relates to the TCP/IP model.
- Convert decimal, binary, and hexadecimal number formats.
- Understand network addressing.
- Understand different network security controls such as recommended security settings, firewalls, IDS/IPS systems, and honeypots.
- Describe certain tricks that you can use to develop strong, complex passwords.
- Understand the importance of patch and vulnerability management.

7.1 Host Security

> Security is like a linked chain. It is only as strong as the weakest link.
>
> **Jay Trinckes**

We are now ready to talk about technical controls. Although every type of control is important, many individuals put a lot of emphasis on technical controls. Much money and time and many resources are allocated to different types of technical controls. Some technical controls can be very simple, like automated devices designed to turn systems off at designated times or when they are not in use. Other technical controls can be very complex and have a lot of configurations, like firewalls or routers.

One type of technical control is host security. When we talk about host security, we are primarily talking about the security controls in place for the users on their local systems. Although all devices on a network are considered hosts, we will primarily be discussing workstations and servers. We will discuss other types of hosts, such as routers, switches, gateways, etc., in Section 7.4 because they primarily make up the network infrastructure.

One of the most important layers of protection that an organization can implement involves locking down workstations or your local systems utilized by end users (i.e., your employees). What we mean is that these systems should never be placed on the network without going through a tested and approved system hardening checklist. Through my experience, this area of security is probably one of the most overlooked; however, as mentioned earlier, it is one of the most important and I will explain why.

Let us imagine that you provide administrative-level access or full access to all of your users on your local systems. Now imagine that your IT staff provides troubleshooting support or assistance to your users on a daily basis. For the sake of argument, we are working within a Microsoft network utilizing the Microsoft Windows operating systems on our workstations in a domain environment. Let us also assume that your IT staff logs on to these systems with domain administrator-level access. Because every user has administrative-level access to the system and the system now contains a domain administrator account due to the IT staff coming to fix a problem, we have set up a perfect scenario for an attacker to take control over the entire network.

The attack will go something like this: The local system (which is usually not as important as servers and normally has a lot fewer security controls in place) will be compromised. Compromising a workstation is pretty easy and can involve vulnerabilities from other software running on the workstation, obtaining the user name and passwords written down at the user's desk, social engineering attacks, different types of attacks that provide some remote access into the local workstation, or even the user leaving his or her desk with the system logged on. A number of different avenues can be utilized against the unwitting individual who is not very aware of security.

Once the local system is compromised, it is very easy to obtain the user accounts of the system and—lo and behold—a user account for the IT staff that has domain administrator rights is found. To put this into perspective, in about 15 minutes or less, a program can brute-force attack one of these accounts and crack even a 14-character password. Once the attacker has this domain administrator-level user name and password, he can take control of your essential servers and ultimately your entire network. If you think this cannot happen, I am here to tell you that I have been able to take over many networks using similar scenarios.

7.1.1 System Hardening Checklist

I cannot emphasize enough how important it is to develop and implement a system hardening checklist. This checklist should be followed for all devices prior to placing them into production. The systems should be tested and validated to verify that they conform to the security practices in place. The system hardening checklist should be updated as necessary and all systems should routinely be checked to verify that they are in compliance with these requirements. The system hardening checklist should include a list of all authorized software, standard user configurations, standard registry edits and other system configurations, verification that all ports are closed and that virus and spyware programs are loaded, and a list of any other customized settings that are specific to your environment.

One of the best sources that your organization can utilize in developing your system hardening checklist comes from the Security Content Automation Protocol Checklist (SCAPC). The SCAPC was developed by the National Vulnerability Database, sponsored by the Department of Homeland Security's National Cyber Security Division/US-CERT. You can view this information and the checklists at http://checklists.nist.gov/. In addition to the checklist, this resource will provide some automated tools that your organization can use to assist in analyzing your local security system posture. SCAPC also recommends some commonly accepted security practices for managed environments that we cover throughout this book.

Some of these recommendations include segmenting internal networks with internal firewalls or routers to include

other defense-in-depth techniques;
centralizing management of systems with highly restricted local user access or least-privilege access;
centralizing management of security-related applications such as antivirus or other malware protection software;
automating installations of systems and application patches and updates to limit the chances of not updating all systems on a regular basis;
restricting access to printers and other multifunctional devices along with their features;

centralizing log monitoring systems; and
centralizing backup systems and recovery facilities.

As described in the preceding scenario, one of the easiest security controls that you can place on any device is to change the default user name and password along with renaming the "administrator" account. It is important that all devices on the network require authentication prior to gaining access to these devices. No device on your network should allow a password to be "password," blank, the same name as the user ID, or a common name such as the name of your company. (Review Section 7.5 for further details on constructing complex and secure passwords.)

7.1.2 Host Services

Attackers can exploit systems through many different services that run on a particular system. The functions that a system provides are considered its services. For instance, a system may be set up to store different files or a system may provide Web pages to other systems on the network. Whatever the system's functions are, it is recommended that any service that is not used for a legitimate business purpose should be considered unnecessary and should not be utilized on the network. Although the service may not be a threat or a risk at the current time, this does not mean that a vulnerability or exploitation of the service will not be found in the near future. If it is not being utilized, the best course of action is to disable the service.

Services are offered to other systems on the network by opening different ports on the system. Over 65,000 ports are available to provide different services. Many services provided by systems are assigned specific ports. This way, other systems can request certain services from these systems on these specific ports. For instance, Web services usually use port 80 to provide Web pages. Because this is normally a standard port, other applications that may require these types of services can be hard coded with this port number in their applications.

As we have already discussed, if the service is not required, it should be disabled. Either the service can be uninstalled on the system or the port that the service utilizes can be closed. Because workstations usually request services from servers and do not necessarily run their own services for other systems to share, review Table 7.1 for a list of some of the more common services or ports that may not be necessary on dedicated workstations.

7.1.3 Other Host Security Controls

Other remote-access control programs should be turned off if they are not being used. I recommend that, if available, your operating system's built-in remote administration be utilized instead of other programs. For instance, Microsoft utilizes terminal services as an integrated remote access service. This is recommended for ease

Table 7.1 Common Unnecessary Workstation Ports

Port	Description
13	Time of day (TOD)
17	Quote of the day (QOTD)
19	CHARGEN
21	File transfer protocol (FTP) (especially on workstations; there may be a legitimate use of an FTP server; however, I recommend that authentication be utilized or secure file transfer protocol (SFTP) be used instead)
23	Telnet (passes user names and passwords in free text across the network. I strongly encourage the use of SSH discussed earlier or other secure protocols over Telnet, if possible)
53	Domain name services (DNSs) (should be closed on all devices other than the assigned DNS servers)
69	Trivial file transfer protocol (TFTP)
79	Finger
80	Hypertext transfer protocol (HTTP) (should be closed on all devices other than assigned Web servers)
119	News
123	Network time protocol (NTP) (should be closed on all devices other than assigned network time servers)
161	Simple network management protocol (SNMP) (I recommend turning this off on devices, especially workstations and servers. Some printers and other devices may require this service and I would recommend changing the community string to something other than public or private if it is required)
5000	Universal plug-and-play (UPNP) (some operating systems may have this port running by default, but I recommend turning it off if it is not being used)
8080	Proxy (should be closed on all devices other than assigned Web proxy devices)

of updating and patch management issues. Instead of having to update another program, most operating systems will automatically update their own remote access services as part of their automatic patch update process.

Other controls relevant to host security are to make sure that asset tags are attached to all devices and that the tags match updated inventory sheets. Make sure that systems have session time-out limits set, and, in case a user forgets to log off the system when he or she leaves a desk, the system should automatically turn into a protective mode by initializing a password-protected screen saver or other mechanism. It is important that antivirus or spyware software be installed on every system. In addition, these protective measures should not be allowed to be circumvented by the user. Systems should have log-on warning banners present upon log-on to limit liability. A sample of a log-on warning banner can be found in Appendix C.

We have already explained why it is important that users not have administrative-level access to their systems and why this access should be restricted following the least privileges rule. In addition, external media devices such as USB memory sticks, CDs/DVDs, or external hard drives should be controlled. (See Section 7.3 for additional information on this topic.)

Software installed on the systems should be licensed to the organization. Controls need to be implemented to prevent users from installing unauthorized software on their systems. If your company allows Internet access to users, it should be restricted and monitored by Web filtering software. (See Section 9.6 in Chapter 9 for further details.)

7.2 Malware Protection

As we have already briefly discussed, we need some technical control implemented to prevent *malware,* which is malicious software. This is software that causes harm to your systems, sucks up resources, or tracks user behaviors. This broad grouping of programs includes viruses, worms, Trojan horses, adware, and other related software. One of the easiest and probably one of the most effective security controls that you can implement into your network environment is antivirus, antispam, and antimalware protection.

7.2.1 Viruses, Worms, and Backdoors

Some malware programs are self-replicating. This means that they can propagate themselves to other systems throughout your network. A *virus* is one such program. A virus usually attaches itself to a file such as an executable file (.exe, for example) or word document file (.doc, for example). A virus requires some sort of user interaction to initiate. This means that a user has to click on or run the virus for it to implement its code.

Another self-replicating program is called a *worm*. A worm may be considered a little more dangerous than a virus because it does not require user interaction to propagate as it moves across a network. Some malware programs are considered to be both a virus and a worm.

Other programs are utilized to gain unauthorized access to a system. One such program is referred to as a *backdoor*. These backdoor programs are used to bypass security controls that have been implemented on the system. They can be triggered by the attacker at will to allow remote access or open other channels into the system.

Another form of this type of program is called a "Trojan horse." A Trojan horse looks like a legitimate program; however, this program has hidden malicious code inside. An attacker may use a Trojan horse program to trick the user into running it by looking like a useful, nonthreatening program. Once the Trojan horse runs, it may allow the attacker to gain unauthorized access into the system. These types of programs may modify the operating system and thus are also known as "rootkits" because they strike at the "root" of the system. The codes give the attacker access to the system and allow him or her to hide his or her activities.

7.2.2 DAT Signatures

One of the most important maintenance functions that you can apply to your malware protection software is to keep the virus signature files, or DAT files, up to date. Because new malware programs are created or variants of existing malware programs are designed daily, it is important that the antivirus solution that you implement is kept up to date against these threats.

It is recommended that the antivirus solution be an enterprise-wide solution. The solution should be centrally administered and should monitor the entire network, rather than just individual systems. It is also recommended, especially for e-mail, that a device be set up at the network boundaries to strip attachments from e-mail prior to its coming into the server. Spyware or adware protection should also be used in conjunction with antivirus on all systems and should be set up to scan and monitor these systems actively.

It is important to stay current on upcoming threats. Here are some sources that can assist you:

■ AusCERT (www.auscet.org.au);
■ CERT Coordination Center (www.cert.org);
■ Internet Storm Center (www.incidents.org); and
■ Security Focus Incidents Mailing List (http://www.securityfocus.com/archive/75).

Most of these sources have RSS feeds to which you can subscribe and receive daily notifications of threats.

7.3 Multimedia Devices

In the early days of computers, the system architectures were much different from what they are today. Huge mainframe computers stored and processed all of the transactions transferred to them by "dumb" terminals. Fortunately, as computers advanced, workstations on desks grew to have all the processing power needed without ever having to utilize a mainframe computer. In fact, most mainframe types of computers are primarily just central storage units for databases and files, with all of the processing requirements occurring on the local systems.

Along with the advancement in computers came advancement in multimedia devices. When we talk about such devices, we are talking about CDs, DVDs, removable hard drives, USB media, smart cards, and any and all other types of devices that are portable and are used to store information. These devices have grown to capacities that were only seen in normal hard drives, while getting increasingly smaller in physical size.

These devices have a lot of advantages, but they also raise several major security issues in the process. Entire databases, customer lists, and other sensitive files that were one time too large to be portable can now fit on devices that are smaller than a thumb. Operating systems and programs can even run from these devices without ever being loaded onto the systems. You can now carry every piece of information that you need on these small devices conveniently in your back pocket. These devices can be brought in and out of your facility without ever being noticed. They can carry away your organization's entire client list, financial accounts, trade secrets, and other proprietary and confidential information without your knowledge.

In developing policies and procedures to deal with these removable media devices, your organization must determine the business purposes behind them. It must decide why these types of devices should be utilized and who should be authorized to use them. It must decide what type of information will be stored on these devices and whether encryption of this information would be required.

Next, it must determine what types of controls are currently in place and what types of controls will need to be put in place to enforce the organization's policies. Are these controls administrative (i.e., policies and procedures), or will they be technical in nature? What are the requirements of these controls and what are the controls' limitations?

Will technical controls be hardware or software controls? Can you disable the hardware? If you set group policies to close certain ports, will this affect the use of legitimate business equipment such as keyboards, mice, printers, etc.? Numerous software applications enforce USB policies, and each has its own benefits and limitations. I cannot recommend one solution over another—short of saying that each solution has to be the right match for your specific organization.

In addition, you have to take a look at the devices themselves and the types of devices that will be utilized. Is encryption required on these devices? Again, there are several solutions for USB or removable media encryption, each with its own benefits and limitations. Some USB devices have their own software applications installed, such as those that come with U3 technology or other "smart drives." The organization needs to make sure that it considers the pros and cons of these technologies.

There are some recommended settings that you can use to restrict the use of multimedia devices. A good source is the National Institute of Standards and Technology (NIST) SP800-53, "Recommended Security Controls for Federal Information Systems." This publication shares specific registry settings that you can utilize to lock down these devices. There is a warning related to editing the registry, and it is very important that you are familiar with this prior to editing any registry settings. Improper registry editing can make a system unbootable and unusable. There are some precautions that you should take before editing the registry; as the NIST SP800-53 publication advises, you can follow the links to Microsoft's TechNet resources to learn more.

7.4 Network Security

Buckle your seatbelts, folks; this section is going to be an in-depth session and it is important. Technical controls regarding network security cover a lot of areas. When we talk about network security, we first must understand what it takes to have two systems (computers, servers, and other network devices) talk to each other. To explain this, we use a reference tool to understand data communication known as the Open Systems Interconnection (OSI) model.

The OSI model divides the communication process into seven layers. Each layer performs specific functions and offers services to the layer that is below it. The lowest three layers primarily focus on passing traffic to an end system; the four top layers complete the process of the communication at the end system. Without the OSI model, networks would be very difficult to implement and understand due to all of the different aspects involved in the communications of two systems. The OSI model defines a common standard and provides manageability between the different communication functions. A great computer-animated demonstration of the network communication process and the devices utilized in this communication can be found at the Warriors of the Net site (http://www.warriorsofthe.net/).

7.4.1 Seven Layers of the OSI Model

The seven layers of the OSI model are as follows:

- application;
- presentation;
- session;
- transport;
- network;

- data link; and
- physical.

These layers can easily be remembered using a mnemonic of "*a*ll *p*eople *s*eem *t*o *n*eed *d*ata *p*rocessing."

The first layer of the OSI is the physical layer. This layer specifies the type of medium, or cabling, to be utilized by the interfaces of the system to communicate with each other, as seen in Figure 7.1. This layer also specifies the connectors, electrical requirements, mechanical requirements, functional requirements, and procedural specifications of sending bits of data across the network (as seen in Figure 7.1).

The second layer of the model is the data link layer. This layer includes network interface cards, switches, and bridges, as seen in Figure 7.2. All devices on a network must have a unique address. It is similar to the address of your home. Without this physical address, you would not be able to get mail. Likewise, without a physical address for a computer, it will not be able to talk to other computers on the network. A network interface card, which is used to connect your computer to a network cable, has an embedded hardware address. This address is known as a

NIC   CAT5 UTP Cable   Hub/Switch

Figure 7.1   Physical layer.

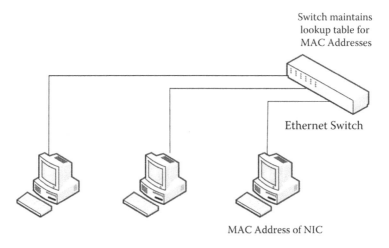

Switch maintains
lookup table for
MAC Addresses

Ethernet Switch

MAC Address of NIC

Figure 7.2   Data link layer.

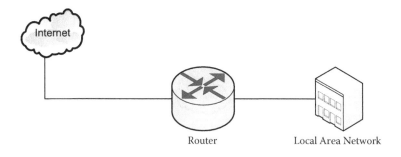

Figure 7.3 Network layer.

Figure 7.4 Transport layer.

Media Access Control (MAC) address. The MAC address consists of 12 hexadecimal characters. The first six characters are known as the Organizationally Unique Identifier (OUI) that is assigned to the manufacturer of the card, and the last six characters identify the serial number of the card.

The data link layer identifies the MAC address that will be utilized for communication and provides some error-detection capabilities. There has been some improvement in security by locking down and filtering at this data link layer through more intelligent switches.

The third layer of the OSI model is the network layer. This layer deals with an end-to-end logical addressing of system so that data can be routed across different types of networks, as seen in Figure 7.3. Internet Protocol (IP) addressing has come into play as networks have grown to provide traffic routing between different networks. Security has also been implemented through filtering at this router level.

The fourth layer of the model is the transport layer, as seen in Figure 7.4. The most common transport layer protocols are the connection-oriented Transmission Control Protocol (TCP) and the connectionless User Datagram Protocol (UDP). This layer provides many different functions, such as application identification, message arrival confirmation, memory overrun control, transmission-error detection, and sharing of multiple sessions over a single physical link.

The fifth layer of the OSI model is the session layer, which provides to applications the means to establish, manage, and terminate communications through the network, as presented in Figure 7.5. The sixth layer of the model is the presentation layer. This layer is responsible for how an application formats the data across the

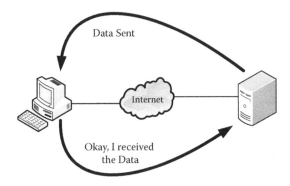

Figure 7.5   Session layer.

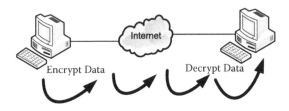

Figure 7.6   Presentation layer.

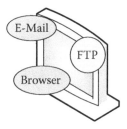

Figure 7.7   Application layer.

network. Encryption is also included in this layer, as seen in Figure 7.6. The seventh layer of the OSI model is the application layer. This layer is primarily what the user sees in terms of loading a Web browser or opening e-mail (demonstrated in Figure 7.7).

7.4.2 Other Layers

Three additional layers are not part of the OSI model, but may be just as important. Layer 8 is considered the "office politics" layer. In most organizations, management favors one group of individuals over another. This group usually has the best equipment and if for any reason this equipment is not working as it should, it is considered a priority for the technology department to fix it immediately.

In addition to layer 8, another layer is called the "blinders" layer. This undocumented ninth layer applies to executives that have decided on the way things should be done without looking into what is being done or what can be done. These executives may have come from organizations that have done things a certain way, so they want to change the way in which the current organization operates. Sometimes this is fine; however, they should not be so "blind" as to bypass planning and make quick decisions that may have detrimental effects on the current organization.

The last network layer that needs to be discussed is the "user" layer. Although users are much more than just a layer, it is important that some understandings and rules between users and technology staff be present. Networks are hard enough to operate without users making changes without consulting the necessary individuals first. IT staff has sometimes referred to issues that arise from users—who "did not do anything," but all of a sudden the network segment that they were working on no longer functioned properly—as layer 10 troubles, or "ID10T" errors.

7.4.3 Protocol Data Units

At each layer of the OSI model, the data that are sent are encapsulated within that layer. This capsule is known as the Protocol Data Units (PDU) for each layer. At the physical layer, bits (0s and 1s) are encapsulated into frames at the data link layer. From there, the frames are encapsulated into packets at the network layer. At the transport layer, packets become segments and are changed into data at the session, presentation, and application layers. The reverse happens to these PDUs when the data are received at the other end of the connection. Each layer at one host communicates with the same layer at the other host, as demonstrated in Figure 7.8.

7.4.4 TCP/IP Model

To go further into our discussion of networks, we have to review a key component that involves the TCP and IP. Although other networking protocols are available, TCP/IP is one of the dominant protocols in use on local and wide area networks. It is also the protocol of the Internet.

TCP/IP was originated as a proprietary Department of Defense protocol. It uses its own model of communication that is slightly different from the previous OSI model that we discussed. In a nutshell, OSI layers 5, 6, and 7 (session, presentation, and application, respectively) map to a single application layer of the TCP/IP model. Transport and network layers are the same for both OSI and TCP/IP. The bottom layer of TCP/IP, the network interface layer, combines both the data link and physical layers of the OSI model, as seen in Figure 7.9.

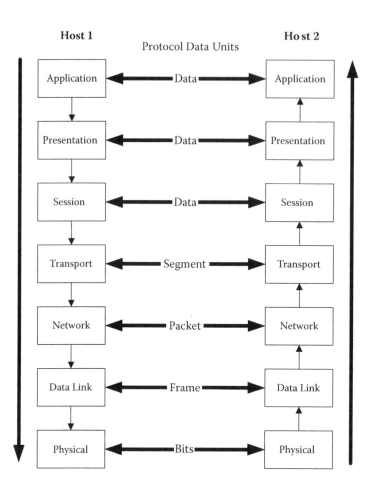

Figure 7.8   Protocol data units.

TCP/IP Model	OSI Model
Application	Application
	Presentation
	Session
Transport	Transport
Network	Network
Network Interface	Data Link
	Physical

Figure 7.9   TCP/IP model mapped to OSI model.

It is important to note that the TCP/IP model is a logical model, even though it defines some physical layers, because TCP/IP essentially will touch this layer at some point. In reality, TCP is essentially an OSI layer-4 protocol and IP is an OSI layer 3 protocol.

7.4.5 Decimal, Binary, and Hexadecimal Compared

As you might have already heard, computers only speak in 0s and 1s. In basic terms, a computer is made up of multiple switches that take the inputs in 0s and 1s and produce output based upon programming of certain switches. Of course, a computer is more complex than this; however, this is the primary concept behind the processing of a computer. Computers speak in a language called binary. Binary is base 2 numbering. Our numbering system is base 10. That is why we have 10 characters (0–9) that represent different values based on their column position. In base 2, there are only two possibilities: 0 = "off" and 1 = "on." Table 7.2 demonstrates this concept for the decimal number of 190.

To explain this further, columns that have a "1" on the binary value table are added together to make up the decimal value. In our example, binary values of 128 + 32 + 16 + 8 + 4 + 2 are equal to 190. Thus, to translate a decimal value into binary, we look at the values and see whether we can subtract the binary value into our decimal value. We ask ourselves, "Does the first binary value of 128 go into the decimal value 190?" Because it does with a remainder of 62, we put a 1 in the 128 binary value column. We move on to 64; the remainder of 62 is less than 64, so we put a 0 in the 64 binary value column. We move on to 32, which can be taken away from 62 with 30 left over. Thus, the binary value of 32 will get a 1. We continue in this fashion until we get a binary string value of 10111110 for the decimal value of 190. Table 7.3 assists with the binary values.

Hexadecimal works the same way; however, it is a base 16 numbering system. It is represented by 16 possible values, from 0 through 15. Because we would want to represent two-digit numbers in a single character, we use the letters A–F to represent numbers 10–15, respectively. Table 7.4 demonstrates the value relationships of decimal, binary, and hexadecimal values.

The easiest way to convert is through binary. For instance, in our example of decimal 190, we found that the binary value is 10111110. To translate this into

Table 7.2   Decimal Values

100,000s	10,000s	1,000s	100s	10s	1s
0	0	0	1	9	0

Table 7.3   Binary Values

128	64	32	16	8	4	2	1
1	0	1	1	1	1	1	0

Table 7.4 Decimal, Binary, and Hexadecimal Value Comparison

Decimal	Binary	Hexadecimal
0	0000	0
1	0001	1
2	0010	2
3	0011	3
4	0100	4
5	0101	5
6	0110	6
7	0111	7
8	1000	8
9	1001	9
10	1010	A
11	1011	B
12	1100	C
13	1101	D
14	1110	E
15	1111	F

hexadecimal, we split the eight characters into four binary bits: 1011 and 1110. From Table 7.4, we find that 1011 binary is B in hexadecimal. 1110 is E in hexadecimal. We use the expression "0x" to designate a hexadecimal value; thus, the decimal value of 190 will be represented as 0xBE in hexadecimal.

We conduct the reverse actions if we are to convert a hexadecimal value into decimal format. If we have a hexadecimal value of 0xA8, we would first convert hexadecimal A to binary (1010) and then hexadecimal value of 8 (1000). If we string these two 4-bit strings together, we get 10101000; now all we have to do is add the binary values together: 128 + 32 + 8 = 168.

7.4.6 Network Addressing

Now that we can convert decimal, binary, and hexadecimal values, let us move into network addressing. The Internet Assigned Numbers Authority (IANA) has defined five classes of IP addresses; however, we will only be concerned with three classes: A, B,

Table 7.5 Default Masks

Class	Default Mask
A	255.0.0.0
B	255.255.0.0
C	255.255.255.0

and C. This grouping is determined by the high-order bits, which are the highest values of an 8-bit binary string. Therefore, class A is high-order bit 0 with a range of 1–126. Class B has high-order bits of 10 with a range of 128–191. Class C has high-order bits of 110 with a range of 192–223. As a note of reference, 127 is left out because this number is dedicated as the local loop back, 127.0.0.1, and is normally used for testing.

An IP address consists of a network and host. To determine the part of the address dedicated to the network and the part dedicated as the host, you need to know the subnet mask. Each of the classes has a default mask, as seen in Table 7.5. In addition, certain IP addresses have been designated as private IP addresses. They are considered local addresses and are nonroutable on the Internet. These IP address ranges are as follows:

class A (24-bit block): 10.0.0.0 to 10.255.255.255 (16,777,216 possible addresses); class B (20-bit block): 172.16.0.0 to 172.31.255.255 (1,048,576 possible addresses); and class C (16-bit block): 192.168.0.0 to 192.168.255.255 (65,536 possible addresses).

Wherever you see a binary 1 in the subnet mask, it corresponds to the network part of the IP address. For example, if you have an IP address of 192.168.0.190 and a default mask of 255.255.255.0, the network and host part are as follows:

binary IP of 192.168.0.190:   11000000.10101000.00000000.10101000
subnet mask of 255.255.255.0:   11111111.11111111.11111111.00000000

In this example, the network is 192.168.0.X and the last octet of 190 is the host address on the network.

As you can imagine, IP addressing can get a lot more complicated as additional networks and hosts connect together. There is also the concept of subnetting, which allows for the borrowing of bits to expand the size of networks and ranges of hosts; however, this is beyond the scope of this book.

7.4.7 Network Security Controls

Now that we have learned a little about how systems talk to one another, we need to learn about what types of controls we can put in place to protect our networks.

These controls come in many different forms, such as an administrative form with policies and procedures or a technical form with different devices and filtering rules that have been implemented.

As you will notice, a lot of controls cross several different categories. For instance, renaming the default account of "administrator" on all devices, as discussed earlier in Section 7.1, also plays an important role in network access authorization procedures. Likewise, implementing a log-on warning banner should also be a part of your network security controls.

A formal, documented, and auditable process for requesting new network accounts that requires a signature approval of management should be in place. There should also be a formal verification process in place for resetting these network account passwords and removing accounts if someone is terminated or leaves the organization. As discussed under layer 2, filtering known as MAC filtering can be implemented at the switch level to identify authorized equipment being attached to the network. As already discussed, each device that communicates on the network has some sort of network interface card physically installed in it. Each card is programmed with a unique address set by the manufacturer of that card. Once a system is plugged into a network, a device, such as a switch, records this MAC address and provides communication at the data link layer. This MAC address can be filtered and security can be placed to control the devices allowed to connect to the network.

Network accounts should be audited frequently to verify that terminated or disabled users are no longer active. Once an employee has been terminated, his or her account should be deactivated immediately. In addition, the domain administrator groups should be checked and verified. Only individuals that require this type of access should be in this group. Although all groups should be verified, the domain administrator group should have special precautions and review.

7.4.7.1 Network Audit Log Settings

We have already discussed the importance of network logging and monitoring, but I wanted to provide some specific recommended settings here. The Computer Internet Security (CIS) standards utilize NIST SP800-53, "Recommended Security Controls for Federal Information Systems." Table 7.6 shows the recommended settings for audit logs. In addition, a SysLog server should be implemented to centralize the collection of these audit logs, and these logs should be reviewed at least weekly. They should be retained for at least 3 years or as defined by your records retention policy.

7.4.7.2 Network Security Settings

In addition to the network audit log settings, you should have specific network security settings configured. The CIS standards utilizing NIST SP800-53,

Table 7.6   Network Audit Log Settings

Audit Policy (Minimums)	Success and Failure
Audit account management	Success and failure
Audit directory service access	<Not defined>
Audit logon events	Success and failure
Audit object access	Success and failure
Audit policy change	Success (at a minimum)
Audit privilege use	<Not defined>
Audit process tracking	<Not defined>
Audit system events	Success (at a minimum)

"Recommended Security Controls for Federal Information Systems" (Table 7.7), show the recommend settings for network security.

In addition to these network security settings, a group policy should be in effect or other configurations implemented to shut down inactive sessions with a password-protected screen saver after no more than 15 minutes of inactivity. This will mitigate the chance of someone walking away from a desk and forgetting to sign off or lock the system for an extended period of time.

As previously stated, passwords should be unique for each user. They should follow the recommendations laid out in Section 7.5. You should conduct a routine

Table 7.7   Network Security Settings

Minimum password length	8 Characters; 12 characters for specialized security-limited
Maximum password age	42 Days
Minimum password age	1 Day
Password complexity	Enabled
Password history	24 Passwords remembered
Store passwords using reversible encryption	Disabled
Account lockout duration	15 Minutes
Account lockout threshold	15 Attempts; 10 attempts for specialized security-limited
Reset account lockout after	15 Minutes

audit on passwords, utilizing password auditing software that we will discuss later to see how many passwords can be cracked in an hour and also in 2 hours. It should also be noted how many of these accounts have domain administrator privileges because these are the "Holy Grail" of the network.

7.4.7.3 Network Diagrams

Network diagrams visually represent the configuration and architecture of the network. It is important that network diagrams be kept up to date as the network changes. These diagrams should contain all devices—laid out logically so that they can be easily understood—and should have proper classifications as to the type of information each device holds. A firewall should be located between all internal and foreign networks, and all devices housing databases should be located inside the protected network.

Internal IP address ranges should be non-Internet routable or private IP addresses, as noted in Section 7.4.6. This means that any device on the internal network must pass through a router or gateway to obtain access to the Internet and vice versa. There should also be some sort of network perimeter protection for e-mail, which should never enter the mail server without going through some prefiltering, blocking, or stripping of executable types of attachments prior to being introduced to the server.

Finally, network devices should be redundant in nature. If one of the devices fails, the other should automatically take over and continue to route traffic accordingly. There should never be a single point of failure anywhere in your network.

7.4.7.4 Firewalls

One of the required devices that you need on your network is a firewall. This firewall should provide "state-full inspection"; this means that only established connections are allowed to enter the network. These restrictions are set up through firewall rules. Some rules can be very complex, depending on the structure of your network. A formal approval process should be in place—not only to justify all firewall rules but also to document these rules as they change. These rules should be reviewed for accuracy on a regular basis.

7.4.7.4.1 Firewall Rules

Firewall rules should be set to deny all connections except those that are explicitly permitted. Specifically, the last rule of any firewall rule set should be "deny any" or "deny all." Firewall rules should be designed to allow access from one specific source IP address to one specific destination IP address over specific ports or protocols. No external connections should directly access systems on the internal network. In addition, any sensitive information passing through the firewalls into the Internet should be encrypted prior to traversing the public Internet.

7.4.7.4.2 Firewall Audit Logs

Firewall audit logs should keep track of all failed and successful connection attempts. These logs should be monitored on a daily basis, protected from modifications, and retained for at least 3 years or what is dictated by your company's records retention policy.

Most organizations have made the decision to contract with a third-party provider to monitor and assist in the upkeep of firewalls. I would say that this would be a good course of action, especially if your organizational resources are limited. Firewall maintenance is a full-time job if you want the effective protection that you should require for your network. I would recommend that the service provider chosen be thoroughly investigated and that you follow some of the tips provided in Section 6.9 in Chapter 6.

One special consideration that I should share with you at this time regards the storage capacity requirements for the logs that are recommended to be stored. Storage capacity requirements are determined by the following equation:

$$\text{(retention period in days} \times \text{events per day} \times 200 \text{ bytes)}/ \\ 1{,}000{,}000{,}000 = \text{storage size in gigabytes}$$

Log events average around 200 bytes each. Table 7.8 provides an example of the amount of storage capacity required for logging based on a retention period of 30 days. The Payment Card Industry Data Security Standards (PCI-DSS) require that these logs be retained for at least 1 year, with 3 months' worth readily available; the Sarbanes–Oxley Act requires 3 years of log retention.

With all these logs, what can you do about hardware storage requirements? For starters, I recommend implementing a write/read-only SysLog server, as noted earlier, to collect all audit logs from appropriate sources such as internal servers and routers. These servers can be configured to have enough storage space or off-load to a Storage Area Network (SAN). In addition, the software applications utilized should contain

Table 7.8   Storage Required for Logging

Events per Day	Storage Required (Gigabytes)
1,000,000	6
10,000,000	60
25,000,000	150
50,000,000	300

compression technology that will compress the normal log files down to a reasonable level while still keeping the recommended settings and retention policies in place.

7.4.7.5 Intrusion Detection System

Another required device on your network should be an Intrusion Detection System (IDS). An IDS is normally located between an internal network and a publicly accessible network. Its job is to examine all the data that pass through it. It can perform a deep inspection of the data, gather information, log it, and make alert notifications to administrators based on specific criteria. IDSs are passive in that they take no action on any generated alert; it is up to the administrator to make any decisions based on the information provided. The IDS will collect large amounts of information, but it will not block any traffic so that an administrator can get a complete look at what is going on in the network.

An Intrusion Prevention System (IPS), on the other hand, not only examines the data traversing the network, but also can make active decisions to block certain malicious or inappropriate traffic. This relieves some of the work or actions that an administrator may need to take to protect the network. Although it may appear that an IPS is better than an IDS, it can also be a disadvantage to put this responsibility on the IPS instead of the administrator. Because the IPS normally makes decisions very quickly, it may not perform an extensive examination of the data prior to blocking them. This can create some connection issues if legitimate traffic is being picked up as malicious and being blocked (Jackson 2005).

It is recommended that both solutions be utilized and the following be applied:

- Install an IDS/IPS solution outside the Internet firewall.
- Install an IDS/IPS solution inside the Internet firewall.
- Unless the organization has properly trained personnel on staff, outsource IDS/IPS monitoring to a third party that is staffed and trained to monitor activity and react to situations in real time, 24 hours a day, 7 days a week, and 365 days a year.

7.4.8 Honeypots

Honeypots are other devices that may be utilized to provide some security on your network. A *honeypot* is a system that fools an attacker into thinking that it is a "real" server or other system of interest. It can be used to gather information and monitor how an attack occurs and as an early warning system for intrusions.

There are many different types of honeypots. Most of these are described in terms of their ability to interact with an attacker. They are meant to be somewhat vulnerable so as to preoccupy an attacker and lead him or her away from other important network devices. Another type of honeypot is a low-interaction one. It emulates vulnerabilities rather than allowing the attacker to interact with it. These systems are usually safer, but they are less flexible to utilize.

One way that honeypots are utilized is by creating simulated networks of what appear to be live hosts. This, in essence, fakes the attacker out by masquerading real hosts with imaginary hosts. Another way that honeypot tools are used is by using a tool known as a network telescope, or darknet. Instead of faking a network, the tool is used to monitor traffic going to this network segment that has no real machines on it. A tool known as a *honeytrap* is used to monitor unknown attacks. This tool listens on all ports and dynamically loads handlers on these ports. It can record the session information, use replay techniques, download files, and proxy connections to other programs.

Just as there are servers to attract attacks, there are clients that actively search for malicious servers on the network. These clients are known as client honeypots. They can be quite expensive and require a lot of resources in that they actively seek out and attempt to find malicious servers based on state changes. There are also many application-specific honeypots, such as those that mimic open e-mail relays, proxy servers, and even Web application honeypots.

Although honeypots can be valuable tools, they have some potential security issues. One main concern is that a honeypot needs to be kept secret. If individuals know that it is a trap, then attackers will avoid it. Also, if one becomes compromised, this device can be utilized as a stepping stone on the network to gain control of other devices.

7.5 Passwords

Passwords are, by far, one of the most used and easily implemented security controls. They are also, in my opinion, one of the weakest forms of security controls that can be implemented. It is not that passwords themselves are the problem, but rather how they are utilized. Too many times, passwords are weak and contain common elements like dates of birth, relative names, common names, and other elements that make them easy to guess or easy to crack. At other times, because passwords are used so frequently, there are a lot of them to go around and some of them may be forgotten. To overcome this, individuals will write their passwords down and keep them in unsecured locations such as posting them on their monitors or underneath their keyboards. Of course, this defeats the purpose of the password altogether.

Because passwords are not going away anytime soon, let us discuss how we can make these passwords stronger. We focus on strong passwords because they minimize the threat of malicious individuals guessing them or cracking them. A strong password is one that is made up of at least eight characters. The password does not contain the user account name, a real name, or a company name. It should not be a complete dictionary word or even a slang word in any language. The reason for this is that multiple dictionaries can be used to crack these types of passwords. Passwords should be unique and changed on a frequent basis. They should not be similar to previously used passwords such as "password1," "password2," etc. They should also contain characters from at least three of the five following groups:

- uppercase letters (A, B, C,…);
- lowercase letters (a, b, c,…);
- numbers (1, 2, 3,…);
- nonalphanumeric keyboard symbols (~, !, @,…); and
- unicode characters (€, Γ, *f*, λ).

Instead of using a password, I would recommend using a pass phrase, which is a sentence that you can easily remember. For instance, consider the following sentence:

My daughter Traci is 4 years older than my son Brandon.

You can make a pretty strong password by just using the first letter of each word—for example, "mdtifyotmsb." You can make this even stronger by using upper- and lowercase letters, numbers, and special characters that look like letters. Here is my new password using these tricks:

MdT14Y0Tm$B

Pass phrases are not immune to dictionary attacks; however, most password cracking software programs do not check passwords over 14 characters. If you use pass phrases that are easy to remember, rather than conventional passwords, it is less likely that your password will be cracked by one of these programs. A good example of a strong pass phrase is

T0 B3 0r n0t T0 B3, th@t 1s th3 Qu3st10n?

This pass phrase is more than 40 characters long and uses four of the five character groups. It may not be a well-known phrase; however, it may be easier to remember than a 15-character alphanumeric password.

A new way of thinking about passwords or pass phrases is to utilize lyrics from your favorite song. Basically, you would be "singing" your password. For example, I love the movie *Highlander;* in that movie, a song performed by the group Queen is entitled "Who Wants to Live Forever?" Because this is a really good song in one of my favorite movies, I can remember a pretty strong pass phrase using this song title and mixing up some of the letters with symbols and numbers:

Wh0W@nts2Live4ever

Whatever method works best for you to remember a strong and complex password is the best course of action for you.

7.6 Patch or Vulnerability Management

When we talk about patch management, or vulnerability management, we are talking about how, as an organization, we are kept informed and up to date on critical vulnerabilities that have been discovered in the software that our organization utilizes. There are many ways in which you can be notified of these updates. If you are using reputable vendors, they should be providing software updates to you on a regular and automatic basis. You should stay up to date by going to the vendor's Web sites, using vulnerability databases, and staying in touch with user groups that may utilize the same programs you use.

Some resources that keep track of vulnerabilities include

■ The National Vulnerability Database: http://nvd.nist.gov/home.cfm
■ Packet Storm Security: http://packetstormsecurity.org
■ SecuriTeam: http://www.securiteam.com
■ Microsoft's Security Vulnerability Research and Defense (SVRD): http://blogs.technet.com/swi/default.aspx
■ SecurityFocus: http://www.securityfocus.com

No matter how you go about getting the information, one thing remains clear: You need a way to track and keep up with these patches. Some operating systems do a great job in automatically updating their software, especially for critical security patches. These types of updates should be installed on all of your systems within 30 days of their release and should be thoroughly tested in a test environment prior to deployment throughout your production environment.

You can keep track of these patches in many ways. One simple way is to create a list of all software that your organization uses. On this list, you should note the manufacturer of the software and the manufacturer's contact information, such as phone numbers, e-mails, or Web sites. You should note how your organization receives information on updates and patches for each of these software applications. If you are not sure how these updates are communicated to your organization or the application does not have its own automatic update feature, you should contact the software vendor to determine how this is done. You should track when updates come out, when they are tested, the results of the testing, and when they are deployed into production.

7.7 Summary

In this chapter we discussed several different types of technical controls. We described different types of controls surrounding host security to include the importance of standardizing host configurations and utilizing well-documented system hardening checklists. We emphasized that services not required on host devices should be disabled. We then discussed protection against viruses, worms, and backdoors with an emphasis on keeping malware protection software updated at all times. We went on to describe network security controls and provided a background in how computers communicate with each other by describing the OSI and TCP/IP models. We also worked on a little math and how we convert decimal, binary, and hexadecimal numbers.

As part of the defense-in-depth principle, we discussed audit logs, firewalls, intrusion detection, intrusion prevention, and honeypots. All of these items assist us in providing that layered defense mechanisms. We also discussed the importance of passwords and how to create very complex passwords that can be easily remembered. Finally, we ended the chapter on a discussion of patch and vulnerability management. We described the importance of maintaining track of our software and updates to that software.

Reference

Jackson, W. October 24, 2005. IDS vs. IPS: Experts say use both. Retrieved February 17, 2008, from Government Computer News: http://www.gcn.com/print/24_31/37334-1.html

Chapter 8

Application Controls

Objectives

- Describe the different general phases of the Software Development Life Cycle (SDLC).
- Understand the different types of SDLC methods.
- Understand the advantages and disadvantages of using e-mail.
- Understand the importance of encryption.
- Describe the different types of encryption, such as symmetric key, asymmetric key, and digital signatures.
- List different types of private key encryption algorithms.
- Determine how to choose the best private key encryption algorithm for your needs.
- List different types of public key encryption algorithms.
- Determine how to choose the best public key encryption algorithms for your needs.
- List different types of e-mail encryptions.
- Determine how to choose the best e-mail encryption for your needs.
- Understand the different types of Internet encryption available.
- Determine how to choose the best Internet security method for your needs.
- Understand the importance of encrypting hard drives.
- Understand different types of encryption attacks.
- Understand the factors that go into multifactor authentication.

8.1 Application and System Development

This chapter is dedicated to application controls. This section specifically examines the decision-making process involved in application and system development. The formal process or steps taken to develop a piece of software are known as the Software Development Life Cycle (SDLC). The SDLC process may vary slightly in different frameworks or standards; however, it generally encompasses the following:

- conceptualization;
    - requirements and cost/benefits analysis;
    - detailed specification of the software requirements;
    - software design;
    - programming;
    - testing;
    - user and technical training; and finally
- maintenance.

There are several methodologies or models that can be used to guide the software development life cycle. Some of these include

- the linear or waterfall model (which was the original SDLC method);
    - Rapid Application Development (RAD);
    - Joint Application Development (JAD);
    - the prototyping model;
    - the fountain model;
    - the spiral model;
    - build and fix; and
- synchronize and stabilize.

Usually, a few models are combined into a hybrid methodology to make the best fit for the project. (MKS, Inc. 2007)

Most of these methodologies are self-explanatory and others go beyond the scope of this book; however, we will cover the typical steps involved in a system development project.

To expand on the life cycle phases of a system development project, the first step is project initiation. In this step, we develop the scope of the project and figure out the exact business reason for the system. We will tie in our risk management and analysis procedure to determine possible security vulnerabilities and the mitigating controls that we need to take into consideration.

During the functional design, analysis, and planning phase, we will define the security requirements and develop some checkpoints within the system. We will also define how we are going to handle change control on this project. We need to make sure that appropriate personnel are making authorized changes and make sure that implemented changes work the way we expect them to work.

We then move into the system design and specification phase. We will determine the hardware requirements and what types of data will be utilized by the application, as well as look at the function of the application and the triggers that the application will utilize to make it work.

Once the planning part of the development cycle is complete, we must then write the code. This is considered the software development phase, and the programming begins here. We need to include thorough testing throughout this phase, at specified intervals, to make sure that our security controls are in place. We should also make sure that duties of individuals that write or program the system and individuals that conduct the testing on the system are separated.

When the programming is complete, we will then install and implement the application. We run the application through a complete functionality test, performance test, and security test to make sure the program is working as designed. Now that we have the application in place and everything is working, we will continue to maintain the operation of the system and implement changes as necessary, following our change management procedures.

As the system becomes obsolete, we will make a decision as to keeping the system updated or replacing the system with something new. During this final phase, we will take into consideration the complete destruction of any media, data, hard copy documentation, etc. if we decide that the system will no longer meet our business needs. See Figure 8.1 for a general description of how the SDLC works.

One method of software development that we spoke about earlier is the waterfall software development model. This method of design has defined phases with required formal completion reviews. Once one phase is complete, it will be reviewed prior to moving on to the other phase. If this phase was not successful in meeting its predetermined goals, that phase will be redone prior to moving to the next. Changes to the system are only allowed to be done within the current phase or one previous phase. This method may also incorporate verification and validation into each phase.

As previously described, it is extremely important that information security be integrated into the beginning design or project initiation phase. We want to make sure that adequate controls are in place and security requirements are explicitly stated. We also want to make sure that data inputs and outputs will have validation checks and are protected from accidental or deliberate acts. Program source code should always be restricted to authorized individuals only and audit trails should be logged for every type of successful or failed access or important transaction.

Software dealing with sensitive information should have built in authorization controls containing the following requirements:

■ Passwords should be a minimum of eight characters in length. Carried over from the Microsoft Windows operating system, this number has been set

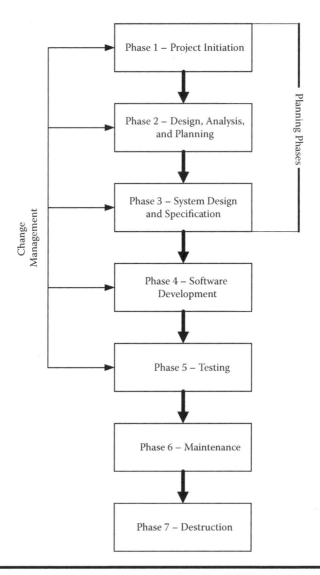

Figure 8.1 Phases of the software development life cycle.

as best practice. Without getting very technical, the hashing processes used by Microsoft to authenticate users involved breaking the hashes into seven character groups. If a password was seven characters or less, widely available cracking programs were able to crack them with ease. Adding an additional character significantly increased the amount of time it took these programs to crack the password because they were now dealing with two groups of hashes instead of just the one seven-character group.

■ Maximum password age should be less than 90 days. This requires passwords to be changed at least every 3 months. The reason this is best practice is to keep the passwords fresh and new. Over time, passwords may be written down or given to other people that may no longer be with the company; maybe the same passwords are being used for several different applications. All of these items raise the risk of passwords being compromised. To mitigate some of this risk, users are normally required to change their passwords on a frequent basis.

■ The software should remember at least the last 10 passwords. For some of the reasons already stated, passwords should be changed to new ones on a frequent basis. Password history settings require the users not to use the same passwords that they used in the past. This requires them to use different passwords; setting the level to 10 requires them to go through 10 different passwords before allowing them to utilize the same ones again.

■ The software should lock accounts out after three failed attempts and should be reset only by an administrator. This control mitigates the risk behind cracking programs using brute force on the user's passwords. Most cracking programs will attempt to guess all possible character and number combinations of a password. After three guesses, the account will lock out and become temporarily disabled. Once the account is locked out and requires a reset from the administrator, this creates an alert mechanism for the administraor to follow up on why the account was locked out in the first place. If the password resets after a certain amount of time instead of requiring administrator action, this may allow a malicious individual to resume the cracking process without creating alerts for the administrator.

■ User templates should be utilized to set up new accounts based on roles of the individuals. Using templates is an effective and efficient way to set up new accounts based on the duties and responsibilities assigned to that individual. Time can be spent up front creating the accounts, instead of re-creating them, by making sure that the least number of privileges are assigned to them. Checklists can be used to make sure that the accounts are not given more rights than they need; these templates become the standard security policies for the users.

■ The software should have a connection time limit set based on session inactivity. This best practice is utilized to maintain control of the program resources and limit the footprint the program has in operations. If a program is left open for a period of time and no activity occurs, the session will terminate and the user of the program will have to reauthenticate. Session termination closes ports and services that may have been used so as to limit the risk that malicious individuals may utilize these vectors to compromise the systems. It also makes the programs more efficient by not wasting resources on sessions that have no activity.

System and application developers should provide easy communication channels to their clients to keep them updated on new development, security updates, and new vulnerabilities that may be found in their systems. Someone in the company should be assigned responsibility to keep updated on any vulnerabilities or updates to these applications. In addition, any critical security updates should be fully tested before deployment to the system and should be installed within 30 days of official release from the application vendor.

8.2 e-Mail

It seems that no one talks face to face anymore and a lot more communication is taking place through e-mail. It is amazing to note that the protocols utilized in sending and receiving e-mail were set up as an unreliable communication channel; however, if you go to any business, e-mail is considered to be one of the most critical business processes. Businesses have spent millions of dollars to maintain their e-mail systems and on litigation or settlement of lawsuits that have arisen from the misuse of e-mail. Without appropriate computer use policies that include e-mail and Internet access, organizations are leaving themselves open to some legal risks and a host of other potential issues, such as spam and viruses being introduced into their networks.

As you are probably already aware, some of the advantages of e-mail include

- *Wide use and accessibility:* almost everyone has an e-mail account.
- *Speed of delivery and ease of forwarding:* with just a click of a button, communication is broadcast instantly to those that are on the list.
- *Economics:* e-mail is cheap as opposed to parcel mail or "snail mail."
- *Attachments:* e-mail can contain attachments of other documents.

Although using e-mail has many advantages, it is not without its costs:

- *Security:* most e-mail, unless encrypted, transfers across the wire in clear text and can be captured by unauthorized individuals.
- *Informal treatment:* how many times have you seen or even written items in e-mails that you would not have written in other forms or reports. Even grammar, spelling, and sentence structure are overlooked in writing e-mail as opposed to other formal documents.

■ *Ease of circulation and copying:* although this was noted as an advantage earlier, it is also considered a problem in the form of copyright infringement.

■ *Sexual harassment and discrimination:* how many times have you heard of cases or even been involved in cases where e-mail was utilized as a form of sexual harassment or discrimination?

■ *Ease of misaddressing:* how many times have you accidentally sent an e-mail to a wrong addressee and then had to "eat crow" because you were not able to stop the e-mail before it was sent?

■ *e-Mail forgery:* e-mails can be easily forged and utilized in phishing attempts.

■ *"Spam" attacks:* e-mails are utilized in creating spam or unwanted e-mail attacks. These types of attacks can bring down e-mail servers and fill up user in-boxes with a lot of garbage.

■ *Viruses:* one of the avenues by which viruses enter a network is through e-mail. Viruses can enter a network through a couple of different ways, including user intervention, or tricking a user into activating a malicious e-mail attachment or possibly entering a network through outdated virus scanners.

To reduce, and possibly eliminate, some of these negative factors [with e-mail], businesses can take three steps:

1. Adopt written policies on computer and e-mail use that specifically define the rights and obligations of employees regarding computer resources.
2. Conduct training and awareness seminars for employees regarding proper use of their computers and Internet and e-mail access.
3. Install appropriate monitoring and filtering software to prevent access to inappropriate material and to identify problem employees. (Overly 1999)

Another major issue related to e-mail comes from the amendments to the Federal Rules of Civil Procedures (FRCP) effective on December 1, 2006. In essence, the courts have taken a stronger stance with organizations that have not appropriately dealt with e-mail.

It is difficult to identify a single U.S. entity that could not feel the Federal Rules of Civil Procedure. There are no exceptions for company size, nonprofit status, or foreign organizations. The FRCP apply to lawsuits that cross state lines and many court cases that involve federal regulations, such as workplace safety, immigration, and discrimination. States are also starting to adopt the major provisions of the FRCP for state courts. (Roger Matus 2007)

In addition, with the new technology available for e-mail retention and retrieval, the courts have no tolerance for companies that cannot retrieve their e-mail in an accurate and timely matter. Limited resources and staff is no excuse, even for small companies. It is no longer enough to have a policy for retention and legal holds; the company must now prove that it is in compliance and following these policies at all levels.

In most cases, it is less expensive to implement a system for e-mail retention and retrieval as opposed to taking the risk of failing to meet the FRCP requirements. Penalties and fines can be severe (Roger Matus 2007).

The important things to remember related to the FRCP amendments are that the amendments differentiate between Electronically Stored Information (ESI) and other types of records. The amendments to the FRCP require early attention to electronic discovery. There should be discussion regarding such discovery efforts. The amendments also address the inadvertent production of privileged or protected materials. There is a two-tiered approached for discovery. The first deals with reasonably accessible information and the second deals with inaccessible data. The amendments provide for "safe harbor" against penalties if the company acted in "good faith" and was not able to provide required information under discovery requests (Tolson 2007).

Another important factor to consider when an organization selects between a backup or archiving system involves being able to provide e-mail in its original form per FRCP Rule 26(f)(3). Archiving or backup systems need to ensure that someone cannot change any of the original messages and that no additional information is added to an e-mail. It is also necessary to be able to export messages in their original format easily.

Under FRCP Rule 37(f) (the safe harbor provision), a company is protected from sanctions for deleting e-mail as part of "routine, good-faith operation." However, this rule also includes the obligation of organizations to ensure that employees cannot delete messages once a litigation hold has been enforced.

Litigation holds are normally placed on documents (and e-mail) when it is "reasonably foreseeable" that litigation will occur. An indicator that may require a hold would be you or your company receiving a notification of a lawsuit. This may be in the form of a sworn complaint or subpoena or in the form of a verbal threat of litigation if someone tells you that he or she is going to sue you or your company. Other good indicators of a hold requirement include a governmental entity beginning an investigation or an attorney requesting some facts related to an incident. If someone is injured or an employee makes a formal complaint to management, it may be a good time to place a hold on relevant documents or information (Roger Matus 2007).

The preceding recommendations or suggestions in no way should be construed as legal advice and legal counsel should be consulted for a professional legal opinion and interpretation of the FRCP. The information in this book is presented to make you aware of some of the legal issues that may be present in your environment, but it should not be used as a basis for legal opinion.

In deciding on a possible e-mail archiving and retrieval solution, you may want to ask the following questions:

1. Would a hosted solution or an in-house solution be better for my organization?
2. Is the system scalable or can the number of mailboxes archived be increased?
3. How much e-mail can I archive and for how long?
4. Do I need journaling or log shipping capabilities?
5. How are searches handled in response to e-discovery requests?
6. What do I need to know in regard to "litigation holds"?
7. What type of employee access should I give related to e-mail or mailbox archiving?
8. Should I incorporate personal storage table (.pst) files into the archive?
9. What are the server backup requirements for e-mail archive solutions?
10. What are the storage requirements for e-mail archiving?

Some of the benefits achieved by archiving e-mail as described in the book *Email Archiving for Dummies* include

1. meet federal and state regulatory requirements;
2. respond to e-discovery orders and litigation hold requirements;
3. increase your server's performance;
4. reduce your server backup and recovery times;
5. reduce storage requirements to lower your overall storage costs;
6. increase employee productivity;
7. adopt internal corporate governance processes;
8. more effective corporate knowledge management;
9. lower migration costs; and
10. eliminate personal storage table (.pst) files.

In addition to e-mail archiving, something else to consider is the amount of time that these types of records need to be stored, as described earlier in Section 6.6 in Chapter 6.

On the technical side, several controls should be implemented on e-mail servers. For instance, mail exchange records that may be publicly available should not disclose the internal networking scheme or IP addresses. It should not be possible for e-mail originating from the Internet to be relayed through the organization's servers back out to the Internet. Protocols related to e-mail, such as Simple Mail Transfer Protocol (SMTP), Post Office Protocol (POP3), or Internet Message Access Protocol (IMAP) services, should not provide the type or version information of the services running on the mail servers.

Furthermore, specific e-mail addresses should be guarded from distribution or made available as business needs require. For instance, if you list specific e-mail addresses of your executives on Web sites, a malicious individual might attempt to use this information in spamming or social engineering types of attacks. It may be better to use general e-mail accounts, such as administrator or Webmaster, or names of departments, such as Accounting, Human Resources, or IT. e-Mail addresses should be utilized within predefined policies and procedures of your company for business purposes only. If specific e-mail accounts are required, you may want to spell out the word "at" instead of using the symbol "@" and "dot" instead of "." as in this example: email[at]yourwebsite[dot]com. This may provide some mitigation over spider software that could be used to mine e-mail accounts from publicly available Web sites.

8.3 Encryption

Encryption is a very important control to implement on your data. Numerous security breaches have involved organizations not utilizing encryption to protect their sensitive data. Although you are not expected to become an expert in encryption by reading this book, it is my intent to summarize and provide some details regarding the process behind encryption and some of the different types of encryptions currently available.

Before we start talking about encryption, let us review a few terms related directly to encryption that you must understand. First, *authentication* is to provide proof that you are who you say you are. This can be done by something you know (like a password), something you have (like a security token or, in the case of encryption, a key), and something you are (usually a fingerprint). Second, *encryption* is intended to keep information confidential. This means that encryption is intended to prevent the unauthorized disclosure of the information. Third, when we speak of *integrity,* we are talking about the assurance that the information has not been changed by an unauthorized individual. Finally, *nonrepudiation* means that someone is not able to deny that he or she committed an act or that a transaction took place on that person's behalf of which he or she was not aware.

Encryption is a way to mask data using a mathematical algorithm to convert the data, or *plaintext,* into an unintelligible form, called *ciphertext,* and convert it back again to its original form by someone who is authorized to view these data or this information. Encryption has been around for many years and has been used in many different forms. Throughout history, forms of encryption were used to transfer information between military leaders. These orders could not be passed in "clear text" because the messenger bearing the order might be captured in the line of duty.

The same still holds true today. Many types of protocols, such as File Transfer Protocol (FTP), Password Authentication Protocol (PAP), Post Office Protocol (POP), Simple Network Management Protocol (SNMP), and Telnet, transmit information in clear text by default; thus, encryption plays a key role in protecting sensitive data utilizing these types of protocols.

Here are some additional terms that you need to know before we discuss some of the different types of encryption available today:

- An *algorithm* is a set of rules or a mathematical formula used to encrypt and decrypt data.
- *Block ciphers* function by dividing the message into blocks for processing.
- A *cryptographic key* is a piece of information that controls how the cryptographic algorithm functions.
- *Stream ciphers* function by dividing the message into bits for processing.
- *Substitution cipher* is a simple method of encryption in which units of plaintext are substituted with ciphertext according to a regular system.

8.3.1 Private Key Encryption (Symmetric Key Encryption)

There are many different types of encryption methods and many different algorithmic formulas. A few common methods of encryption in use today are private key encryption (or symmetric key encryption), public key encryption (or asymmetric key encryption), and the use of digital signatures. Private key encryption (or symmetric key encryption) uses a single "private" key that both encrypts and decrypts a message. This method is primarily used when high performance is required. The key distribution of this encryption method only provides confidentiality. Each of the many types of algorithms has its own pros and cons. We will discuss some of the more common symmetric encryption algorithms here and give you a little detail about each.

8.3.1.1 Blowfish

Blowfish is a quick and secure secret key cryptography that utilizes a 256-bit key and breaks the plaintext down into 64-bit chunks before it encrypts it. It is a general-purpose symmetric algorithm that was intended as a replacement for DES. The algorithm uses a block cipher method with block lengths encrypted through 16 iterations of 64 bits, and it can have key lengths of up to 448 bits.

8.3.1.2 IDEA

IDEA is utilized in "pretty good privacy" (which we will detail later) using a block cipher with block lengths of 64 bits divided into smaller 16-bit units and encrypted through eight iterations. Key lengths are 128 bits.

8.3.1.3 RC2, RC4, RC5, and RC6

RC2, RC4, RC5, and *RC6* algorithms were created by RSA Data Security in Redwood City, California. RC2 is a block-based cipher that uses a variable key size and 64-bit block. RC4 is a stream-based cipher that uses a variable-length key and a 40-bit block. RC4 is commonly used in Wired Equivalent Privacy (WEP) encryption for wireless networks. (Note: 128 bits is becoming more popular and will be discussed further under the wireless section in this book.) RC5 is slower than RC4, but allows for greater security. RC5 (created by Ron Rivets and patented by RSA) uses block ciphers with variable blocks (32, 64, or 128 bits) and has key lengths up to 2,048 bits. RC6 is a block cipher based on RC5 and uses a minimum of 128-bit block size and two working registers. It complies with the Advanced Encryption Standard (AES).

8.3.1.4 Twofish

Twofish algorithm uses block cipher with 128-bit block lengths and encrypted through 16 iterations. Key lengths can be up to 256 bits. It may also use a Feistel network and subkeys for additional security. (Note: A Feistel network is a framework for designing block ciphers developed by Horst Feistel at IBM in 1974.)

8.3.1.5 Data Encryption Standard

Data Encryption Standard (DES) was developed by the National Bureau of Standards (NBS), now known as the National Institute of Standards and Technology (NIST). This algorithm uses a 56-bit key for symmetric key encryption and the remaining 8 bits are used for parity. This method breaks the plaintext into 64-bit chunks before it is encrypted. DES is a commonly used encryption and is very fast; however, it only offers a few hours of exhaustive key search to those trying to crack it. It has been phased out due to this issue and replaced by Advanced Encryption Standard (AES). There are four modes of DES:

- *Electronic Codebook Mode* (ECB) is a native DES encryption mode with the highest throughput, but it is the easiest mode to crack.
- *Cipher Block Chaining Mode* (CBC) is widely used and similar to ECB. It takes data from one block to be used in the next—in essence, "chaining" the blocks together. It is more secure than ECB; however, any errors produced by processing in one block will be propagated to the next block.
- *Cipher Feedback Mode* (CFB) emulates a stream cipher and is used to encrypt individual characters.
- *Output Feedback Mode* (OFB) emulates a stream cipher; however, errors do not propagate throughout the process because OFB uses plaintext to feed back into a stream of ciphertext.

8.3.1.6 Triple Data Encryption Standard

The *Triple Data Encryption Standard (3DES)* algorithm takes longer to encrypt than DES, but raises the key used to 168 bits. It uses two or three keys to encrypt data and performs multiple encryptions. It uses a 112-bit cipher key and encrypts a message a total of three times.

8.3.1.7 Advanced Encryption Standard

The *Advanced Encryption Standard (AES)* algorithm was developed by NIST as a replacement for the previous versions of DES. It uses a Rinjdael block cipher that incorporates a block and key length of variable sizes. AES implementations use key sizes of 128, 192, or 256 bits and a fixed block length of 12 bits. It has been approved for use by the U.S. government because it has been able to withstand all known encryption attacks. It uses a four-step, parallel series of rounds:

Step 1 (byte sub). Each byte is replaced by an S-box substation.
Step 2 (shift row). Bytes are then arranged in a rectangle and shifted.
Step 3 (mix column). Matrix multiplication is performed based on the rectangle arranged.
Step 4 (add round key). The round's subkey is "cored in."

8.3.1.8 SkipJack

The *SkipJack* algorithm is quite involved and was declassified by the National Security Agency (NSA) in June of 1998. It uses an 80-bit key to encrypt 64-bit chunks. The encryption key is also encrypted with another two escrow keys. Lost keys cannot be recovered, and this algorithm has not been able to be reversed engineered.

8.3.2 Choosing a Symmetric Key Cryptography Method

With so many methods available, how do you choose the best one? Here is a guideline that you can use to determine an appropriate symmetric key cryptography method.

1. Review the security and cryptography requirements. If a large volume of information requires fast encryption, symmetric key cryptography would be the best encryption method. If the encryption requires authentication or non-repudiation, then you will need to choose something other than symmetric key cryptography because it does not fulfill the requirement of authentication and nonrepudiation.
2. Review approval requirements. If a simple symmetric key is enough, then you can use DES encryption. If the encryption method needs to be approved by the U.S. government, then 3DES and AES would work. If the information being encrypted is sensitive and unclassified, but still needs government-approved encryption, you should consider using AES.
3. Determine the key bit size and the level of security required. If a 64-bit key is appropriate, then use DES. If you need 112 bits or higher security, choose

3DES. If, on the other hand, the encryption requires larger than 112 bits, you can use AES, which will accommodate 128-, 192-, and 256-bit keys.

Special note: We said that one of the concerns utilizing encryption is the protection of the keys. We must also consider the issue of the number of keys required when we use symmetric encryption. The key management formula to determine how many keys are needed is [N * (N – 1)]/2, where N is the number of people using symmetric encryption. For example, if 10 people are using symmetric encryption, the formula will be [10 * (10 – 1)]/2. This equals (10 * 9)/2 = 90/2 = 45; thus, we require 45 keys. As you can see, keeping track of and protecting all of these keys may create a key management nightmare. For this reason, key management must be taken into consideration.

8.3.3 Public Key Encryption (Asymmetric Key Encryption)

The *public key encryption (or asymmetric key encryption)* method involves two keys. One key is a public key and the other is a private key. The public key and private key are paired together; when the public key encrypts data, only the paired private key can decrypt these data. This is analogous to a metal key and lock. The lock is paired to the key and only that specific paired key should be able to open the lock it is cut to. Asymmetric key encryption can provide confidentiality and authentication, but it is slower than symmetric key encryption.

Asymmetric key encryption utilizes two keys (a public key and a private key) to encrypt a message. If we consider the two keys as A and B, then B decrypts what A encrypts. Likewise, A decrypts what B encrypts. We talk about three types of messages when dealing with asymmetric key encryption:

A signed message is encrypted with the sender's private key and provides message authentication.

The secure message is encrypted with the receiver's public key and provides confidentiality to the message.

The signed and secured message is first encrypted with the sender's private key and then again with the receiver's public key. This type of message provides both authentication and confidentiality.

Digital certificates are used to prove identity when performing electronic transactions. They contain identification information such as user names, serial numbers, and valid dates of the certificate. They also contain the public key of the certificate holder and the digital signature of the signature authority. The signature authority is a critical part of the digital certificate because it validates the entire package.

Before we go any further with our discussion on asymmetric key encryption, let us talk about what makes up the public key infrastructure. This infrastructure works on the basis of trust and three types of trust models are utilized. The single authority trust uses a single third-party central agency. In the hierarchical trust, individuals at different levels know that they can trust one ultimate entity, and this trust is passed down from level to level. The web of trust consists of everyone signing each other's certificates.

The public key infrastructure consists of the Certificate Authority (CA), the Certificate Revocation List (CRL) and the Registration Authority (RA). The CA issues certificates to authorized users and is maintained by the organization for this purpose. The CRL is maintained by the CA. Certificates are checked against the CRL to verify that they are valid. The CRL is used to maintain accuracy and report any problems with certificates issued. The RA assists the CA by accepting certificate verification requests and verifying the certificate owner's identity. The RA will pass this verification along to the CA to generate a certificate. The RA, by itself, cannot generate certificates. The certificate server maintains a database on all certificates using the X.509 standard for digital certificates.

Just like symmetric keys, there are many different types of algorithms for asymmetric keys. The following subsections describe some of the more popular ones.

8.3.3.1 Diffie–Hellman

The *Diffie–Hellman* asymmetric key algorithm allows for the secret key to be sent over an insecure communication line. It does, however, require key agreement prior to sharing this secret key. This key exchange does not authenticate the participants by default; thus, it can be vulnerable to "man-in-the-middle" types of attacks. However, this can be overcome by using digital signatures. Diffie–Hellman is used in SSL and IPSec, which we will talk about in a moment.

8.3.3.2 El Gamal

The *El Gamal* algorithm uses a finite field and discrete logarithm that function on the encryption and digital signature. It works off the difficulty of solving this discrete logarithm problem and is composed of three components: the key generator, the encryption algorithm, and a decryption algorithm. For this reason, El Gamal is a slow method of encryption.

8.3.3.3 Elliptic Curve Cryptosystem

The *Elliptic Curve Cryptosystem (ECC)* method uses a finite field and analog of the discrete logarithm problem over the points of an elliptic curve. It functions on the encryption, digital signature, and keys. It is sometimes difficult to implement, but is capable of functioning with limited resources such as power and bandwidth. For this reason, ECC can be useful in cell phones, PDAs, and other devices where resources are limited.

8.3.3.4 Merkle–Hellman Knapsack

The *Merkle–Hellman knapsack* method applies weights to each set of items; the total defines the items in the "knapsack." This method is commonly used with "trap doors" to one-way functions.

8.3.3.5 RSA

The *RSA* method was named after its inventors, Ron Rivest, Adi Shamir, and Leonard Adleman, and was one of the first public key encryption systems invented. It has now become the standard for public encryption. The algorithm is performed by factoring large prime numbers while encrypting and verifying the digital signature in one direction and decrypting and creating the digital signature in the opposite direction. It also functions on encryption, digital signature, and the key exchange mechanisms.

8.3.4 Choosing an Asymmetric Key Cryptography Method

Again, with different methods available, how do you choose the best one? Here is a guideline that you can use to determine an appropriate asymmetric key cryptography method:

1. Review the security and cryptography requirements. If a large volume of information requires fast encryption, you probably want to use a symmetric key cryptography method instead of asymmetric key cryptography. If the system needs to be scalable and capable of encrypting and sending messages, then stick with asymmetric key cryptography.
2. Determine the authentication and encryption requirements. If the message requires encryption and a digital signature, then use RSA, El Gamal, or ECC. If the message needs to perform key agreement, use Diffie–Hellman or El Gamal. If you have limited resources, you may want to consider using ECC because it can function with limited resources.
3. Determine the intended use of the information. If you know you have limited bandwidth or power available for sending and receiving messages, stick with ECC.

8.3.5 Digital Signature

A *digital signature* is like a written signature and is used to identify the sender of a message. Digital signatures prove integrity and authentication. They are far less susceptible to forgery or fraud and can be easily attached to e-mail. These signatures follow the X.509 standard that specifies information and required attributes for identification. Version 3 of the X.509 standards is the most current. Let us take a second to explain how digital signatures work and the process involved in creating

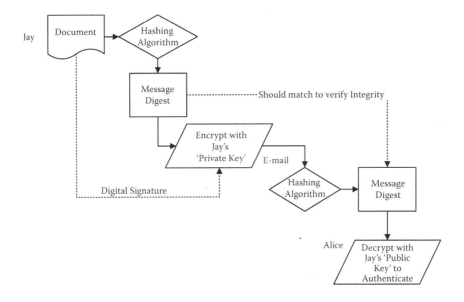

Figure 8.2   Digital signatures.

a digital signature. For this example, look at Figure 8.2. Jay is digitally signing a document to send to Alice. Jay passes his document through a hashing algorithm to produce a message digest. He then encrypts the message digest with his private key (signature) and e-mails the document to Alice. Alice uses the same hashing algorithm on the document to create a new message digest. She then decrypts Jay's signature using Jay's public key to authenticate Jay. The two message digests that were created are compared and should match to verify the integrity of the message.

8.3.6 One-Way Encryption

We have discussed mechanisms by which a message is encrypted and decrypted, but what if we only want to encrypt a message without decrypting it? What would we utilize this type of encryption for? To answer these questions, we look at another form of encryption called one-way encryption. To go into a little detail on this type of encryption, we must first understand a "message digest." This is a message that contains cryptographic data that verify the contents of another message to determine whether or not it has been altered.

A message digest can be keyed or nonkeyed. If it is keyed, the original message is combined with a secret key sent with the message. Keyed messages are known as Message Authentication Codes (MACs). They usually perform a littler more slowly than nonkeyed messages. A nonkeyed message digest consists of the original message that is hashed without any other mechanisms. Nonkeyed message digests are also known as Message Integrity Codes (MICs) or Modification Detection Codes (MDCs).

To elaborate a little further, a message hash is a set-length signature created from a variable-length message. If you compare two message hashes of the same message, they should be the same; however, if any slight change occurs with the original message, the resulting hashes will be different. This answers the second part of the question presented earlier as to why we would want to have one-way encryption. This is to verify the integrity of a message so as to confirm that the original message was not altered in any way.

A couple of examples of one-way encryption algorithms are Message Digest 5 (MD5) and the Secure Hash Algorithm (SHA). MD5 is used to create a message digest for digital signatures. It creates a fixed 128-bit output that, when summed, totals 32 characters long. SHA is used to create digital signatures. It is similar to MD5 and is considered the successor to MD5. It produces a 160-bit message digest that is considered to be more secure than MD5. SHA is used in challenge and response authentication; because the actual password never has to cross the network, the secrecy is preserved. One of the most common challenge and response protocols is the Windows NT Challenge/Response Protocol (NT CHAP). SHA also comes in a couple of different versions, such as SHA-0 and SHA-2.

As a key point of reference regarding encryption, the greater the size of the key that is used to encrypt the data, the stronger the encryption of these data is. Strong encryption is considered to be any key greater than 40 bits. Because it is very hard to break good encryption and would take a lot of time and resources to attempt to crack such algorithms forcibly, the weakest point of any encryption is in the protection of the keys, especially the private keys. If an attacker is able to steal these keys, he or she will eventually be able to crack the algorithm and access the information.

8.3.7 e-Mail Encryption

One of the main reasons that encryption is used is to protect messages in the form of e-mail that are in transit across public networks such as the Internet. There are many methods of e-mail security and the following lists some of the more popular ones.

8.3.7.1 Pretty Good Privacy

Pretty Good Privacy (PGP) e-mail security uses a "web of trust" to certify valid users. In this web of trust, public keys are shared and signed by all to designate that the messages are trusted. PGP is unlike the common public key infrastructure in that it does not utilize a CA. Instead, one portion of the paired key is held within a "key ring" and kept by the user. This is PGP's own form of digital certificates. PGP uses an IDEA cipher for encryption and RSA for key management. It also uses MD5 to ensure integrity and digital signatures to ensure nonrepudiation.

8.3.7.2 Privacy-Enhanced Mail

The *Privacy-Enhanced Mail (PEM)* e-mail security method handles both Internet and local message transmission. It commonly uses RSA and 3DES for encryption and is compatible with other various key management mechanisms. PEM uses a standard certification authority to verify digital certificates, which are created using X.509 standards. PEM is extremely structured and although compliant with the Public Key Cryptography Standard (PKCS), it is not often implemented.

8.3.7.3 Multipurpose Internet Mail Extension

Multipurpose Internet Mail Extension (MIME) is a common e-mail standard that contains specifications on how attachments of files and multimedia data are handled. Although it is not an inherent security mechanism, it does include indication of file type for recognition by the receiving system. It is a good choice for internal systems.

8.3.7.4 Secure/MIME

Because MIME does not have security built in, *Secure/MIME (S/MIME)* was created as a secure counterpart. It utilizes user-specified encryption and message digests along with the X.509 standard for authentication. It utilizes digital signatures for nonrepudiation.

8.3.8 Choosing e-Mail Encryption

Just as before, you can choose from many solutions to protect messages through e-mail. Here are some guidelines to assist you in your choices:

1. Determine the sensitivity of the information being transferred via e-mail. If the information is classified or requires more stringent security, consider using either PEM or PGP. If the information is available to the public, MIME will be the simplest form of e-mail security to implement and will provide some security through S/MIME.
2. Determine other security protocols that the e-mail system must use to function properly. If the e-mail is part of a stand-alone system, all choices will usually meet this requirement, but MIME will probably be the most effective. If the e-mail system needs to provide message integrity, then your best solution would be PGP because this is one of the only mechanisms that use MD5 for message integrity.
3. Consider the functional area of the e-mail system. If the system is for internal use, all solutions will work; however, if the e-mail system is for both internal and Internet use, then PEM will provide the best security. If a large number of users require e-mail encryption capabilities and they would benefit from being able to differentiate between users sending

trusted messages and those that do not, PGP will fulfill these requirements. If the system will be utilized to send multimedia data along with messages, then MIME may be necessarily implemented with another security method like S/MIME.

8.3.9 Internet Encryption

Companies have moved to the Internet to provide different types of services to their customers. They have gone to great efforts to provide different levels of Internet applications to assist their customers and make their businesses more efficient. In the process, security has been raised to include different methods by which personal information is protected as these applications are being utilized on the Internet. A few of the more common methods involved in providing Internet security are discussed next.

8.3.9.1 Internet Protocol Security

Internet Protocol Security (IPSec) handles the protection of data from server to server or from remote access user workstations to servers. IPSec is one of the most widely used standards for protecting IP datagrams across the Internet. It is able to perform encryption, access control, and authentication. It can be implemented via two different security protocols: Authentication Header (AH) protocol, which provides authentication, and Encapsulating Security Payload (ESP), which provides authentication, encryption, and message integrity. IPSec functions in two different modes: transport mode, which ensures messages are protected from intrusion, and tunnel mode, which protects the message, header, and other routing information.

8.3.9.2 Point-to-Point Tunneling Protocol

The *Point-to-Point Tunneling Protocol (PPTP)* type of Internet security is widely used for Virtual Private Networks (VPNs). It comprises two components: the transport, which maintains the connection, and the encryption, which ensures data confidentiality.

8.3.9.3 Secure Electronic Transaction

Secure Electronic Transaction (SET) is an Internet security protocol used for transmitting credit card data on e-commerce sites.

8.3.9.4 Secure Hypertext Transfer Protocol

The *Secure Hypertext Transfer Protocol (S-HTTP)* Internet security protocol can protect single Web pages.

8.3.9.5 Secure Shell

The *Secure Shell (SSH-2)* protocol handles remote access over a network by authenticating the client to the server and providing confidentiality and integrity of the transmissions.

8.3.9.6 Secure Sockets Layer

You have seen this protocol utilized when you go to a Web site with an https extension. *Secure Sockets Layer (SSL)* was developed by Netscape to provide security over the Internet between clients and servers. This Internet security protocol is compatible with many different encryption types, such as RSA, IDEA, DES, 3DES, and MD5. It handles the client-to-server authentication and requires both server and the Web browser to be compatible with each other. When SSL is utilized, it will protect the entire session created by the user request.

Special note: Some Internet security methods utilize "cookies"—simple programs that are normally readily available through most programming languages and Internet browsers. They are generally used to track user activity on the Internet, but they can also be utilized in providing security. This is done by embedding session keys or other time-stamping items to assist users in maintaining a secure session while they are visiting a Web page or Web site. Unfortunately, users can manually disable these cookies and even transfer cookies from one computer to another. It is recommended that security mechanisms that utilize cookies not be used when sensitive information is involved.

8.3.10 Choosing an Internet Security Method

What Internet security method is right for you? Follow this guideline:

1. Determine what devices will be used to make the Internet connection. If the connection is straightforward Internet communications, SSL, SET, and S-HTTP are probably the best suited, although many protocols may work. If the connection involves remote access, two protocols that specialize in remote access are IPSEC and SSH-2. If the connection is network to server or server to server based, then use IPSEC; if it is client to server based, use SSH-2.
2. Determine what level of security is required during the communication. If the communication requires the entire session be secure, use SSL. If it only requires that certain pages within a Web site be secured, S-HTTP will work on this page-by-page basis.
3. Attempt to look into the future and predict what other types of applications may be used because it may be difficult later if you need to change to another Internet security protocol. If the application involves or will involve Internet e-commerce transactions, you will probably want to use SET. If your

company is deciding on possibly utilizing wireless, consider using some of the wireless security protocols that we will talk about later in this book.

8.3.11 Encrypting Hard Drives

Another factor to take into consideration when we talk about encryption is that some major security breaches related to lost or stolen laptops, hard drives, and backup tapes have occurred. Any time that sensitive information is involved—no matter what form it is in—security controls should be in place around that information. In the case of laptops, hard drives, and backup tapes, encryption should be required for these devices if sensitive information is maintained on them. Multiple solutions for each device include commercial and publicly available encryption methods. Because these encryption methods are so widely available, there is no excuse for not having this information encrypted.

In fact, some operating systems include their own encryption capabilities built into the software. Microsoft's Encrypted File System (EFS) is an example of a built-in encryption system. EFS allows users to encrypt NTFS files, folders, and directories.

8.3.11.1 TrueCrypt

Another freely available encryption program that I would recommend is TrueCrypt, which is advertised as

> Free open-source disk encryption software for Windows Vista/XP, Mac OS X, and Linux
>
> Main features:
>
> - Creates a *virtual encrypted disk* within a file and mounts it as a real disk.
> - *Encrypts an entire hard disk partition* or a *storage device* such as USB flash drives.
> - Encryption is automatic, real time (on the fly) and transparent.
> - Provides two levels of plausible deniability, in case an adversary forces you to reveal the password:
>   – hidden volume (steganography)
>   – no TrueCrypt volume can be identified (volumes cannot be distinguished from random data)
> - Encryption algorithms: AES-256, Serpent, and Twofish. Mode of operation: XTS. (http://www.truecrypt.org/)

8.3.12 Encryption Attacks

Encryption is not without its sources of trouble. Most criminals would think that if the information is important enough to encrypt, it must be worth something to steal it. This leads us into a quick discussion on some attack methods that malicious individuals can utilize in an attempt to gain unauthorized access to your information. As stated before, one of the weakest components of encryption involves protecting the encryption keys. If the keys are not protected and an individual with malicious intent gets hold of them, any amount of encryption you place on the data is worthless.

The following is a list of some of the more common types of attacks against encryption:

- *Known plaintext attack* is a type of attack that requires that a malicious individual have plaintext and ciphertext of one or more messages. With these two pieces of information, an extraction of the cryptographic key can occur.
- *Ciphertext-only attack* requires that a malicious individual obtain the encrypted messages that have been encrypted using the same encryption algorithm.
- *Man-In-The-Middle (MITM) attack* is a type of attack based on the ability of the malicious individual to place himself or herself within the middle of the communication flow. From there, the individual may be able to obtain enough of the messages to carry out another type of attack or trick one of the communicators into believing the malicious user is the other authenticated party.
- *Replay attack* occurs when the malicious individual attempts to repeat or delay transmissions. Use of session tokens to combat the delay times or replay attempts can prevent this type of attack.
- *Chosen plaintext attack* occurs when the malicious individual can trick one of the communicating parties into encrypting a known message. Because the individual now has the plaintext for the known message and also the encrypted message, he or she may be able to extract the cryptographic key from this information.
- *Chosen ciphertext attack* is similar to the chosen plaintext attack; however, the malicious individual somehow tricks the communicating parties into decrypting known ciphertext messages and then analyzes this against the plaintext output. Some of the earlier versions of RSA and SSL were vulnerable to this type of attack.
- *"Rubber hose" attack* is not a technical type of attack; however, it is important to note that extortion or threatening someone with bodily harm may be methods by which a criminal could obtain the keys to crack encryption.

8.4 Multifactor Authentication

Authentication, as we have already discussed, is providing proof of someone's identity. In real life, a driver's license would be utilized to prove that a person is who he says he is. In the digital world, we use passwords. This is something that only the user would know and it is assumed that, along with the user ID or account number, the individual attempting to log on to a system is the authorized user if the correct password is provided.

As we have learned, passwords are a weak form of authentication and, in many situations, it is inappropriate to rely only on a user name and password to authenticate an individual. This is usually the case in financial transactions and accessing sensitive information. Therefore, systems have been developed to require multifactor authentication.

Normally, someone's identity can be verified or authenticated in three ways. We have already touched on the first way: providing passwords. This is something that the authorized individual "knows." Another way that someone can prove his or her identity is with something that he or she "has." This is usually in the form of a security token. The last way that someone can prove identity is with something that he or she "is," such as a fingerprint. For multifactor authentication to be effective, the system must have at least two of these three methods.

A common multifactor authentication system is with ATM cards. In this type of system, in order for an individual to access a bank account, the individual must have a card that is embedded with information pertaining to the card holder and a PIN number. This is something that you have (the card) and something that you know (the PIN).

Unfortunately, in the online banking environment, a pseudoform of multifactor authentication is utilized. In most of these systems, a user enters an account number, a PIN number, and provides an answer to a secret question to access the online account. In essence, all of these items are single factor in that they are just something a user knows. In an attempt to prove that the system is multifactor, the online service may load a "cookie" or provide a security certificate to the local system. This, in essence, acts as a second factor authentication of something that a user has. The fallacy or weakness in these types of systems is that it still only takes what the user knows to prove the user's identity. In some situations, the secret questions are the same question for all users such as "what is your mother's maiden name?" or "what is your favorite pet's name?" Unless there was another method by which the cookie or certificate was securely passed to the user or verified by other methods, this online banking system is not a true multifactor authentication system.

8.5 Summary

In this chapter we discussed some of the specific application controls that we can use to protect a company's information. We described the application and system development process in detail and the importance of information security being included in the initial phases of development. We went on to discuss security around e-mail or the lack thereof. We also discussed the importance of encryption and detailed different types of encryption methods. Furthermore, we detailed steps of how to choose the best encryption available for your needs and requirements. We explained the importance of encrypting data on local hard drives, especially mobile type devices. We also looked at different types of attacks surrounding encryption. Finally, we described the importance of multifactor authentication and what it means to have multifactor authentication implemented into your systems.

References

MKS, Inc. 2007. Software development life cycle (SDLC) resources from MKS. Retrieved February 2, 2008, from MKS: http://www.mks.com/sdlc

Overly, M. R. 1999. *e-Policy: How to develop computer, e-mail, and Internet guidelines to protect your company and its assets.* New York: SciTech Publishing, Inc.

Roger Matus, S. T. 2007. The new federal rules of civil procedure: IT obligations for e-mail. Retrieved February 7, 2008, from Inboxer: http://www.inboxer.com/downloads/Whitepaper_FRCP.pdf

Tolson, B. S. 2007. *Email archiving for dummies.* Hoboken, NJ: Wiley Publishing, Inc.

Chapter 9

Perimeter Controls

Objectives

- Understand the differences between traditional and modern computing environments.
- Describe some internal controls that should be implemented in your security architecture.
- Describe some external controls that should be implemented in your security architecture.
- Understand the different types of cables and specifications of each used in telecommunications.
- Describe the differences between the different types of dedicated lines.
- Understand some of the security controls surrounding telecommunications.
- Understand the security controls and risks involved in Voice over IP (VoIP) solutions.
- Understand the benefits of a Virtual Private Network (VPN).
- Understand the risks and security controls around wireless access solutions.
- Describe the importance of Web filtering and list sites that should be filtered.

9.1 Security Architecture

Computing environments have been described in terms of two broad categories: *traditional* and *modern*. Figure 9.1 illustrates an example of the differences between

217

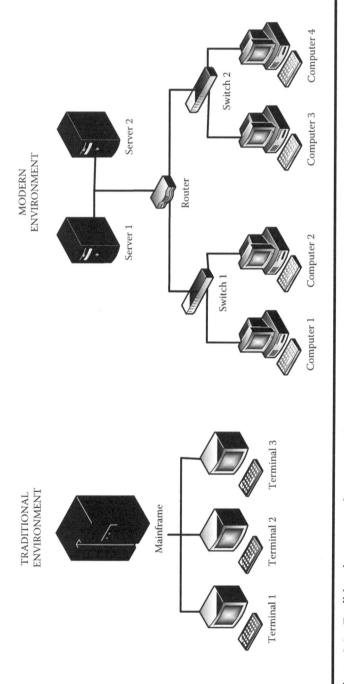

Figure 9.1 Traditional versus modern computing environments.

these two computing environments. The traditional computing environment is considered easier to secure than the modern computer environment. This is because the modern computing environment contains multiple security threats. These threats come in the form of the number of nodes that are in place where the traffic flows. In a traditional computing environment, there was a hierarchy of information flow—usually in a vertical, top to bottom approach. In the modern computing environment, information is laid out in a more horizontal method and multiple hubs, switches, and routers are utilized to forward the information to where it needs to go. There is an inherent security threat in this method when information can be viewed at any point along the path along which it flows.

With the complexity of computing environments, more administrators are required to maintain these systems. If a set procedure is not in place, administrators may resort to insecure methods of logging and overcoming the needs of multiple log-ons and passwords. They may also circumvent security by introducing systems onto the network with default settings due to the time it takes to lock these systems down or because of the lack of knowledge or procedures in place.

In addition, modern systems may lack appropriate monitoring and logging mechanisms. Management may deem these systems unnecessary because the organization may not have had penetrations or security incidents that would raise awareness of this need for monitoring. As organizations grow, importance is placed on new applications to make business more efficient; however, these applications may not have a good underlying security framework built into them. For these reasons, it becomes more difficult to regulate security in a flat modern environment with several control points.

"Information security architecture" describes the number of staff members involved, the roles of these staff members, and the resources required to maintain a proper security environment adequately. Information security architecture will depend on the current information technology environment, and all of these components will depend on the risks to the organization.

9.1.1 Internal Controls

The following are some internal controls that you should consider when implementing your information security architecture:

■ An authentication server, or a server used to identify and authenticate users, should be connected to its client by a trusted path. This path could be network cables physically attached to the devices or through secure tunnels through publicly accessible channels such as a virtual private network. These paths are considered trusted and secured if your organization has control over them or if formal controls in place comply with your organization's security policies.
■ There should be a centralized point of administration in a network with several points of control. This centralized point can be considered your IT

department or possibly a domain controller in an active directory environment. The points of control can be considered to be individuals responsible for different roles such as security or technical support in your IT department. These controls can also be the network devices that direct the flow of data throughout your network, such as switches, routers, and firewalls.

■ Users should be assigned to groups and their unique identifiers should be stored in a protected database. In most organizations, access control, rights, and privileges are determined by an individual's job roles or functions. One of the more efficient ways to manage these rights is to classify users into similar groups of roles or functions. Resources are also normally grouped or classified together and these groups are assigned access to these resources accordingly. For instance, you may have a group of users that work in the front office and will utilize the printers nearest to their locations. Under this example, these users would be assigned to a group that has access to these printers. Once these access levels are assigned to these different groups, the individual users are then assigned to their respective groups based on the resources they need to perform their jobs. These users will all be assigned a unique identifier that will be associated to their assigned groups. This information will then be secured in a database. Rule-based access control, which handles more data and requires less administration than a list-based format, should be used.

■ Groups should have one responsible owner, and administering group membership should reduce administration overhead. Each group that we discussed previously should be assigned an individual responsible for this group. If members of a group of service representatives in your company all have the same types of access levels, then there should be a responsible owner or administrator that will manage and maintain this service representative group. He or she will be responsible for assigning the necessary resources required for members of that group to do their jobs. Assigning a responsible owner over these groups will also alleviate a lot of administrative overhead on other system administrators.

■ Each user should have a single user name for all resources. For management and tracking purposes, it is a good idea for all available resources to use a single user name for each user. For example, if a user is named John Doe and he uses a user name of "jdoe" to access the system, then he should use the name "jdoe" to access the accounting program or other resources to which he has access. It will get very confusing and very hard to maintain if the user name for the accounting program is "doej." If reports are produced from each of the applications and are alphabetically sorted by user name, obviously a lot of time would be wasted looking through these reports to track and identify a specific user if he is working with two different user names.

■ Multifactor authentication should be used to verify all users' identities. We discussed this in detail in Section 8.4 in Chapter 8.

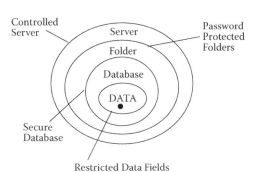

Figure 9.2   Points of control.

■ The same interface should be used for monitoring, logging, and access control. Whether it is at the network level or at the application level, your systems should have a centralized interface for your monitoring and access control functions. These should be integrated and will improve security with minimal effort. For instance, it will be very burdensome if you have to use one program for logging, another program for monitoring, and another program for access control. Each one of these programs uses different identifiers to recognize certain events or user names to identify specific individuals. As you can imagine, it may take a long time to go through all the information you have collected to find the specific information for which you are looking. It could be like looking for a "needle in a haystack."

■ Points of control should be placed as close to the data that need protection as possible. For example, if you have a database on a server, you should put access controls, such as user name and password, on the database itself. You should then put controls around the folders or portions of the hard drive that house the database. You should also have access controls around the server itself. This is an ideal example of defense in depth. You should not solely rely on controls around the server because anyone that may have access to the server could have unauthorized access to your database. See Figure 9.2 as an example. In addition, access controls should be placed on the files and data rather than the application using them. For example, if you have a sensitive Word document, you may consider password protecting the document rather than trying to place restrictions on the Word application that opens up this document.

■ To prevent expanding attacks, firewalls and packet-filtering routers should be deployed on network segments. Although an attacker may be able to gain access to a portion of the network, these firewalls and packet-filtering routers will limit the attacker to this area only and thus prevent the attacker from moving to other areas of your network or digging deeper into your network. In addition, data should be separated and hidden from connecting subnets and only the data required by an application should travel between subnets.

This will also limit the exposure the company faces if an attacker is able to compromise a segment of your network.

■ Encryption should be utilized as much as possible. We discussed in detail the different types of encryption throughout Section 8.3 in Chapter 8. In addition, as we discussed, a public key server should be used and keys should be referred to only by name and never duplicated or transmitted in plaintext.

■ To guard against installation of unauthorized programs, access control procedures should be implemented on the workstations. Users should not be given full administrative access to their systems. They should have only limited access to the Internet to perform their jobs. They should also not be allowed to use USB or external hard drives. These restrictions can be enforced through formal policies and training or the use of technical controls, such as software applications that enforce controls on users' desktops in accordance with your company's policies.

9.1.2 External Controls

The system architecture that we have talked about has been primarily focused on the internal network. Let us take a few minutes to discuss some security controls that we should have in place on the external network. One of the first and most important controls that we can have on our external network (Internet facing) is a managed, third-party Intrusion Detection System (IDS)/Intrusion Prevention System (IPS) service. If your company conducts a lot of business via the Internet, it is essential that this type of service be utilized. I recommend a third-party service provider in this situation because it is very unlikely that a company would have the expertise, equipment, and resources available to provide an effective IDS/IPS solution. Therefore, a third party that can provide protection 24 hours a day, 365 days a year, is recommended.

You should have external penetration tests conducted at least on a quarterly basis, and in some industries this is a requirement. This testing should be conducted by highly respected professionals under a formal scope of conduct to perform these types of tests. When the tests are conducted, it would be beneficial to test your IDS/IPS solution as well. These tests should create alarms and you should be notified that such tests are being conducted on your external facing devices. If they do not create such an alarm, I would recommend that follow-up be done to determine why this was the case.

Penetration testing should look at domain name registrations to verify that these entries do not contain specific information about your organization. Bandwidth on the devices should not be degraded or the quality of the services diminished in any way during these types of tests. A free service that provides really good information regarding the security of your domain can be found at http://clez.net. This Web site allows you to perform different types of tests against your registered domain and Web site.

Your external network should not provide any unnecessary services. For instance, the penetration test should determine whether or not a trace route can be performed and devices can be identified along the data path. A trace route is a diagnostic test to determine the path that packets take as they cross the Internet or other network. In most cases, the trace route will provide information on each of the devices that the packets touch getting to their destination. There may be some countermeasures for your specific environment to prevent divulging information relayed in a trace route.

Another example of some unnecessary services that may be enabled on your externally facing or public devices is Simple Network Management Protocol (SNMP). Systems that are externally facing should not have SNMP enabled because this protocol divulges information about your devices. This protocol was intended, as its name implies, to provide network management to devices. A few upgraded versions have been implemented for this protocol; however, not all devices are compatible with these newer versions. You should attempt to use the latest versions or upgrade to any protocol that has a business requirement. If there is no business purpose for these services or protocols to be enabled, then turn them off on your devices.

Telnet is an administrative management protocol. It is normally utilized to control or configure different types of network devices. Telnet should not be utilized in managing your devices because user names and passwords are transported across the Internet in plaintext. Instead, you should use a more secure protocol for device management, such as Secure Shell (SSH), that encrypts traffic between devices.

Special care should be given to administering any externally facing devices remotely. If this administration is not required for business purposes, then terminal services or other remote access tools should be disabled.

Another protocol that should be turned off if not utilized is File Transfer Protocol (FTP). This protocol allows for the transfer of files between two devices. If this type of service is required, you should utilize a secure protocol such as Secure File Transfer Protocol (SFTP) because user names, passwords, and data can be sent in plaintext across the Internet using FTP.

One of the best safeguards for external facing devices—and I cannot emphasize this enough—is not to divulge or give away information about your devices. The more information an attacker can get about your systems or devices, the easier it is for him or her to find possible vulnerabilities for that device. A good rule of thumb to follow is that if the services are not used, disable them.

As part of the penetration test, you will want to make sure that your Web applications are secure. Penetration testing should include tests to verify vulnerabilities for at least the following:

- *Cross-Site Scripting* (XSS) involves malicious users injecting code into Web pages viewed by other users.

- *Injection flaws* (including SQL injections, LDAP injections, Xpath injections, and other injection flaws) allow malicious users to relay code through a Web application to another system.
- *Malicious file execution* works on applications that improperly trust certain inputs. If a malicious user is successful in this type of attack, he or she could execute remote code, install rootkits, or gain a complete system compromise.
- *Insecure direct object references* attacks occur when a developer of an application exposes a reference to an internal object such as a file, database record, key, etc. If an access control check is not in place, an attacker may be able to manipulate this object directly or gain unauthorized access to other objects.
- *Cross-Site Request Forgery* (XSRF) is also known as one-click attack, session riding, or CSRF ("sea–surf"). In this type of attack, a malicious user exploits a Web site by sending commands pretending to be a user that the Web site trusts. Unlike XSS, where the exploit comes from the trust a user has in a Web site, XSRF exploits the trust a site has in a user.
- With *information leakage and improper error handling,* as we discussed earlier, you should not divulge any information about your systems or devices. Sometimes, applications can unintentionally leak information about their configurations, programming, or other information. Information can be obtained from the error codes that are received from entering invalid data inputs into the system if these applications are not configured correctly.
- *Broken authentication and session management* includes all aspects of user authentication and active session management. Most secure applications require some form of token to authenticate users and maintain session connections. If these session tokens are stolen, an attacker could hijack an active session and pretend to be an authorized user. For this reason, it is important that session management also requires reauthentication even if the user appears to have a valid session ID.
- *Insecure cryptographic storage* revolves around not encrypting the data or using weak or insecure algorithms as part of the application's encryption framework. It could also include hard coding encryption keys within the program or storing these keys in unprotected storage areas that could be accessed by unauthorized or malicious users.
- *Insecure communications* involves failing to encrypt sensitive data as previously discussed in Section 8.3.9 in Chapter 8.
- *Failure to restrict Uniform Resource Locator (URL) access* involves a malicious user who is able to gain access to links or Web pages that were not presented to users in authorized ways such as links on the main page.

It is important that different types of tests with different types of tools be utilized to check the preceding vulnerabilities. A code review is also essential to discover some of these flaws because most automated testing will not be able to discover them.

You will also want to make sure that your Web server software is kept up to date with all of the security patches installed. In addition, it is important that error codes and headers be configured with general information so as not to give away server types and versions. If your Web services provide this type of information publicly, it is much easier for an attacker to search for and attempt certain known vulnerabilities for these systems, as mentioned earlier. If an attacker is unsure what type of Web server is being used, it will make it that much more difficult to attempt certain exploits.

9.2 Telecommunications Security

For our discussion of telecommunications security, let us start at the beginning and talk about the cables that make up our telecommunications and network systems. Common telecommunication cable utilizes Shielded Twisted Pair (STP) and Unshielded Twisted Pair (UTP)—normally 24-gauge American wire gauge (AWG) wiring. Another common type of cabling is coaxial cable, which comes in two grades. *Polyvinyl chloride (PVC)* is used for outer cover and the insulation, but it can give off poisonous smoke and gas when burned. *Plenum* is insulated and jacketed in special materials that give off a minimum amount of smoke and fumes when burned.

Cable has some characteristics such as bandwidth, which measures the amount of data that can transmit on the wire and is usually measured in megabits per second (Mbps); the maximum number of devices that can be connected to the network; and the maximum cable runs or length normally measured in meters. Table 9.1 shows some of the common cabling types along with bandwidth, nodes, and cable

Table 9.1 Summary of Cabling

Media	Bandwidth (Mbps)	Nodes/ Segment	Maximum Nodes/ Network	Maximum Cable Length (Meters)
Unshielded twisted pair (UTP)	4–100	1	1024	100
Shielded twisted pair (STP)	16–155	Varies	260	100
Coaxial thicknet	10	100	300	500
Coaxial thinnet	10	30	90	185
Fiber optic	2000	1	1024	2000
Infrared	1–10	NA	Varies	32

Table 9.2   Line Types

Line Type	Description
1	Basic voice
2	Voice with some quality control
3	Voice/radio with tone conditioning
4	Data applications below 1,200 bps
5	Basic data
6	Voice and data over trunk circuits
7	Voice and data over private lines
8	Voice and data over trunks between computers
9	Voice and video
10	Application relays

lengths. Cabling is also classified by line types. See Table 9.2 for a description of the different types of cables.

Cabling can sustain different modes of communication. Simplex transmission is one-way communication only. Half-duplex sends transmission in both directions, but only one at a time. Full-duplex allows for two-way simultaneous transmissions. Cables can be described as baseband or broadband. Baseband is digital, bidirectional cabling that uses the entire capacity of the cable by utilizing Time Division Multiplexing (TDM). TDM occurs when two or more bit streams use subchannels in one communication channel, but take turns using this channel. Broadband, on the other hand, is analog, unidirectional cabling that allows two or more channels to share the capacity of the cable by utilizing Frequency Division Multiplexing (FDM). FDM occurs when nonoverlapping frequency ranges are assigned to separate users of the channel.

Voice and data lines have been integrated together into larger, dedicated connections. Companies no longer need to have separate lines for data and voice; now, all of these channels can be combined into one "pipeline." Table 9.3 shows the different dedicated lines and the number of voice channels and data rates available for each. T1 and T3 are the American standards; E1 and E3 are the European standards.

No matter what technology your company decides on, special attention should be given to protecting the physical cabling of your environment. Cable drops should be terminated in secured rooms and protected from unauthorized interception or damage. Locks should be utilized on cable cabinets, and they should have restricted access.

Table 9.3 Dedicated Lines

Connection Type	T1/E1/OC1 Channels	Voice Channels	Data Rate (Mbps)
T1	1	24	1.544
T3	28	672	44.736
E1	1	32	2.048
E3	16	512	34.368
XDSL	N/A	N/A	Varies depending on ISP; faster download than upload
OC-1	1	N/A	51.8
OC-3	3	N/A	155.52
ATM	N/A	N/A	Either 155.520 or 622.080 (can reach 10 Gbps)

9.3 Voice over IP Security

Advancement in technologies has brought us to the point that voice calls are now transmitting over the Internet. This technology is known as Voice over IP (VoIP). Although VoIP is more of the protocol that has been optimized and designed to enable digital voice data to be transmitted over the network, the term has been used abstractly to describe the actual transmission of voice. Voice over IP offers a lot of improvements in reliability and quality of service. It has now become a viable option and alternative to the Plain Old Telephone Service (POTS). With this new technology, however, come new security threats. Because voice data are transmitted over the public Internet, they need to be encrypted and secured from prying eyes. Companies that provide this type of service have gone to great lengths to supply the security that their clients are looking for and to raise confidence in voice over IP technology.

As more and more companies move to use new technologies such as VoIP phones, it has become increasingly important to consider security in the configuration of these solutions. There are many best practices for implementing a VoIP solution. The following discussion offers a few recommendations or considerations when a VoIP solution is implemented.

VoIP security best practices recommend a firewall to separate the voice network from the data network. Some vendors assume that because the corporate network is considered a "trusted" network and users already have access to the data, the users would not be expected to attack the internal VoIP network. Some vendors are not aware of specific attacks against the VoIP network. It is possible to "sniff"

VoIP traffic and hear confidential conversations on the VoIP network if the recommended security controls are not implemented.

An attack such as "VoIP hopping" can allow a PC on the internal network to jump into the voice Virtual Local Area Network (VLAN) and run several different types of attacks against the IP phone network. These attacks can include eavesdropping on unencrypted phone calls or interrupting services.

One of the most effective ways to mitigate the VoIP "hop" is to use layer 2 network controls such as enabling MAC address filtering and enabling 802.1x. With MAC address filtering in place, IP phones can be statically configured on the switch. If a PC attaches to the port on the switch with the voice VLAN ID, it will not be able to pass traffic unless it is authorized. MAC addresses can be dynamically learned to assist in the administration and management of this control, along with setting limitations on the Ethernet port. Limits, such as "1," can be specified; therefore, the first MAC address that is dynamically learned (IP phone) is the only MAC address permitted on the switch for the voice VLAN.

Phones that support 802.1x would require clients to authenticate to the switch port with the proper credentials. Cisco recommends configuring two VLANs over the shared network switch port. The first VLAN should be used for voice traffic and the other for data traffic.

If layer 2 controls cannot be implemented, layer 3 solutions should be undertaken. If the current internal network cannot be redesigned to separate the voice and data networks with a firewall, the VoIP solution can be placed within a "VoIP DMZ network." Because IP phone services should be treated as an external (untrusted) network, a new VoIP DMZ network can be created that allows only the IP phones access to servers on the data signaling and media stream ports allowed for IP phones. This would involve creating a new firewall interface and implementing Access Control List (ACL) filtering on the firewall so that only the IP addresses of IP phones are allowed at specific destinations on specific port ranges. IP phones can be configured with static IP addresses and Dynamic Host Configuration Protocol (DHCP) disabled on this separate subnet. This configuration would eliminate the need for a firewall on the internal VoIP network because traffic would be limited utilizing the firewall interface of the VoIP DMZ network. The disadvantage in this type of configuration would be that the IP phones may still be directly attacked.

A few additional recommendations or considerations include the following:

■ Consideration should be made on how the IP phones receive their configuration files. If this is done by Trivial File Transfer Protocol (TFTP), then the server relaying the configuration files should be "locked down." This means that the server should be tested for vulnerabilities and that the IP phones are required to be authenticated with the server prior to releasing any configuration files to them.
■ Consideration should be made on how the IP phone software is "locked down." In a number of networks, I have seen IP phones running Web

services that require no authentication. Although most of these interfaces only provide limited information on the phones, it is still important to note the type of information revealed and to verify that administrative control or management of the phones cannot be done by unauthorized individuals. Furthermore, Telnet should be disabled on all VoIP devices and a more secured protocol such as Secure Shell (SSH) should be utilized.

■ Encryption capabilities should be utilized, if available, to secure all voice traffic traversing the network. Strong encryption is an ideal mitigating control for a lot of the known attacks of VoIP. See Section 8.3 in Chapter 8 for further details.

■ Physical access to the VoIP management servers should be restricted. An ideal location for the VoIP servers would be in the dedicated secured server room with other critical systems.

9.4 Virtual Private Network

A Virtual Private Network (VPN) is a way to provide secure transmission and connect a host or network to another host or network through other types of networks such as the Internet. A VPN establishes a "tunnel" for one computer to connect to another computer that provides secure communications between the two systems.

You should implement several security controls when you allow remote access to your network. First, all remote access points and lines available for remote access should be monitored. They should be audited on a periodic basis to verify that no unauthorized access has occurred. All remote users should be authenticated and have a business purpose for their remote access. Although it may be a great privilege to work remotely, some risks are associated with such capabilities. Remote access should be limited to tasks that need to be performed remotely and static addresses should be reserved for each remote user. The company can mitigate some risks by enforcing these limited functions and static assignments for remote users. Static assignment will also allow for ease in auditing remote access.

Multifactor authentication should be implemented for all remote use. It is not adequate to protect your remote access capabilities only with a user name and password. You should implement some sort of token- or certificate-based authentication. This token or certificate should be loaded on an authorized system for an authorized user by an authorized IT individual. It should expire in a certain time frame designated by your company's security policy. It should be able to be revoked at any given time for suspected abuse or compromise. It should also be changed on a frequent basis just like passwords.

Encryption should be implemented. Because remote users may be dealing with sensitive information traversing publicly available channels, encryption is a requirement. Review Section 8.3 in Chapter 8 to determine the best type of encryption to utilize for your needs.

Although having dial-up connections for remote access is not recommended, if you have a business need for such connections, then you should definitely follow these recommended actions. If your remote access utilizes a dial-up connection, make sure that it uses a callback or caller ID feature to assist in authentication. This dial-up connection should be limited to specific remote numbers that can be verified by the caller ID function or by the callback function. In addition, dial-up lines should only be "up" when in use. If the dial-up connection is not being used, it should be turned off or the telephone line should be unplugged.

Because dial-up connections use older technologies, the risk of exploitation is greater; numerous programs can be utilized to break into these dial-up connections. One such attack is known as "war dialing." In this type of attack, ranges of phone numbers are tested for a targeted victim. If a system with a dial-up connection picks up on the line, the war dialing program will attempt to make a connection or crack the security controls in place. Because most dial-up connections are only secured by user name and password, it may not take long for these types of systems to crack the connection and gain remote access to your system. Centralizing modem banks to prevent these types of war dialing attacks is also recommended.

System access should only be provided to a predetermined list of IP addresses assigned to the remote systems. This will mitigate some of the risk of remote access; however, it is not foolproof. Because the IP address, rather than the user specifically, is verified, the IP address could be "spoofed" or forged and an unauthorized individual may be able to gain access to the system. This control should be implemented with other controls to build a defense in depth control over your remote access solution.

9.5 Wireless Security

The Institute of Electrical and Electronics Engineers (IEEE) is the professional organization for the development of communication and network standards. With the increase in wireless technology, standards such as IEEE 802.11b became important to provide a mechanism for authentication and encryption in wireless communication. Wireless security provides for the encryption and message security to ensure the confidentiality and integrity of broadcast transmissions. Wireless security is also concerned with securing the sending and receiving devices. One of the first network security protocols defined by the 802.11b standard was *Wireless Encryption Protocol (WEP),* also called wired equivalency privacy. WEP is a key-phrase-based network security protocol used to encrypt transmissions being broadcast. Unfortunately, WEP uses a weak key and can be cracked using tools that are freely available on the Internet.

To strengthen wireless security, *Wi-Fi Protected Access (WPA)* was developed. Created by the Wi-Fi Alliance, WPA was designed to enhance the security of wireless networks. There are two flavors of WPA: *enterprise* and *personal.* The enterprise method uses an authentication server to distribute different keys to each user; the personal method is less scalable and uses *PreShared Key (PSK)*, where every authorized computer on the wireless network is given the same password or passphrase.

WPA encrypts data using the RC4 stream cipher with a 128-bit key and a 48-bit *Initialization Vector (IV)*. One major improvement WPA had over WEP is the *Temporal Key Integrity Protocol (TKI)*, which changes the keys dynamically as it is being used. This, combined with the larger initialization vector, effectively defeats the key recovery attacks that WEP faces.

Another wireless security method used by mobile devices such as PDAs and phones is the *Wireless Application Protocol (WAP)*. WAP is a wireless security method that provides protection for mobile devices accessing the Internet. It provides session, transaction, and applications services while having low resource requirements. WAP provides security through the *Wireless Transport Layer Security Protocol (WTLS)*, which performs through anonymous authentication, server authentication, or client and server authentication. WTLS is a security protocol based on the industry standard *Transport Layer Security (TLS)* protocol that is optimized for narrow bandwidth communication channels. WTLS provides data integrity, privacy, and authentication as well as denial of service protection.

Although most of the wireless security methods employed today are good, they are still not guaranteed to protect all wireless access. The types of attacks on wireless network connections revolve around authentication. An attacker can pretend to be an authenticated user by conducting a "man-in-the-middle" type of attack or an attacker may attempt to crack the wireless security method itself. Although the algorithms utilized in the encryption are pretty strong, there has been some recent advancement in cracking capabilities. Using "brute force" on passwords or authentication methods is processor intensive.

Although all passwords and encryption would eventually be cracked, the amount of time it takes to accomplish this task is the primary control over most, if not all, password and encryption security controls. With the advancements in video card technology and installing graphical processors on cards, system designers are now working on ways to utilize these processors to perform tasks other than rendering images on monitors. Therefore, not only are computers able to utilize their processors on their main boards, but they also are now able to utilize the processors that have been installed on graphic cards to increase overall processing time by factors of 10. This decreases the amount of time it takes to use brute-force and crack the wireless security methods in place. This new technique ultimately requires vendors to come up with new and more secure wireless security methods.

To limit your exposure to risks that wireless access can bring, it is recommended that a limited number of wireless devices be used and that a business purpose be associated with such devices. A firewall should be configured between all wireless access points and other network segments. In addition, all wireless access points should have their default settings changed. This includes any preloaded WEP keys, default Service Set Identifiers (SSIDs), and, of course, default passwords.

To clarify, an SSID is a 32-character unique identifier that is attached to the packets sent over a Wireless Local Area Network (WLAN). This SSID acts like a password to connect to the access points; all the devices that are trying to communicate on the WLAN must have the same SSID. By default, this SSID usually broadcasts itself to everyone in the WLAN, but it is recommended that this broadcast be disabled. This will provide a little more security, albeit through obscurity.

In addition, it is recommended that WPA be utilized over WEP due to the added security that WPA provides. WPA provides improved integrity through its use of Cyclic Redundancy Check (CRC) and secure message authentication code, or message integrity code, which uses a frame counter that prevents replay-type attacks.

Furthermore, if you do allow wireless access in your organization, you should equip your wireless access with a disclaimer to protect your organization against possible liability. The disclaimer should be written by your legal counsel and reference the fact that your organization will not be responsible or liable for any damage, malware, or viruses that the user may get on his or her computer by utilizing the wireless connection. It should also state the terms of use and prohibition of use of the wireless access service provided.

Finally, it is important that a rogue wireless checker be utilized on a regular basis. A site survey should be conducted by walking throughout the entire facility and surrounding areas to look for wireless access points. You never know when a disgruntled employee or other individual that has had physical access to your facility might plant a wireless gateway device. This device would enable someone to access your network from outside your building's walls. Numerous software applications or hardware devices can test for these rogue wireless devices. Some of these are free and some are commercial; each has its own benefits and limitations.

9.6 Web Filtering

Due to the liability and other security issues that your organization could face by providing Internet access to your employees, it is recommended that a Web filtering solution be implemented to restrict the types of Web sites that can be visited. Web filtering solutions should log Web browsing activity by user ID and block access not only by the specific site, but also by the category of the site. Web filtering should be in place for anonymizer (or proxy avoidance) sites, nudity/pornography sites, chat sites, Web mail sites, hacking-related Web sites, or any other site that may violate the company's Internet use policy.

9.7 Summary

In this chapter we discussed some perimeter controls and, more specifically, the internal and external controls of security architectures. We discussed the security controls that we can implement on telecommunication. With the advancement of technology, we have moved to voice over IP telecommunications, which brings other types of security risks to your company. We discussed some important security controls and brought to light some elements of a VoIP solution. We then discussed the ability and functionality of remote users with the use of virtual private networks. We described some of the security controls surrounding these VPNs and why it is important to implement them in your environment. Wireless security has become a major issue and as wireless capabilities are enhanced, so are the different attack techniques used to break into these communication channels. Finally, we discussed the importance of Web filtering and liabilities that may be inherent to allowing unrestricted access to the Internet.

Chapter 10

Audit and Compliance

Objectives

- Understand the three types of events under an audit: system-, application-, and user-level events.
- Understand the objectives of a security audit.
- Describe security monitoring.
- Understand the different types of security governance metrics and describe a good metric using the "SMART" system.
- Describe the phases involved in a vulnerability assessment.
- Understand why reconnaissance is important.
- Describe the importance of testing systems in place to monitor or track unusual activities.
- Describe the term "soft targets" and the importance of protecting all systems on the network equally as opposed to only the critical systems.
- Understand how attackers can maintain access to a system and cover their tracks.
- Describe the importance of documenting and reporting.

10.1 Audit and Compliance

Auditing is the practice of checking or testing current activities against the organization's established policies and procedures. Auditing can be done internally or externally. A security audit generally focuses on three types of events: system-, application-, and user-level events. These types of audits utilize logs that are generated by the operating system, application, or other security-related systems. The logs are used to provide a transaction history or audit trail, which is a chronological record of a system's performance or activity. Audit trails should be sufficient to examine the sequence of events from the start of a transaction to the final results of that transaction.

System-level security audit events include the following:

■ auditing and logging of system startup and shutdown;
■ successful and unsuccessful log-on attempts;
■ log-on ID and time stamp;
■ operating system performance;
■ user and session lockouts;
■ activities involving an administrator;
■ device access; and
■ changes to configuration files.

Application-level security audit events include:

■ auditing and logging of files that have been opened, modified, or closed;
■ application security violations;
■ error messages; and
■ application services that fail to execute.

User-level security audit events include:

■ auditing and logging of user identification and authentication;
■ user commands that have been initiated;
■ user security violations; and
■ resources that have been accessed, services that have been accessed, files that have been accessed, or any attempts to access these resources.

There are three objectives of a security audit, as seen in Figure 10.1. The first objective is to assess the operational security controls in place to support a financial audit. The next is to assess software applications and operating system security controls that are in place to support information technology audits. The final objective is to identify unauthorized access and verify whether any unauthorized changes have been made to sensitive information to support forensic audits.

A great resource for standards followed when conducting an audit is provided by the Information Systems Audit and Control Association (ISACA), the governing body for auditing and control professionals that defines standards, guidelines, and procedures for information systems security audits. ISACA professionals must also

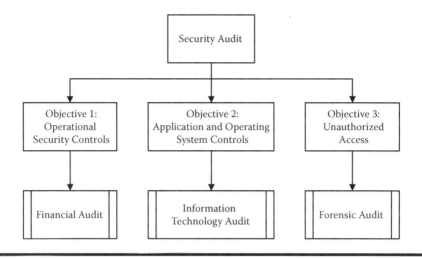

Figure 10.1   Security audit objectives.

agree to abide by a professional code of ethics and concentrate on the audit charter, independence, competence, planning, performance, reporting, and follow-up areas of interest. You can refer to www.isaca.org for a current copy of the ISACA's standards.

10.1.1 Security Monitoring

Security monitoring refers to the practice of monitoring operational controls to identify unusual activities. A few security monitoring techniques are the use of intrusion detection systems, penetration testing, and analysis of violations to determine whether an unusual or unauthorized event has occurred. *Violation analysis* is a technique that tracks unusual user activities. It is sometimes referred to as *violation processing* or *violation tracking* and uses an established clipping level to form a baseline of normal or routine user activities. Users that exceed this level or activities that fall outside this normal expected range are flagged for further follow-up and may indicate a possible intrusion attempt.

Some security threats that should be monitored are as follows:

■ *Inappropriate activities* are unusual activities that violate organizational policies. These types of activities may include storing entertainment, pornography, or offensive content on company computers; downloading unauthorized applications or copyrighted materials; wasting computer or network resources; distributing harassing e-mail; or even abusing user access rights and privileges.

■ *Illegal computer operations* include theft, fraud, and unauthorized surveillance that utilizes the organization's computer and network resources for personal gain.

■ *Intentional attacks* include sabotage and external attacks that occur from malicious individuals with the intent to disrupt or shut down systems. Examples of these types of attacks include denial of service attacks, work stoppage attacks, or even data modification or integrity types of attacks.

■ *Unauthorized entry* includes the unauthorized modification, destruction, manipulation, or prevention of access to systems.

■ *Initial Program Load (IPL)* is an inherent threat to a system when an initial application or program is being loaded onto a system for the first time. At this point, the operator can turn off security features, load unauthorized software, reset passwords, change date and time stamps, or even move or rename files. It is important that only trusted and authorized individuals conduct the IPL and that the procedures followed are verified by another independent party.

10.2 Information Security Governance Metrics

Good management is arguably one result of good governance.

Unknown author

Metrics is a term used to denote a measure based on a reference. Security, in its most basic form, is the protection from or absence of danger. Combining security and metrics together should give you the state or level of security your organization has as it relates to certain reference points. The only activities that can provide this type of information to your organization are full audits and comprehensive risk assessments. Unfortunately, these audits and assessments are a snapshot in time. Even though your organization may seem to have an effective information security management program one day, this does not mean that a zero-day exploit is not spreading across the Internet that makes your organization's entire network vulnerable. What organizations really need is a way to measure the effectiveness of their information security management programs on a day-by-day trending basis.

There is a strong correlation between good security management and practices producing relatively fewer incidents and losses. To determine whether it is meeting its goals and objectives, your organization can use Key Goal Indicators (KGIs) and Key Performance Indicators (KPIs). A KGI is a measure of *what* has to be accomplished in your organization to make it successful. KGIs are usually expressed in terms of availability of services, cost efficiency of processes, or the absence of certain risky activities. Some specific examples of KGIs may be the achievement of targeted return on investments, standardization in processing, or compliance with standards.

Key performance indicators are metrics that help determine or define the progress toward your organizational goals. KPIs are usually tied to your company's strategies and can be expressed through a technique known as the Balance ScoreCard (BSC). A BSC attempts to provide a comprehensive view of your company not only financially, but also in terms of operational, developmental, marketing, and other areas. The BSC attempts to measure the specific operational activities and how they align to the overall strategy of your company.

Although using the balance scorecard approach provides valuable information to your company, you may want to look at other effective security metrics, such as the following:

- downtime due to viruses;
- number of system penetrations or attempted system penetrations;
- impact and losses over time from security incidents;
- time it takes to recover systems;
- number of vulnerabilities discovered during penetration tests; and
- percentage of servers patched or unpatched.

No matter how your organization wants to measure or go about determining its effectiveness, it is important that the data reflect a SMART approach. *SMART* is an acronym for *s*pecific, *m*easurable, *a*ctionable, *r*easonable, and *t*ime based. This approach states that data collected must be specific and measure one and only one metric at a time. The metric has to provide actionable information that is put in understandable terms. In addition, the metric needs to be reasonable; it needs to make sense. Finally, metrics need to cover a certain time frame or be time based. This will allow for more accurate trend analysis over time.

For example, the time it takes to recover a particular system is a good metric to use in your disaster recovery planning. This metric is specific covering a particular system. It can be measured, normally in hours spent on recovering the system. It is actionable because there should be defined procedures on how to recover the particular system. It is reasonable and may be required to test in certain industries. It is also time based because you can track each time and the amount of time it takes to recover your particular system.

Many different types of metrics can be utilized; a few of the more common ones used in measuring information security include:

- NIST special publication 800-55, "Security Metrics Guide for Information Technology Systems," is an excellent source that builds each metric, one on top of another. This resource covers results-oriented metric analysis, quantifiable performance metrics, practical security policies and procedures, and strong upper level management support.
- Balance scorecard, as already discussed, is not only a measurement system, but also a management system that attempts to clarify an organization's goals and strategies into actionable items. Metrics are developed, data are collected, and analysis of the data is conducted against four different perspectives: learning and growing, business processes, customers, and finances.
- Systems And Business Security Architecture (SABSA) focuses on the business. The security architecture is dictated by the business strategy, objectives,

relationships, risks, constraints, and enablers. The method uses "contextual security architecture," which is the analysis and description of the business. SABSA emphasizes the flow from business strategy to execution and uses a matrix of business attributes to describe the objectives of security.

10.3 Testing—Vulnerability Assessment

Now that we have an understanding of metrics and what we are trying to measure, let us look at how we may conduct testing and, more specifically, at a vulnerability assessment or penetration test as it may sometimes be called. A *vulnerability assessment* can be internal or external. In an internal assessment, the evaluator has access to the facility and can physically connect to the local area network. An external vulnerability assessment looks at devices that are available to the public, such as a Web site. The evaluator's goal is to test or validate the effectiveness of the controls that we have been discussing throughout this book that are in place at your organization.

A vulnerability assessment is a security measure that exposes your network to a simulated attack. This type of testing is fairly sophisticated and this book is in no way meant to make you an expert; however, we will go through some high-level steps and the methodology behind conducting a vulnerability assessment. We will also provide some tools that you can look at to assist you in conducting a self-assessment. I recommend that you hire a professional, experienced, and competent company that can independently verify and conduct these types of assessments and analyses of your network and systems.

You should know some essential terms in regard to conducting a vulnerability assessment. Although we have already gone through some of these terms, we provide them here as a review:

- *Threat* is a potential violation of security.
- *Vulnerability* is a weakness in design or implementation of a system that can lead to an undesirable compromise of a system.
- *Target of evaluation* is an information system resource that is being evaluated.
- *Attack* is any action that violates security and can come in four different varieties:
  - *Active attacks* modify the target of evaluation.
  - *Passive attacks* violate confidentiality without affecting the state of the system.
  - *Inside attacks* are initiated by someone from inside the organization.
  - *Outside attacks* are initiated by someone outside the organization.
- *Exploit* is a specific way to breach the security of the target of evaluation through a known vulnerability.
- *Exposure* is the loss realized from an exploit.

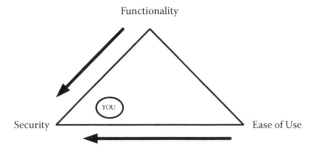

Figure 10.2   Security trade-off.

Your organization wants to be in a state of security in which the possibility of a successful, undetected theft; tampering; or disruption of the information systems or services is kept to a tolerable level. The rule of security is that security increases when the number of exploits is minimized, and this comes as a direct result of the reduction in the number of weaknesses discovered. Thus, a trade-off takes place with security, functionality, and the ease of use of information systems, as seen in Figure 10.2. As the organization moves toward more security, it is moving away from functionality and ease of use. Functionality is reduced as it takes more effort to conduct the same task through different security controls, such as entering user name and password combinations for different applications or systems.

The methodology behind conducting a vulnerability assessment has five phases, as seen in Figure 10.3:

1. reconnaissance;
2. scanning;
3. gaining access;
4. maintaining access; and
5. clearing tracks.

10.3.1 Phase 1—Reconnaissance

In this phase, the evaluator uses passive or active means to gather as much information about the target of evaluation as possible. This phase is referred to as "rattling the door knobs" and has only a negligible amount of business risk. The evaluator will utilize the information in this phase as a future reference point to carry on more in-depth attacks. The reconnaissance phase usually involves social engineering, which we discussed in Section 4.3 in Chapter 4, or maybe even "dumpster diving," where the evaluator looks in the trash for discarded sensitive information.

To conduct reconnaissance on the Internet, I utilize a program called *Maltego* (http://www.paterva.com/web2/Maltego/maltego.html). This program provides a lot of information about your target of evaluation and presents it in a nice graphical

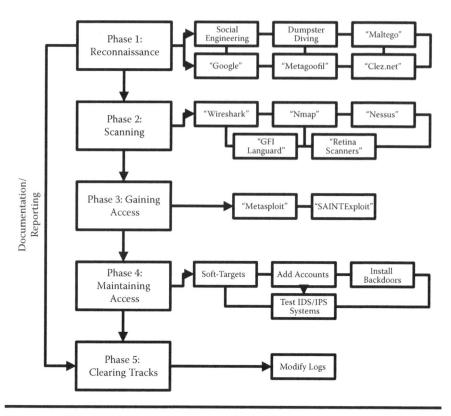

Figure 10.3 Vulnerability assessment methodology.

user interface. Google (http://www.google.com) is also your reconnaissance friend. I will not go into details on how you can utilize Google for recon activities because the Internet already contains a lot of information about Google. The final tool I utilize is Clez (http://clez.net). This online tool provides trace route information, *WhoIs* information, and a lot more to assist in gathering information on your target.

You may be asking why it is so important to conduct reconnaissance. The answer is that reconnaissance is probably one of the *most* important parts of an assessment. You need to know your enemy better than you know yourself. The more information you can gather on your target, the better your assessment will be. Knowledge is power, and with power comes a lot of responsibility. Be aware that the information gathered can be used for malicious intent, so it is very important that you trust the individuals conducting your assessments.

10.3.2 Phase 2—Scanning

After some information has been gathered, the evaluator will normally begin actively to probe the target of evaluation for known vulnerabilities to exploit. The evaluator will utilize sniffing programs like *Wireshark* to see what traffic can be monitored on the network. He or she will also utilize *Nmap* to see what types of ports may be open on the devices and what types of services these devices may be offering.

As the assessment progresses through this phase, the evaluator will want to determine what type of operating systems each device on the network is running. This is done by probing the ports or services to enumerate what type of operating system or application is running on the target. Responses to certain types of inquiries or requests against these services or ports can help determine the types of applications running. Although this enumeration is not perfect, the tools utilized to perform it are pretty accurate.

The evaluator will also run scanning tools such as *Nessus, GFI Languard,* or *Retina Security Scanners.* These tools assist in determining known vulnerabilities that may be affecting certain devices on the network. Numerous tools are available and each has pros and cons. For example, some tools provide better and faster results for different environments, such as Windows and Unix environments. No matter what scanner the evaluator uses, they are all used to footprint the network and to develop a plan of action for further evaluation.

10.3.3 Phase 3—Gaining Access

After the scans have been performed and the evaluator has a plan of action, it is time to perform penetration tests. After analyzing the information obtained in phase 2, the evaluator will have a good idea as to the vulnerabilities and vectors that can be exploited to obtain access to the system. As can be inferred, the goal of this phase is to obtain access to a system or, better still, administrative level or root access to the system.

Access to a system can be achieved at the operating system level, the application level, or even at the network level. As far as business risk is concerned, this phase poses the highest level of risk and is the most important phase of an evaluation in terms of potential damage. It is essential that the individuals conducting this type of evaluation be skilled and highly trained in conducting vulnerability assessments. Some of the exploits that may be verified in this phase can cause serious damage or potentially take down critical systems on the network.

Several different tools can be used to perform exploits and really good penetration testers have developed their own exploits. Also, exploit frameworks have been designed to assist individuals in developing these exploits easily. Tools such as *Metasploit* and *SAINTExploit* are just a couple of the exploit frameworks available.

Just as quickly as software developers fix or secure their applications, individuals with malicious intent are finding ways to circumvent these security controls. It is a game of cat and mouse; the security environment we live in today is very dynamic and fluid. Exploits termed "zero-day" exploits are released into the public almost on a daily basis. These are the exploits that most concern software vendors because they are not given any type of notice to fix their vulnerabilities. If the exploit is serious enough, the vendors must be able to assign the necessary resources to fix the problem. .

This goes back to the root of our discussions in that security needs to be considered up front in any type of software or application development in an effort to mitigate some of the effects that these zero-day attacks can have.

10.3.4 Phase 4—Maintaining Access

Once access to a system has been obtained, the evaluator should not stop there. He or she should attempt to obtain access or jump off into other systems. The evaluator should look for sensitive information that can lead to other areas of the network.

I have found that, in most cases, servers are normally locked down tightly because they normally have dedicated staff members watching over them. They house important data and are considered to be critical components of the company's infrastructure. Although good penetration testers will examine these servers, they will also concentrate their efforts on "soft targets."

When I speak of soft targets, I am describing devices such as workstations, laptops, printers, and other noncritical systems. These soft targets are sometimes considered the "low-hanging fruit." To hone their skills, penetration testers may try to see how fast they can get access to your network. They will look for these "low-hanging" or "low-lying" soft targets that may have minimal to no security controls in place. Once they are able to compromise these systems, they will attempt to use them to gain further access into the network.

Here is an example of how this occurs. Your company probably has multiple workstations. At some point, one of your system administrators probably had to work on or help your user out with a workstation. This system administrator probably logged on to the workstation using an administrator account. Some systems keep a log or cache this account information. Because these workstations are not usually as secure as servers or may not be maintained with proper patches or updates, it is normally just a matter of time before they are compromised. Once these systems are compromised, the cached accounts can be retrieved. Again, it is just a matter of time to crack these accounts, and once someone has compromised the accounts, he or she can then use these credentials to access other systems or gain full control of the network. I also create my own accounts on these systems so that I can maintain control of the systems throughout the evaluation.

During this phase, the evaluator may test the different notification or alert systems in place. Because the evaluator is creating a simulated security breach or incident, it may be helpful to see how well the organization's intrusion detection systems or log monitoring systems have worked. Did they pick up the unauthorized access? Do the logs indicate that any unusual event has occurred? Is your IT staff able to tell what the evaluator is doing or how the evaluator may have compromised the system without anything being said?

It is important to determine how well your controls work. If you cannot pick up penetration activity or tell what is going on at any point in time on your network, it will be very difficult for you to determine whether you have fallen victim to an attack. It will also be very difficult for you to investigate or bring charges against malicious individuals if you have no way of telling what they did to you. In my experience, incident management or tracking has probably been one of the weakest areas; however, it is probably one of the most important areas to consider.

10.3.5 Phase 5—Covering Tracks

Although the evaluator may not cover up actions performed during a vulnerability assessment, if an actual attack were to occur, the attacker would attempt to hide or cover his steps. The attacker may attempt to alter logs. This can be accomplished by accessing areas of the system that store the logs or by utilizing specialized programs that can edit or delete these logs.

The attacker can also plant "backdoors" for further use of the system. These backdoors can consist of key logging or monitoring programs that monitor or store all key strokes that occur on the systems. The backdoors may also provide hidden communication or remote access tunnels so that the attacker can enter and leave systems at his or her leisure.

The attacker can also tunnel out sensitive information through covert channels. These covert channels can be through the use of encryption or *steganography* (the art of disguising or hiding messages in other forms such as picture files or other document files). When information is hidden in this fashion, the organization has very little chance to determine to what extent it has become a victim. Because most information is stored electronically these days, huge amounts of sensitive or proprietary information can be sent through these covert channels without anyone knowing.

10.3.6 Documentation and Reporting

One of the most important parts of the evaluation is good documentation. Throughout the assessment, the evaluator should be taking careful notes and documenting all steps and procedures that he or she followed. At the end of the evaluation, a detailed report should be generated that notes all of the findings or observations made during the process. Experienced penetration testers should also be able to provide actionable recommendations on how to tighten the security and correct vulnerabilities that may have been found during the assessment. Although it will be up to the organization to determine what recommendations to follow or actions to take to mitigate any risks or findings noted, it is important that it be open to these professional suggestions or recommendations. The organization will obtain more value from these types of assessments if it is not already predisposed and management is open to change and enhancing its current security state.

10.4 Summary

In this chapter, we completed the book by discussing audit and compliance issues. We emphasized the importance of these activities as they relate to documenting the adequacy of an information security program. The auditor can be your best friend or may be your worst enemy, but in either case he or she is an important element in implementing your program. We discussed information security governance and provided a step-by-step procedure on conducting testing. Finally, we explained the five phases of a vulnerability assessment and the steps involved in conducting a comprehensive vulnerability assessment.

Appendix A: Information Security Policy

The following is an example of an information security policy. This policy incorporates the minimum required components that should be included in any information security policy. Your specific company's policy may require including additional regulatory elements, and legal counsel should be consulted in developing an information security policy customized for your organization.

A.1 Purpose

The purpose of this policy is to provide the necessary requirements to ensure that ABC Company's information is handled appropriately by employees and technology.

A.2 Objectives

ABC Company's security goals concentrate on the following objectives.

A.2.1 Confidentiality of Information or Systems

Protect against the unauthorized access or use of ABC Company's information.

A.2.2 Integrity of Information or Systems

Protect ABC Company's information from any compromise by individuals that may accidentally or with intent manipulate such information. ABC Company will at all times maintain accountability of information by tracking events to their source and destination. ABC Company will also ensure the accuracy and reliability of its information by conducting compliance testing assurance.

A.2.3 Availability of Information or Systems

Protect against the accidental or intentional attempts of individuals to gain access to information or systems owned and maintained by ABC Company.

A.3 Responsibilities

A.3.1 Security Committee

To fulfill ABC Company's information security objectives, a security committee will be designated for organization-wide information security responsibilities including, but not limited to, establishing, maintaining, and implementing information security policies and procedures.

A.3.2 Chief Information Security Officer

A chief information security officer will be designated and will report to the security committee. The chief information security officer will administer the information security policies and procedures. The chief information security officer is also assigned the duties of risk management, contingency planning, vendor management, incident handling, security awareness training, and consulting on information security matters. The chief information security officer will assign responsibilities to audit compliance on information security policies and procedures, as necessary. The chief information security officer will work with employees to maintain and interpret the objectives of related information security policies and procedures.

A.3.3 Information Security Department

Information security responsibilities will be centralized in ABC Company under the Information Security Department headed by the chief information security officer. The Information Security Department is assigned the following tasks: perform information security risk assessments, testing, evaluations, and perform other tasks assigned by the chief information security officer, as necessary, to implement the information security program efficiently and effectively.

A.3.4 Chief Technology Officer

A chief technology officer will be designated and report directly to the chief executive officer. The chief technology officer will lead the Information Technology Department in its responsibilities to configure, monitor, and document activities as they relate to information security.

A.3.5 Information Technology Department

The Information Technology Department is responsible for the specific hands-on matters related to software applications, operating systems, intrusion detection and prevention systems, firewall configurations, and other technology components of ABC Company.

A.3.6 Network Services Group

The Network Services Group under the Information Technology Department will act as information security coordinators. This group will serve as the internal information security liaison implementing the requirements of the information security policies and procedures. The Network Services Group will be responsible for assigning user access, monitoring access logs, and performing the hands-on administration of security devices. The group will report any suspicious activities to the chief information security officer.

A.3.7 Department Heads

Each and every department head will be responsible for ensuring that the information security policies and procedures are observed in his or her respective areas. Department heads are also responsible for ensuring that all their employees are made aware of ABC Company's policies and procedures related to information security. It is the responsibility of all employees to carry out information security on a day-to-day basis.

A.3.8 Employees

Employees are responsible for complying with ABC Company's information security policies and procedures. Employees are required to sign an acknowledgment of understanding with regard to ABC Company's technology resource policy. Employees are also required to attend annual information security awareness training administered by the Information Security Department. This training, at a minimum, will discuss ABC Company's information security policies and procedures for employees. Employees are required to report any suspicious activity or other related security issues to the chief information security officer immediately.

A.4 Security Processes

The following processes will be followed to develop comprehensive information security plans that are designed to meet ABC Company's security objectives. These plans will be approved by the chief information security officer and security committee. They will also be reviewed by business owners.

A.4.1 Information Security Risk Assessments

Information security risk assessments will be performed on all business functions and systems. The risk assessment will identify threats, vulnerabilities, and possible attacks to these functions. It will determine the probability of the occurrence of the attack and potential impact or damage that may be sustained if an attack occurs. The information security risk assessment will rank these findings and develop strategies to mitigate these risks to an acceptable level determined by the security committee.

A.4.2 Security Strategies

Defense-in-depth controls will be formulated to mitigate risks against business assets.

A.4.3 Implementing Controls

Physical, administrative, and technical network security controls will be implemented. Department heads and employees will be assigned specific duties and responsibilities for these controls, as necessary. These controls will be deployed on a risk-appropriate basis and department heads and employees will be assigned relevant duties based on their knowledge and skill sets concerning these controls.

A.5 Portable Devices

Portable devices are defined as any portable electronic devices, laptops, notebook computers, palmtops, USB drives, external portable hard drives, or any other transportable electronic device that can store data. Encryption will be utilized on any of these devices that contain ABC Company's sensitive information.

A.6 Logs and Systems Security Tools

Every information system, including but not limited to computers, servers, and other portable electronic devices, will include adequate tools to verify security settings, configurations, and logging functions. All security-relevant events will be securely logged to the extent possible for any information system considered sensitive or critical to ABC Company. These logs must be stored in a secure fashion so that they cannot be modified and can only be read by authorized persons for at least 5 years. All relevant security patches will be installed by system administrators in accordance with ABC Company's change management procedures.

A.7 Security Information Management

Information concerning any security controls implemented at ABC Company is considered confidential. This information should not be released to anyone at any time without the express permission of the chief information security officer.

A.7.1 Reporting Problems

Employees should immediately report any security-related issues or potential issues to the chief information security officer. Employees are prohibited from forwarding this type of information to any other individual either internal or external to ABC Company.

A.8 e-Mail and Computer Use

ABC Company's computer and electronic assets should be used only for business purposes in accordance with the technology resource policy. Any illegal or unauthorized use of these assets is strictly prohibited.

A.8.1 Configuration Control

A.8.1.1 Changes to Application Software and Operating System Configurations

The Information Technology Department is responsible for installing updates or making any configuration changes to ABC Company's electronic assets. Employees are prohibited from installing any additional software, upgrades, changes to the configurations, or changes to the operating systems on any of ABC Company's electronic assets without the express permission of the Information Technology Department. The Information Technology Department will be responsible for the centralized and coordinated efforts to distribute software patches, manage software licenses, and automate backups on all systems used to process ABC Company's information. These systems may or may not be owned by ABC Company, but they may be used on a regular basis for business activities. A clear indication of such systems are those that are reimbursed for by ABC Company.

A.8.1.2 Changes to Hardware

The Information Technology Department is responsible for maintaining and making changes to any hardware on computer equipment owned by ABC Company. Employees are prohibited from making any alteration or changes to this hardware without the express permission of the Information Technology Department. Any hardware or magnetic media that are no longer being used must be destroyed or formatted by the Information Technology Department with a Department of Defense-approved software application.

A.9 Backups

A.9.1 Archival Copies

ABC Company will store at least one original copy of all computer software in a secured location. These original copies will not be used on a regular business basis; however, they will be reserved for use as part of the security incident recovery procedures. To document licensing requirements and obtain valid technical support, all software license documentation will be accurately maintained by the Information Technology Department.

A.9.2 Copyright Protection

Any unauthorized copying of licensed or copyrighted software is strictly prohibited. ABC Company adheres to software licensing agreements and copyright holders' notices. ABC Company only allows copying of materials to the extent legally considered "fair use" or with the express permission of the author of such material. All material, unless otherwise noted, should be assumed to be under copyright. Employees should seek assistance from their department head if they have any question about copyrighted material. Department heads should refer these questions to ABC Company's legal counsel.

A.9.3 Periodic Backup

The Information Technology Department will perform a full backup at least weekly on all information deemed sensitive or critical. The information on these backups will be encrypted and stored in a secured off-site location. Employees are required to store their information on network shares. Any information stored on local systems may or may not be recovered in case of a hard drive failure. The Information Technology Department has no expectation of restoring such information stored on local systems. The Information Technology Department will conduct routine restores of selected files on a periodic basis to demonstrate the effectiveness of the backup process.

A.10 Networking

A.10.1 Installation of Communications Lines

The chief information security officer will oversee any installation of communication lines. Employees and vendors are prohibited from making any arrangements or conducting any installation of voice or data lines without obtaining prior approval from the chief information security officer.

A.10.2 Establishing Networks

ABC Company maintains security controls on all networked systems. Employees are prohibited from establishing any types of network communications with ABC Company's network that have not been expressly permitted by the Information Technology Department. This includes electronic bulletin boards, other local area network connections, modem connections, wireless connections, or any other multiuser communication connections.

A.11 Physical Security

ABC Company will implement physical security access controls on restricted areas to protect sensitive and critical electronic assets. These areas include, but are not limited to, data centers, telephone wiring rooms, switching rooms, development servers, and other work areas that contain sensitive information or devices.

A.11.1 Custodians of Equipment

A custodian of equipment is defined as the primary user of that equipment. Equipment should not be moved or relocated without the knowledge or approval of the Information Technology Department.

A.11.2 Use of Personal Equipment

The use of personally owned equipment to conduct ABC Company business is strictly prohibited. This equipment should not be brought into ABC Company's facility without prior authorization from an employee's department head.

A.11.3 Safeguarding Information

Any information considered sensitive that is contained on hard copies should be secured at all times when not in use. Any information considered sensitive that is contained on electronic storage media should also be secured at all times when not in use. Information is secured when it is locked in filing cabinets, desks, safes, or other security-type furniture.

A.11.4 Environmental Controls

ABC Company will utilize environmental monitoring controls to monitor for temperature, humidity, and other related environment hazards within the data center.

ABC Company will also utilize Uninterruptible Power Systems (UPSs) on systems classified as critical and at least surge protectors on all other electronic assets.

Appendix B: Technology Resource Policy*

ABC Company
Technology Resources Policy
Version 1.0

B.1 Purpose

The ABC Company and its divisions, subsidiaries, and affiliates (collectively, "ABC") have adopted this technology resources policy (the "policy") to ensure uniform and appropriate use of their networks, computers, and telecommunication resources (the "technology resources," defined later). The rules, obligations, and standards described in this policy apply to all ABC employees, temporary workers, independent contractors, agents, and other computer or telecommunication users (collectively, the "users," as defined later), wherever they may be located.

It is every user's duty to use the technology resources responsibly and in a professional, ethical, and lawful manner. In addition, every user is responsible for ensuring the security of ABC's technology resources and its valuable proprietary and confidential information. Users agree to assist ABC in investigating any potential or actual violations of this policy.

Violations of this policy may result in disciplinary action, including termination, and potential civil and criminal liability. Use of the technology resources is a privilege that may be limited or revoked at any time, with or without cause and without notice, at the sole discretion of ABC. If a user does not accept the terms of this policy, including particularly the provisions regarding collection and use of personal information, the user may be denied use of the technology resources, may be denied employment, or may be terminated, to the full extent permitted by applicable law.

---

* This technology use policy was reproduced here with permission from Michael R. Overly, Esq.

255

B.2 Definitions

As used in this policy, certain terms are defined as follows:

"Confidential/proprietary information" includes, but is not limited to, any information owned, licensed, or possessed by ABC that (1) ABC is contractually obligated to protect (e.g., third-party information that is the subject of a confidentiality or nondisclosure agreement), or (2) is not generally known to the public, especially if such information gives ABC a competitive advantage or its disclosure would harm ABC. Confidential/proprietary information includes, but is not limited to, trade secrets, proprietary information, and all other information, documents, or materials owned, licensed, developed, or possessed by ABC or any employee or agent of ABC, whether tangible or intangible, relating in any way to ABC's customers, prospective customers, business plans and activities, business relationships, costs or profit information or data from which that information could be derived, human resources (including internal evaluations of the performance, capability, and potential of any ABC employee), business methods, databases, and computer programs whether or not marked as "confidential" or "proprietary."

"e-Mail" means messages sent and received via electronic media, either through an internal network or over an external network (e.g., the Internet, America Online, or MSN), including any file attachments.

"Internet gateway" means a hardware and/or software system placed between the technology resources and the Internet to limit unauthorized access to and use of the technology resources.

"Listserv" means an automatic distribution method for e-mail on the Internet. Users can subscribe to a listserv, typically a discussion list, and receive copies of e-mail sent to the list by other subscribers.

"Online forums" means online discussion groups, news groups, bulletin boards, chat rooms, blogs (a form of online diary in which individuals may post descriptions of their activities), and other similar forums on the Internet and other public networks (America Online and MSN).

"Policy" means this technology resources policy, including all attachments.

"Portable technology resources" means those technology resources that are portable or mobile in nature. By way of example only, portable technology resources include laptops, personal digital assistants (PDAs), palmtop computers, portable/handheld telecommunications devices (e.g., cellular telephones, pagers, and radios), cameras (both digital and analog), and other similar devices.

"Removable media" means portable or removable hard disks, floppy disks, USB memory drives, zip disks, optical disks, CDs, DVDs, digital film, memory cards (e.g., secure digital [SD], memory sticks [MS], compactFlash [CF], smartMedia [SM], multimediaCard [MMC], and xD-picture card [xD]), magnetic tape, and all other removable data storage media.

"Server" means a computer running administrative software that controls access to a network and its resources, such as printers and disk drives, and provides resources to computers functioning as workstations connected to the network and code that provides a service on the network.

"Technology information" means all information, data, and communications created, received, or stored on or passed through the technology resources, including all user files and e-mail.

"Technology resources" means ABC's entire computer and telecommunications network, including, but not limited to, the following: fax machines, host computers, file servers, application servers, communication servers, mail servers, scanners, fax servers, Web servers, workstations, stand-alone computers, laptops, PDAs, palmtop computers, portable/handheld telecommunications devices (e.g., cellular telephones, pagers, and radios), cameras (both digital and analog), software, applications, data files, removable media, and all internal and external computer and communications networks (e.g., intranets, extranets, Internet, commercial online services, value-added networks, e-mail systems) accessed directly or indirectly from ABC's computer network.

"Users" means all employees, independent contractors, consultants, contract employees, temporary workers, and other persons or entities using the technology resources, wherever located or however deployed.

"Virus" means a program that infects computer files and systems, often with destructive results (e.g., loss of data, unreliable operation of infected software and systems).

"Workstation" means the individual computers assigned to one or more users.

B.3 Policy

In using or accessing the technology resources, users must comply with the following provisions.

B.3.1 Use of Technology Resources in General

The technology resources constitute a valuable business asset of ABC and may only be used for approved purposes. Users are permitted access to the technology resources to assist them in the performance of their jobs. Occasional, limited, appropriate personal use of the technology resources is permitted when the use does not: (1) interfere with the user's work performance, (2) interfere with any other user's work performance, (3) unduly impact the operation of the technology resources, (4) result in any material expense to ABC, (5) violate any law or regulation of any jurisdiction, or (6) violate any other provision of this policy or any other policy, guideline, or standard of ABC.

Users are strongly discouraged from using the technology resources to store, send, or receive information that is personal to them (e.g., online account passwords and activities, communications of a personal nature, visiting Web sites that may identify personal information about the user, etc.). As discussed later, all information transmitted through or stored on the technology resources may be reviewed by others. ABC cannot guarantee and does not assume any obligation to protect the security of this kind of user personal information. If a user desires privacy and security for this type of personal information, the user should not use the technology resources. Instead, the user should restrict the information to a computer owned and operated by the user (e.g., the user's home computer).

B.3.2 No Expectation of Privacy

Users understand and agree that

ABC retains the right, with or without cause or notice to the user, to access and monitor the technology information, including user e-mail and Internet usage. Anything created or stored on the technology resources, including the technology information, may, and likely will, be reviewed by others and deleted files may be recovered. Without limiting the foregoing, ABC may record and access any use of the technology resources to measure and set standards for performance of the user's duties, to monitor the user's compliance with applicable laws and this policy, to determine whether specific communications are business or personal communications, and for any other purpose related to ABC's business operations.

Password-protected, encrypted, and deleted files, including those identified as "private," "personal," or the equivalent, may be recovered and reviewed.

Users should specifically expect that their technology information, including e-mail, will be accessed during absences due to vacations, business travel, or otherwise.

Users have no expectation or right of privacy of any kind related to their use of the technology resources or any technology information.

Users expressly consent to the access, monitoring, and recording of their use of the technology resources and any technology information and waive any right of privacy or similar right in their use of the technology resources or any technology information.

B.3.3 Ownership of Technology Information and Technology Resources

All of the technology information and the technology resources are the sole and exclusive property of ABC. Any user files, e-mail, and other technology information stored on the technology resources are the property of ABC.

B.3.4 Prohibited Activities

Inappropriate or unlawful material. Material that is fraudulent, harassing, embarrassing, sexually explicit, profane, obscene, intimidating, defamatory, or otherwise unlawful or inappropriate, including any comments that would offend someone on the basis of race, age, sex, sexual orientation, religion, political beliefs, national origin, veteran status, or disability, must not be sent by e-mail or other forms of electronic communication, including online forums, viewed on or downloaded from the Internet or other online service or displayed on or stored in the technology resources. Users encountering or receiving such material must immediately report the incident to their supervisor or other responsible manager.

Prohibited activities. Users may not use the technology resources for personal financial gain or the benefit of any third party (including the sale of any non-ABC products or services) or to solicit others for activities unrelated to ABC's business or sponsored activities or in violation of ABC policies and applicable laws relating to political activity or lobbying. The technology resources may also not be used to create, store, or distribute any form of malicious software (e.g., viruses, worms, or other destructive code).

Waste of technology resources. Users may not deliberately perform acts that waste technology resources or unfairly monopolize resources to the exclusion of others. These acts include, but are not limited to, sending non-business-related mass e-mailings or chain e-mail, subscribing to a non-business-related listserv, excessive use of technology resources for non-business-related activities (e.g., personal purposes, playing games, engaging in non-business-related online "chat groups"), or otherwise creating unnecessary network traffic.

B.3.5 Use of e-Mail

In general. All user e-mail addresses assigned by ABC shall remain the sole and exclusive property of ABC. Users should endeavor to make each of their electronic communications truthful, accurate, and consistent with the qualities of good business communications. Always allow time to reflect before composing and sending a message. The following guidelines should be followed in drafting e-mail:

- Avoid using all capitals.
- Avoid excessive use of boldfaced type.
- Only mark high-priority items as "priority."
- Avoid copying unnecessary parties with the "reply all" feature.
- Make the subject line for your e-mail descriptive.
- Avoid using graphic backgrounds and ornate type fonts for your e-mail. These will make your e-mail less readable and will require far greater company resources to store and transmit than ordinary e-mail.
- Do not send messages to all users or other large groups within the company unless they are business related and a compelling business reason exists.

Altering attribution information. Users may not alter the "from" line or other attribution of origin information in e-mail or other online postings. Anonymous or electronic communications sent using fictitious names are forbidden. However, a user many specifically grant another user the right to send e-mails on behalf of the grantor (e.g., a manager authorizing her assistant to send an e-mail on her behalf).

Forwarding e-mail. Users should use their good judgment in forwarding e-mail to any other person or entity. When in doubt, request the sender's permission before forwarding the message. e-Mail containing confidential/proprietary information or attorney–client communications may never be forwarded without the permission of the sender or other authorized personnel. All messages written by others should be forwarded "as-is" and with no changes, except to the extent that the changes are clearly indicated in the original text (e.g., by using brackets [ ] or other characters to indicate changes to the text).

Confidential/proprietary information. Each user must take all appropriate precautions, including those described in the attached guidelines for information protection, to ensure that confidential/proprietary information is not improperly disclosed or otherwise compromised. If confidential/proprietary information is transmitted via the technology resources, the sender of the message is responsible for (1) ensuring the message is clearly labeled in the subject line and the body of the message as "confidential," "proprietary," "confidential: unauthorized use or disclosure is strictly prohibited," or "privileged attorney–client communication"; (2) keeping the number of recipients to a minimum; (3) ensuring all recipients are aware of the obligation to maintain the confidentiality of the information contained in the message; and (4) assuring that the transmission of information is in accordance with this policy and applicable law.

Receipt of unsolicited, unintentional, or misdirected confidential/proprietary information. In the event a user receives an e-mail, whether designated as confidential or not, by mistake, the user should stop reading the message and immediately notify the sender or system administrator. It is a violation of this policy to read e-mail intended for another person without the express prior consent of that person or other authorized ABC personnel.

Listserv subscriptions. Users should be selective in subscribing to listservs and other e-mail distribution lists. Some discussion groups are very active and may result in dozens of e-mails every day. Promptly unsubscribe to any listservs that are not actively being read. When subscribing to a listserv, make sure to keep a record of the steps necessary to cancel the subscription. This information is usually contained in an initial message from the listserv, but may not be easily located later.

B.3.6 Internet Access and Use

Authorized uses. Users are encouraged to use the Internet and intranets to assist them in the performance of their jobs. Authorized uses include, but are not limited to, the following:

client and customer services, human resources, education, and research;
electronic communication; and
professional purposes and procurement of information from external sources.

Internet monitoring. ABC has software and systems in place that are capable of monitoring and recording all Internet usage. For each user, these security measures are capable of recording each Web site visited, each online forum or e-mail message, and each file transfer into and out of ABC's networks, and ABC reserves the right to conduct such monitoring and recording at any time. As described in Section B3.2, users have no expectation of privacy as to their Internet usage. ABC will review Internet activity and analyze usage patterns, and it may choose to publicize these data to assure that the technology resources are used in accordance with the provisions of this policy. ABC may use software and other technological means to identify and block access to Internet sites containing sexually explicit or other material deemed inappropriate in the workplace.

Online forums. Online forums are public forums where it is inappropriate to discuss or reveal confidential information, customer data, trade secrets, and any other material described in the attached guidelines for information protection. Users must identify themselves honestly, accurately, and completely when participating in online forums and when setting up accounts on outside computer systems. Only those users who have been duly authorized by ABC may speak or write in the name of the company when making postings to online forums. Other users may participate in online forums, provided (1) participation will assist them in the performance of their jobs, (2) they do not disclose any confidential/proprietary information, and (3) the user makes no attempt to speak or write on behalf of ABC and includes the following footer on all postings or comments: "This posting reflects the individual views and opinions of the author and does not necessarily represent the views and opinions of ABC." Each posting leaves an "audit trail" indicating at least the identity of ABC's Internet servers and, most likely, a direct trail to the user. Inappropriate postings damage ABC's reputation and could result in corporate or individual liabilities and may result in discipline.

Accessing the Internet. To ensure security and avoid the spread of viruses, users accessing the Internet through a computer attached to ABC's network must do so through an approved Internet gateway. Accessing the Internet directly, by modem, from a workstation is strictly prohibited unless the computer is not connected to the network (e.g., a laptop being used remotely). Even if a stand-alone computer with a modem is used to access the Internet or other network, the modem must never be left in auto-answer mode.

Disclaimer of liability for internet use. ABC IS NOT RESPONSIBLE FOR MATERIAL VIEWED OR DOWNLOADED BY USERS FROM THE INTERNET. THE INTERNET IS A WORLDWIDE NETWORK OF COMPUTERS THAT CONTAINS MILLIONS OF PAGES OF INFORMATION. USERS ARE CAUTIONED THAT MANY OF

THESE PAGES INCLUDE OFFENSIVE, SEXUALLY EXPLICIT, AND INAPPROPRIATE MATERIAL. IN GENERAL, IT IS DIFFICULT TO AVOID AT LEAST SOME CONTACT WITH THIS MATERIAL WHILE USING THE INTERNET. EVEN INNOCUOUS SEARCH REQUESTS MAY LEAD TO SITES WITH HIGHLY OFFENSIVE CONTENT. IN ADDITION, HAVING AN E-MAIL ADDRESS ON THE INTERNET MAY LEAD TO THE RECEIPT OF UNSOLICITED E-MAIL CONTAINING OFFENSIVE CONTENT. USERS ACCESSING THE INTERNET DO SO AT THEIR OWN RISK.

B.3.7 Disclosures Regarding Security Issues

Information relating to virus attacks, hacking incidents, and other breaches of security shall be treated as ABC confidential/proprietary information. Unless specifically directed to do so by authorized ABC management, users may not discuss this information with their co-workers or disclose it to any nonemployee. Violations of this provision will be considered a serious breach of trust by the user.

B.3.8 Miscellaneous

Compliance with applicable laws and licenses. In their use of the technology resources, users must comply with all software licenses, copyrights, and all other state, federal, and international laws.

Other policies applicable. In their use of the technology resources, users must observe and comply with all other policies and guidelines of ABC, including, but not limited to, the attached guidelines for information protection procedures.

Amendments and revisions. This policy may be amended or revised by ABC from time to time as deemed necessary. Users will be provided with copies of all amendments and revisions.

No additional rights. This policy is not intended to grant, and does not grant, users any contractual rights.

I have read and agree to comply with the terms of this policy governing the use of ABC's technology resources. I understand that a violation of this policy may result in disciplinary action, including possible termination, as well as potential civil and criminal liability. I agree to assist ABC in investigating any potential or actual violations of this policy.

_____

Signature

_____

Printed Name

_____

Date

Appendix C: Log-on Warning Banner

Note: This is an example of a log-on warning banner that contains the minimum elements of an effective warning banner. You should seek the advice of legal counsel in developing a customized log-on warning banner for your company.

Notice to All Users (Authorized or Unauthorized)*

This computer system is for authorized use only. Users have no explicit or implicit expectation of privacy. Any or all uses of this system and all data on this system may be intercepted, monitored, recorded, copied, audited, inspected, and disclosed to authorized sites and law enforcement personnel, as well as authorized officials of other agencies. By using this system, the user consents to such disclosure at the discretion of authorized site personnel. Unauthorized or improper use of this system may result in administrative disciplinary action and civil and criminal penalties. By continuing to use this system you indicate your awareness of and consent to these terms and conditions of use. STOP IMMEDIATELY!!! if you do not agree to the conditions stated in this warning.

---

* This log-on warning banner was reproduced here with permission from Dave Kleiman.

Appendix D: Penetration Test Waiver

The following is an example of a penetration test waiver that contains some of the minimum elements required. This type of waiver should be completed for any individual, either internal or external, that performs penetration testing or vulnerability type assessments on your company's systems. Legal counsel should assist you in developing this type of waiver.

D.1 Objective

[Individual or company conducting assessment] has been hired to perform a vulnerability assessment [or penetration test] on ABC Company's internal and external security profile. This profile will include networked computer systems and intrusion detection/prevention capabilities.

D.2 Scope of Work

This vulnerability assessment [or penetration test] will consist of four phases: network mapping, identifying vulnerabilities, exploitation or penetration, and documentation or reporting. These phases are detailed later. In conducting this vulnerability assessment [penetration testing], [individual or company] will utilize various tools and techniques to gather information and attempt to penetrate ABC Company's computer and network assets. Although every attempt will be made to preserve the integrity and availability of the systems tested under this engagement, ABC Company understands that there are risks inherent to such testing. ABC Company will hold harmless [individual or company] from liability or damages related to this testing activity.

D.2.1 Footprinting

[Individual or company] will obtain sufficient information regarding ABC Company's network profile, such as IP address ranges, telephone number ranges, and other general network topology information from passive information gathering techniques such as sniffing, Internet registration services, public search engines, telephone directories, etc. Additional detailed information regarding ABC Company's network profile may be obtained through the use of Domain Name Server (DNS) queries and more active types of scanning activities such as ping sweeps, port scans, and trace routing. "Social engineering" types of activities may also be attempted to gather specific information from ABC Company's employees to assist in gaining access to network resources. This information will be organized and analyzed to provide a plan to [individual or company] for further exploitation activities.

D.2.2 Identifying Vulnerabilities

[Individual or company] will be associating operating systems and applications identified on ABC Company's computer assets. This can be accomplished in multiple ways utilizing multiple automated tools such as Nmap, Queso, or other manual techniques through the use of Telnet, FTP, or SendMail log-on banners. Other publicly available or commercially available scanners will also be utilized to assist in identifying vulnerabilities. [Individual or company] will use this information to develop a list of possible vulnerabilities. Research will be conducted and some automated scripts may be collected or developed in an attempt to exploit these potential vulnerabilities. As a point of reference, denial of service types of exploits or those exploits that may have the potential of causing services to become unavailable will not be exploited. These types of findings will be noted in the report as such.

D.2.3 Exploitation or Gaining Access

Any information obtained from the prior phases will be used to attack the targeted systems. These attacks will attempt to test the authentication processes of the systems. Some examples of the types of attacks in this phase include, but are not limited to, buffer overflow or remote code execution attacks, system or application configuration issues, modem or remote access issues, firewall or routing problems, DNS attacks, MAC or IP address spoofing, unauthenticated share or file access, and exploitation of system trust relationships inherent to the systems. [Individual or company] will test potential vulnerabilities in a systemic manner, usually in the order of probable success and detection determined by [individual or company]. In addition, any password files obtained will be tested using password-cracking tools. The individual accounts will be tested against common password files, dictionary-based files, hybrids of these files, and brute-force attack methods. The purpose of this testing is to elevate privileges to administrator-level access.

Because it is a goal of [individual or company] as part of the vulnerability assessment or penetration test to determine the extent of vulnerabilities, information discovered about a specific device will be used to gain access to other systems that may be "trusted" by the compromised system. In addition, host-level vulnerabilities may be exploited to gain elevated privileges on the compromised system. If this privilege is achieved, [individual or company] may install "sniffers" or other utilities in an attempt to determine how deeply [individual or company] can go within ABC Company's network. [Individual or company] will insert a small text file at the highest level of compromise on each system or plant an administrator level account, if possible. If read-only access is available, [individual or company] may opt to copy sensitive files obtained or take a screen shot of information available. In either case, a review of the information will be conducted to determine the sensitivity of that information contained on the compromised system.

D.2.4 Documentation or Reporting

[Individual or company] will maintain detailed records of attempts and compromises throughout all phases of this vulnerability assessment or penetration test. [Individual or company] will provide a briefing report that outlines the findings discovered during the vulnerability assessment or penetration test. The final results will be compiled and provided to the ABC Company representative provided to [individual or company]. [Individual or company] will also provide specific details of vulnerabilities exploited to ABC Company's technical staff.

D.3 Special Considerations

[Individual or company] will coordinate vulnerability assessment or penetration testing activities with a "trusted agent" or ABC Company representative. This individual should be designated prior to any activities being performed. There may be a need for more than one individual to be appointed by ABC Company; however, the number of representatives should be set to the minimum possible required. Any and all individuals involved in the vulnerability assessment or penetration test should maintain confidentiality of the information provided to ensure test validity and security.

ABC Company will notify [individual or company] of any critical systems that should be excluded from the vulnerability assessment or penetration test. These systems may be security or safety systems, testing systems, or other systems deemed by ABC Company to be of a critical or sensitive nature that may have issues if tested. Again, it is the goal of [individual or company] to cause no harm to ABC Company's computer assets in the course of conducting the vulnerability or penetration test. These exempt systems should be noted and reasons for not testing them should be provided as an attachment to the signed agreement. In addition, ABC Company will note any systems that are not under the direct control or responsibility of ABC Company. These systems will also be excluded from the vulnerability assessment or penetration testing unless prior permission is obtained from the system's owner and another separate waiver is signed for these specific systems by the owner.

[Individual or company] will provide ABC Company with information regarding the systems used for vulnerability assessment or penetration testing activities. This will be done to ensure that the testing activities are not confused with real attacks. On external tests, [individual or company] will provide the DOE Computer Incident Advisory Capability (CIAC) with this relevant information.

As indicated earlier, [individual or company] will not attempt to exploit denial of service types of attacks unless requested by a competent authority of ABC Company. [Individual or company] will make every effort to prevent damage to any information system or data that the system holds. Some attempts may cause service interruptions due to the inherent risk involved in the activities being performed. In the unlikely event that service interruption occurs, [individual or company] will work with the ABC Company representative or other technical support personnel to determine the cause of the issue and assist in the restoration of the system to its desired state of operation.

[Individual or company] will ensure the protection and security (to the extent possible) from unauthorized access of any and all information obtained as a result of the vulnerability assessment or penetration test.

If ABC Company employees identify the penetration testing activity (excluding ABC Company trusted agents), the ABC Company's personnel should document such activity and take initial actions that would normally be expected under the case of a real attack. These may include notifying the CIAC. Once the CIAC or other trusted agent has been notified of such activity, the ABC Company's personnel will be informed that the activity was identified as part of the vulnerability assessment or penetration test. Logs or other evidence of this detection should be provided to ABC Company's independent oversight team for analysis. [Individual or company] will be allowed to continue with internal or external vulnerability assessment without blocking, filtering, or any other restrictive access.

ABC Company is responsible for restoring its computer assets to a secure configuration following the vulnerability assessment or penetration testing activity. [Individual or company] will document all changes made to ABC Company computers and will assist the company, if necessary, in "cleaning up" the systems. Cleanup may include deleting programs or files added to the systems, removing user accounts, identifying accounts that were compromised, and restoring systems to a secure configuration to ensure that no systems are left in a compromised state.

With the undersigned permission by a representative of ABC Company with full authority to execute such agreement, ABC Company certifies that ABC Company has a banner and warning policy implemented on ABC Company's computer assets and network and the undersigned grants constructive consent to [individual or company] to conduct vulnerability assessment or penetration testing activities in accordance with this agreement.

D.4 Approvals

Appendix E: Tools

The following is a list of tools for specific areas of testing. This is not a complete list because new tools are being developed all the time. The asterisk in front of the tool indicates that it may do a combination of scanning or testing. Some of these tools are free; others are commercial software applications. Some work on Windows and others work on Linux platforms. You will have to determine what tools are right for your organization.

Port scanners:
> Advanced Port Scanner, Angry IP, AW Security Port Scanner, Blaster Scan, *Firewalk, Floppyscan, Fscan, *HPing2, ICMP Scanning, IPSecScan, MingSweeper, NetScan Tools Pro, *Nmap, Ping Sweep, PortScan Plus, ScanLine, *Scanrand, Strove, *Superscan, THC Scan, War Dialer

Host scanners:
> CIS Scripts, HFNetchk/Pro, *Manual Scanning, *MS Baseline Security Analyzer

SNMP scanners:
> Braa, GetIF, SNScan, SNMP Scan, *Solarwinds

Network device scanners:
> CISCO, *Firewalk, Foundscan, *Manual Scanning, NetRecon, RAT, *SAINT, *SARA, SecureNet Pro, SecureScan, STAT Analyzer, VigiENT

Enumeration programs:
> AD Enumeration, *DumpSec, Enum, Fscan, GetAcct, *hping2, ISS, *Manual Scan, *NBTScan, *nbtstat, *Nessus, *Netcat, Netcraft, *Nmap, RING V2, *Saint, snmputil, SNScan, *SolarWinds, *Superscan, *Telnet, User2sid-Sid2user, Winfingerprint, *XPROBE

Password testing:
> Brutus, ISS, *John the Ripper, *L0phtCrack, *Manual, OPHCrack, SamInside

Wireless:
> Aerosol, *Aircrack, Airmagnet, *Airopeek NX, *AirSnort, AirTraf, AP Scanner, BSD-airtools, DriftNeit, *Ehtereal (Wireshark), EtherPEG,

FakeAP, *Kismet, MacStumbler, *MiniStumbler, Mognet, NAI Wireless Sniffer, NetChase, *Netstumbler, PrismStumbler, Redfang, SSID Sniff, StumbVerter, THC-RUT, THC-War Drive, VPNmonitor, VxSniffer, Wavemon, WaveStumbler, Wellenreiter, *WEPCrack, WifiFinder, WinDump, *WinPcap, Wireless Security Auditor

Application scanners:

Achilles, AppDetective, AppScan, BlackWidow, *Burp, Carnivore, *cURL, *IKE-Scan, Instant Source, kOld, *Manual Scanning, SPIKE Proxy, SQL Lock, WebInspect, WebSleuth, *Wget, *Wikto, WindowBomb

Vulnerability scanners:

Cerberus Internet Scanner, Cybercop Scanner, *GFI LANGuard, HackerShield, IdentTCP Scan, ISS Security Scanner, *Manual Scanning, *Nessus, NeWT, *NIKTO, *Retina, SAFEsuite Internet Scanner, *SAINT, SATAN, Typhoon III, VLAD the Scanner

Network sniffers:

Aldebaran, arpspoof, Cain and Abel, DNS Poisoning, dnsspoof, dsniff, EffeTech, EtherApe, Ehtereal, EtherFlood, Etherpeek NX, Ettercap, filesnarf, Hunt, iptables, IPTraf, Iris, MaaTec Network Analyzer, Mac Changer, Macof, mailsnarf, msgsnarf, MSN sniffer, Netfilter, NetIntercept, Network Probe, NGSSniff, Ntop, Nwreader, Packet Crafter, Password Sniffer, pf, SMAC, Sniffer, Sniffit, Snoop, Snort, sshmitm, tcpdump, tcp-kill, tcpnice, urlsnarf, webmitm, webspy, WinDNSSpoof, Windump

Forensic tools:

EnCase to acquire evidence and to do the bulk examinations: http://www. guidancesoftware.com

NetAnalysis for internet usage examinations: http://www.paraben-forensics. com/index.html

FTK for email examinations: http://www.accessdata.com

Forensic tool kits:

Portable forensic labs: http://www.icsforensic.com/index.cfm/action/ product.show/id_product/be25c798-2838-4d18-8bce-bb6c53eec7fa/ id_category/4d134fea-0fbb-4a6a-9542-13490b262404

Regular laptop computers in conjunction with proper hardware write-protection devices: http://www.icsforensic.com/index.cfm/action/catalog .browse/category/DriveLock/id_category/c14d69f1-dcb6-47ab-8be6-1b13217f5b84

Hard drive duplicators: http://www.logicube.com/products/hd_duplication/ sf5000.asp

Appendix F: How to Report Internet Crime*

Internet-related crime, like any other crime, should be reported to appropriate law enforcement investigative authorities at the local, state, federal, or international levels, depending on the scope of the crime. Citizens who are aware of federal crimes should report them to local offices of federal law enforcement. The primary federal law enforcement agencies that investigate domestic crime on the Internet include: the Federal Bureau of Investigation (FBI), the United States Secret Service, the United States Customs and Border Protection, the United States Postal Inspection Service, and the Bureau of Alcohol, Tobacco, Firearms [and Explosives] (ATF). Each of these agencies has offices conveniently located in every state and to which crimes may be reported. Contact information regarding these local offices may be found in local telephone directories. In general, federal crime may be reported to the local office of an appropriate law enforcement agency by a telephone call and by requesting the "Duty Complaint Agent." Each law enforcement agency also has a headquarters (HQ) in Washington, D.C., which has agents who specialize in particular areas. For example, the FBI and the U.S. Secret Service both have headquarters-based specialists in computer intrusion (i.e., computer hacker) cases. (http://www.usdoj.gov/criminal/cybercrime/reporting.htm)

---

* References provided by Dave Kleiman, with permission: http://wiki.castlecops.com/Reporting_Internet_Crime; http://wiki.castlecops.com/Reporting_Internet_Crime:_The_United_States_of_America; http://wiki.castlecops.com/Reporting_Internet_Crime:_International. Page created by Dave Kleiman.

F.1 International Organizations

Interpol official site—International Criminal Police Organization—ICPO
https://www.interpol.int

IT crime—regional working parties (https://www.interpol.int/Public/
TechnologyCrime/WorkingParties/Default.asp):

1. European Working Party on Information Technology Crime
2. American Regional Working Party on Information Technology Crime
3. African Regional Working Party on Information Technology Crime
4. Asia-South Pacific Working Party on Information Technology Crime
5. Steering Committee for Information Technology Crime

Virtual Global Taskforce http://www.virtualglobaltaskforce.com/

F.2 United States

As a general reporting process, begin with the main three: Internet Crime
Complaint Center (IC3), Internet Fraud Complaint Center, and How to Report
Internet-Related Crime:

1. The Internet Crime Complaint Center (IC3) (http://www.ic3.gov) is a part-
   nership between the Federal Bureau of Investigation (FBI) and the National
   White Collar Crime Center (NW3C). IC3's mission is to serve as a vehicle to
   receive, develop, and refer criminal complaints regarding the rapidly expanding arena of cybercrime. The IC3 gives the victims of cybercrime a convenient
   and easy-to-use reporting mechanism that alerts authorities to suspected
   criminal or civil violations. For law enforcement and regulatory agencies at
   the federal, state, and local level, IC3 provides a central referral mechanism
   for complaints involving Internet-related crimes.
2. The Internet Fraud Complaint Center's (http://www1.ifccfbi.gov or http://
   www.ifccfbi.gov/index.asp) mission is to address fraud committed over the
   Internet. For victims of Internet fraud, IFCC provides a convenient and
   easy-to-use reporting mechanism that alerts authorities to a suspected criminal or civil violation. For law enforcement and regulatory agencies at all
   levels, IFCC offers a central repository for complaints related to Internet
   fraud, works to quantify fraud patterns, and provides timely statistical data
   of current fraud trends. Note: The Internet Crime Complaint Center and
   the Internet Fraud Complaint Center are a joint venture that takes international complaints.
3. The How to Report Internet-Related Crime (http://www.cybercrime.gov/
   reporting.htm) link will provide you with a table of links to resources for
   reporting different types of electronic crime.

A next step is to find your local FBI InfraGard chapter and seek its advice in reporting the crime (http://www.infragard.net/chapters/index.htm). Follow that up by contacting your local Electronic Crimes Task Force agency. These are headed up by your local Secret Service agency (http://www.treas.gov/usss/fcd_ecb.shtml). Another option to locate them is to perform an Internet search using Google with the state or major city in which you reside (e.g., Electronic Crimes Task Force Miami). If an agency cannot be found locally, contacting one of the ECTFs listed on this site can point you in the right direction: http://www.ectaskforce.org/Regional_Locations.htm.

Many state Department of Law Enforcement agencies have a computer crime reporting facility—for example:

Florida Department of Law Enforcement FDLE Computer Crime Center: http://www.fdle.state.fl.us/Fc3).

The attorney general's computer crime National Association of Attorney General's Computer Crime Point of Contact List (all state-related cyber questions): http://www.naag.org/issues/20010724-cc_list_bg.php

OJP Information Technology Initiatives http://it.ojp.gov/topic.jsp?topic_id=46 (a resource provided by the U.S. Department of Justice's Office of Justice Programs that gives justice professionals access to information sharing resources, initiatives, and technological developments).

DHS threats and protection http://www.dhs.gov/dhspublic/display?theme=73 Information Sharing & Analysis Centers.

F.3 Well-Known Government Reporting Agencies

1. Cross-border e-commerce purchase complaint form: http://www.econsumer. gov/english/index.html
2. National Fraud Information Center: http://www.fraud.org/info/contactnfic. htm
3. Consumer information from the Federal Government: http://www.consumer. gov
4. Consumer Know Fraud: http://www.consumer.gov/knowfraud
5. FTC—your national resource for identity theft: http://www.consumer.gov/ idtheft
6. FTC—consumer information security: http://www.ftc.gov/infosecurity
7. FTC—report spam: uce@ftc.gov
8. IRS procedures: reporting fraud: http://www.irs.gov/faqs/faq1-13.html
9. USPS—fraud: http://www.usps.com/websites/depart/inspect/fraud/MailFraud Complaint.htm http://www.usps.gov/
10. U.S. Postal Inspection Service (USPIS): http://www.usps.gov/websites/ depart/inspect
11. USPS Office of Inspector General: http://www.uspsoig.gov

12. Securities and Exchange Commission—U.S. investment scams: http://www.sec.gov/enforce/comctr.htm
13. DOJ—Office for Victims of Crime: http://www.ojp.usdoj.gov/ovc
14. DOJ—National Institute of Justice: http://www.ojp.usdoj.gov/nij
15. Financial Crimes Enforcement Network: http://www.treas.gov/fincen
16. U.S. Secret Service: financial crimes division, 950 H Street, NW, Washington, D.C. 20001, or telephone (202) 406-5850; fax: (202) 406-8203; http://www.secretservice.gov/contact_fcd.shtml
17. http://www.treas.gov/usss/ 419 Fraud: 419.fcd@usss.treas.gov
18. U.S. Secret Service: field offices: http://www.secretservice.gov/field_offices.shtml
19. FBI tips and public leads: https://tips.fbi.gov
20. FBI field offices: http://www.fbi.gov/contact/fo/fo.htm
21. Bureau of Alcohol, Tobacco, & Firearms: http://www.atf.treas.gov
22. U.S. Sentencing Commission: http://www.ussc.gov
23. Better Business Bureau online complaint system: http://www.bbb.org/complaint.asp
24. Association of Government Accountants (AGA): http://www.agacgfm.org
25. Commodity Futures Trading Commission (CFTC): http://www.cftc.gov/
26. Federal Deposit Insurance Corporation (FDIC): http://www.fdic.gov
27. FedWorld FTP file archive: http://www.fedworld.gov/ftp.htm
28. FinanceNet: http://www.financenet.gov
29. Government Finance Officers Association (GFOA): http://www.gfoa.org
30. Justice Information Center (JIC): http://www.ncjrs.org
31. National Technical Information Services (NTIS): https://dmf.ntis.gov
32. Nonprofit Gateway: http://www.nonprofit.gov
33. Small Business Administration (SBA): http://www.sba.gov
34. U.S. General Accounting Office (GAO): http://www.gao.gov
35. U.S. General Services Administration (GSA): http://www.gsa.gov
36. U.S. Health Care Financing Administration (HCFA): http://www.hcfa.gov
37. U.S. Patent and Trademark Office (PTO): http://www.uspto.gov

F.4 Scams

US-CERT at soc@us-cert.gov or SANS ISC at handlers@sans.org

F.5 Europe

EUROPOL (http://www.europol.eu.int) is the European law enforcement organization that aims at improving the effectiveness and cooperation of the competent authorities in the member states in preventing and combating terrorism, unlawful drug trafficking, and other serious forms of international organized crime.

F.6 Italy

Italian Cybercrime Polizia Postale Informatica http://www.poliziadistato.it/pds/informatica/contatti.html

F.7 United Kingdom

1. National Hi-Tech Crime Unit: http://www.nhtcu.org
2. National Infrastructure Security Co-ordination Centre (NISCC): http://www.niscc.gov.uk
3. UNIRAS: http://www.uniras.gov.uk

F.8 Australia

1. Australian High Tech Crime Centre (AHTCC): http://www.ahtcc.gov.au
2. Australian Federal Police: http://www.afp.gov.au

F.9 Canada

1. Canadian cybercrime—reporting economic crime online: https://www.recol.ca
2. Canada's national tipline: http://www.cybertip.ca

Acronyms

3DES: triple data encryption standard
AAFS: American Academy of Forensic Sciences
ACL: access control lists
AES: advanced encryption standard
AH: authentication header
AIR: adjusted impact rating
ASC: appraisal subcommittee
ASIS: American Society of Industrial Security
AWG: American wire gauge
BC: business continuity
BCP: business continuity plan
BIA: business impact analysis
BSC: balance scorecard
CA: certificate authority
CBC: cipher block chaining mode
CCE: certified computer examiner
CCTV: closed circuit television
CD: compact disc
CEH: certified ethical hacker
CEO: chief executive officer
CERT: computer emergency response team
CF: compact flash
CFB: cipher feedback mode
CFE: computer forensics expert
CFTC: Commodity Futures Trading Commission
CHAP: challenge/response protocol
CIA: confidentiality, integrity, and availability
CIAC: computer incident advisory capability
CIO: chief information officer
CIS: computer Internet security
CISA: certified information security auditor

CISM: certified information security manager
CISO: chief information security officer
CISSP: certified information systems security professional
CMM: capability maturity model
COBIT: control objectives for information and related technology
CRC: cyclic redundancy check
CRL: certificate revocation list
CSA: Computer Security Act
CVE: common vulnerabilities and exposures
DAC: discretionary access controls
DES: data encryption standard
DFCB: Digital Forensic Certification Board
DFE: digital forensic experts
DHCP: dynamic host configuration protocol
DHHS: Department of Health and Human Services
DMS: digital and multimedia sciences
DMZ: demilitarized zone or demarcation zone (perimeter zone)
DNS: domain name services/server
DoD: Department of Defense
DOE: Department of Energy
DPDP: deter, prevent, detect, prosecute
DR: disaster recovery
DRP: disaster recovery plan
DVD: digital video disc
DVR: digital video recorder
EAP: emergency action plan
EASI: estimate of adversary sequence interruption
ECB: electronic codebook mode
ECC: elliptic curve cryptosystem
ECPA: Electronic Communications Privacy Act
EFS: encrypted file system (Microsoft)
EPIC: electronic privacy information center
ESI: electronically stored information
ESP: encapsulation security payload
FAR: federal acquisition regulation
FBI: Federal Bureau of Investigation
FDA: Food and Drug Administration
FDIC: Federal Deposit Insurance Corporation
FDM: frequency division multiplexing
FERC: Federal Energy Regulatory Commission
FFIEC: Federal Financial Institutions Examination Council
FIRA: Financial Institutions Regulatory Rate Control Act
FIRREA: Financial Institutions Reform, Recovery, and Enforcement Act

FISMA: Federal Information Security Management Act
FRB: Federal Reserve Bank
FRCP: Federal Rules of Civil Procedures
FTP: file transfer protocol
GAISP: generally accepted information security principle
GASSP: generally accepted security system principle
GLBA: Gramm–Leach–Bliley Act
GUI: graphical user interface
HCDA: Housing and Community Development Act
HIPAA: Health Insurance Portability and Accountability Act
HMDA: Home Mortgage Disclosure Act
HTTP: hypertext transfer protocol
HVAC: heating, ventilation, and air conditioning
IAM: INFOSEC assessment methodology
IDS: intrusion detection system
IEEE: Institute of Electrical and Electronics Engineers
IEM: INFOSEC evaluation methodology
IMAP: Internet message access protocol
IP: Internet protocol
IPL: initial program load
IPS: intrusion prevention system
IPSEC: Internet protocol security
ISAC: information sharing and analysis center
ISACA: Information Systems Audit and Control Association
ISC²: International Information Systems Security Certification Consortium
ISFCE: International Society of Forensic Computer Examiners
ISO: International Organization of Standardization or International Standards Organization
ISSA: Information Systems Security Association
ISSMP: information systems security management professional
IT: information technology
IV: initialization vector
JAD: joint application development
KGI: key goal indicator
KPI: key performance indicator
MAC: media access control or mandatory access control (depending on context)
Mbps: megabits per second
MCSE: Microsoft certified systems engineer
MD: message digest
MDC: modification detection code
MIC: message integrity code
MIME: multipurpose Internet mail extension
MITM: man in the middle

MMC: multimedia card
MS: memory stick
MSA: metropolitan statistical area
MTD: maximum tolerable downtime
NARA: National Archives and Records Administration
NBS: National Bureau of Standards
NCUA: National Credit Union Administration
NIPC: National Infrastructure Protection Center
NIST: National Institute of Standards and Technology
NSA: National Security Agency
NTFS: new technology file system
NTP: network time protocol
OCC: Office of the Comptroller of the Currency
OCTAVE: operationally critical threat, asset, and vulnerability evaluation
OFB: output feedback mode
OPSEC: operations security
OSI: open systems interconnection
OTS: Office of Thrift Supervision
OUI: organizationally unique identifier
PAP: password authentication protocol
PCI-DSS: payment card industry data security standards
PDA: personal device assistant
PDCA: plan, do, check, act
PDU: protocol data unit
PEM: privacy-enhanced mail
PGP: pretty good privacy
PI: private investigator
PIG: passive information gathering
PKCS: public key cryptography standard
P of O: possibility of occurrence
POP3: post office protocol version 3
POTS: plain old telephone service
PPTP: point-to-point tunneling protocol
PRM: percentage of risk mitigated
PRR: percentage of residual risk
PSK: preshared key
PVC: polyvinyl chloride
QOTD: quote of the day
RA: registration authority
RAD: rapid application development
RBAC: role-based access control
RFP: request for proposal
ROI: return on investment

RSA: Rivest, Shamir, and Adleman
RTM: requirements traceability matrix
RTO: recovery time objective
SABSA: systems and business security architecture
SAN: storage area network
SAR: suspicious activity report
SCAPC: security content automation protocol checklist
SD: secure digital
SDLC: software (system) development life cycle
SEC: Securities and Exchange Commission
SET: secure electronic transaction
SFTP: secure file transfer protocol
SHA: secure hash algorithm
S-HTTP: secure hypertext transfer protocol
SLA: service level agreement
SM: SmartMedia
SMART: specific, measurable, actionable, reasonable, and time based
S/MIME: secure multipurpose Internet mail extension
SMTP: simple mail transfer protocol
SNMP: simple network management protocol
SOX: Sarbanes–Oxley Act
SP: special publication
SSH: secure shell
SSID: service set identifiers
SSL: secure sockets layer
STP: shielded twisted pair
SVRD: security vulnerability research and defense (Microsoft)
TCP: transmission control protocol
TDM: time division multiplexing
TEP: technical evaluation plan
TFTP: trivial file transfer protocol
TKI: temporal key integrity protocol
TLS: transport layer security
TOD: time of day
UDP: user datagram protocol
UPNP: universal plug and play
UPS: uninterruptible power systems
URL: uniform resource locator
USB: universal serial bus
UTP: unshielded twisted pair
VLAN: virtual local area network
VoIP: voice over Internet protocol (IP)
VPN: virtual private network

WAP: wireless application protocol

WEP: wired equivalent privacy or wireless encryption protocol (depending on context)

WHID: Web hacking incidents database

WLAN: wireless local area network

WPA: Wi-Fi protected access

WTLS: wireless transport layer security protocol

xD: xD-picture card

XSRF: cross-site request forgery

XSS: cross-site scripting

MyISAT

If you like the format and step-by-step procedures to assist you in managing your information security program found in this book, then you may be interested in a software application called MyISAT that takes these recommended steps and puts them into action. I have a working beta version of MyISAT; however, it is currently undergoing some redevelopment as a software-as-a-service or a stand-alone application. I believe an application like MyISAT is a necessity to document and track your efforts in conducting an effective information security management program. This application integrates all of the concepts of information security discussed in this book. Although I am not able to provide MyISAT in its current form, as I noted, it is under development and plans are to make it available to the public following the same methodology and framework that has already been established.

I am looking for financial support, programmers, marketers, and an executive team that would like to become involved in this project to enhance MyISAT. MyISAT was designed to assist executives, like you, in running their information security management program. The intent behind MyISAT is that it would be easy to use, provide customization, and be geared toward managing an effective information security program. It is modular so that only modules that a company needs can be used. MyISAT is also intended to be affordable and scalable to handle the increasing requirements of information security. The modules will integrate with each other so that duplication of work is reduced and a lot of the manual documentation is automated. MyISAT is based on a program produced for a former employer of mine that assisted the company in establishing an effective information security management program.

I will admit that I am not an expert software programmer. I have delved into programming out of necessity and have learned as I went. I asked questions of others that would assist me in coding certain functions that I needed after describing to them what I wanted. I do admit to having expertise in information security and knowing what is required by a company to implement an effective information security management program. I am not rich, but I am an entrepreneur with a vision and driven to reach certain goals. One of these goals is to write this book and to produce a program that puts the concepts discussed into practice.

The predevelopment and design of this program have already been completed. It is now ready to move to the next phase. If you are interested and have the resources to assist in the production of MyISAT, please log on to http://myisat.com or contact admin@myisat.com for further information.

Note: I have shared some of the concepts of MyISAT with you in this book, but I cannot share the coding or the beta version of this application. I have provided a high-level synopsis of what MyISAT currently does or what the redevelopment of the program will do, but MyISAT requires more development to become a viable commercial application.

Synopsis of MyISAT

Background

As part of my job responsibilities for former employers, I was tasked to complete a gap analysis on their policies and procedures. The first step of the gap analysis was to identify the regulatory requirements of the specific industry that I was working in at the time and then to identify all of the policies and procedures that linked to or correlated with these requirements. It was apparent to me that a relational database would assist me in this task. Through my previous experience in law enforcement accreditation, I had been introduced to and was familiar with a program that assisted our department in the proper documentation of regulations and codifying them into policies. From there, the program would assist in assessing and validating that the department was following these policies. I found it reassuring that the same principles we used in law enforcement accreditation were also being applied to certain areas of business. Unfortunately, I was not able to find a software program that would do exactly what I wanted it to do; programs that were close to the functionality were very expensive. I decided to create my own program, which I now call MyISAT (my information security assessment tool).

As the project grew, it became clear to me that the information already present in the database could also be utilized to assist in the completion of some of my other tasks, such as conducting risk assessments, vendor management reviews, and incident management.

There are currently seven modules in the MyISAT program:

- policies and procedures (PP);
- prerisk assessment (PRA) or change management (CM);
- information security risk assessment (ISRA);
- mitigation of information security risks (MISR);

- vendor management (VM);
- incident management (IM); and
- business impact analysis (BIA) and business continuity (BC)/disaster recovery plan (DRP).

Overall Purpose

The overall purpose of MyISAT is to automate repetitive documentation tasks and provide ease-of-use tracking for the seven modules that reflect the core responsibilities of the information security management program. MyISAT is a comprehensive and inexpensive information governance and compliance application.

Benefits and Use of the Program

The program offers the following:

- automatic report writing;
- standardization;
- tracking;
- integration of relational databases;
- module programming;
- integration with Word, Excel, and other office products; and
- customizable reports.

Future Development

This program needs

- to be redeveloped for general business use; however, the framework is established;
- to be ported over to a heartier database, such as SQL;
- a better GUI interface—possibly a Web interface; and
- better security and access levels to be designed.

Policies and Procedures (PP) Module

Purpose of the PP Module

The purpose of this module is to organize all policies into a standard form and to compare them against regulatory requirements and best practices. This module will assist in conducting a gap analysis and will validate compliance.

Benefits and Use of the PP Module

The module

- requires policies to be written in a standard form to include:
  - purpose of the policy
  - policy statement
  - background information
  - the actual policy
  - implementation procedures
  - additional documentation
  - additional references
  - appendix;
- provides tracking of review dates and approval dates;
- provides for referential linking between policies;
- provides tracking of controls related to the policy;
- provides a split screen to show policy and then regulations together for easy comparison;
- provides a bottom screen that shows all regulations the policy relates to specific to your industry;
- allows for follow-up notes to track easily the work completed or pending on a policy;
- automatically tracks when policies are up for review and provides for status, assignments, classifications, approval dates, effective dates, etc. in one easy-to-read format; and
- provides integration into procedures and assists in linking procedures to policies.

Standard Reports of the PP Module

The module

- can automatically print policy into Word format following a standardized form;
- reports all policies, codified number, title, approval date, effective date, reviewed date, and "assigned to" information;
- provides a follow up report that lists the title of the report and user notes to identify what needs to be completed or looked at for each policy;
- provides an upcoming review report that lists codified number, title, review date, and frequency of review, sorted by next review date from current to future;
- provides a policy matrix with a pivot table report that shows the interrelational references between policies; and
- can develop custom reports as required.

Further Development of the PP Module

- Provide one central area for easy lookup of all policies (i.e., publish on intranet).
- Provide support for standards.

Prerisk-Assessment (PRA) or Change Management (CM) Module

Purpose of the PRA or CM Module

The PRA or CM module was developed to create a standardized form that could be utilized to do a preliminary risk assessment on a new project or to track changes. Note: This is not a full risk assessment report, but rather a top-level overview of a proposed new project. This module assists in recognizing the need for a risk assessment on a new project and integrates well with the project/change control procedures.

Benefits and Use of the PRA or CM Module

The module provides

- an automatic numbering and tracking system for projects;
- standard areas to look at when evaluating a new project; and
- a way to gather initial information and to have this information stored for easy retrieval in the future.

Standard Reports of the PRA or CM Module

A standardized PRA report to submit as part of the new project proposal packet is automatically printed.

Further Development of the PRA or CM Module

The intent is to integrate the PRA automatically further into the ISRA module.

Information Security Risk Assessment (ISRA) Module

Purpose of the ISRA Module

This module assists the user in conducting a comprehensive information security risk assessment. It takes a step-by-step approach through all areas of the risk assessment process to include the technical evaluation plan (TEP). This module is customizable and contains formulas specific to the organization.

Benefits and Use of the ISRA Module

- It cuts the time necessary to complete a complex risk assessment by at least half.
- Modular programming allows incorporation of information from other assessments.
- All formulas are programmed behind the scenes, so the user only has to fill out certain information and the system automatically calculates the level of risk as specifically defined by the organization.
- It allows for relationship integration of systems, observations, controls, control activities, etc.
- It lists the characterization components of an assessment to include
  - purpose of the assessment
  - description of the technology base
  - system boundaries
  - list of items that make up the systems (hardware, software, etc.); systems are entered into an inventory list that includes the following:
    - description of the asset
    - confidentiality, ranking, and criticality of the system
    - current controls at the system level
    - planned controls at the system level
    - observations specific to the system under review
  - users and their functions in the area under assessment
- It provides a list of IT processes and diagrams to include in the report (diagrams are stored in a central location and can be utilized by future assessments).
- It lists all threats and provides the threat statement (normally global throughout all assessment, but can be modified accordingly).
- It lists all observations for the assessment. All observations are given a description, threat sources, and threat actions related to that observation.
- Observations are traced to current controls and planned controls.
- Observations are given a possibility of occurrence rating.
- Observations are then given an impact of loss for financial, regulatory, operational, confidentiality, integrity, and availability areas.
- Observations are also assigned a percentage of risk mitigated determined by the controls that are in place.
- The system automatically calculates the level based on user input and produces a list of all medium- and high-level observations.
  - These observations are then rated on the effort it would take to bring their rating down to an acceptable level and the benefit that would be produced by these efforts.

- These observations are also assigned an MISR number once approved for mitigation and the program will automatically update the information based on the tracking provided in the MISR module.
- Observations are given recommendations on how they could be mitigated.
- The user enters information for the following:
  - background;
  - executive summary;
  - identified high and medium risks;
  - information risk management/compliance;
  - information security risk assessment;
  - logical and administrative access control;
  - physical security;
  - encryption;
  - malicious code;
  - systems development, acquisition, and maintenance;
  - personnel security;
  - electronic and paper-based media handling;
  - logging and data collection;
  - service provider oversight;
  - incident detection and response; and
  - business continuity.
- Documentation utilized in the assessment is tracked.
- Follow-up tracking and notes for the assessor are kept.
- Tracking of the assessment along with the dates that the assessment was reviewed with the business owners is done.
- Test plans are automatically produced.
- Technical scans are documented.
- A technical evaluation plan is produced to include documented concerns and constraints and summary results of the 10 areas evaluated.
- Technical vulnerabilities and CVE are identified and rated.
- InfoSec posture rating (IPR) is automatically calculated based on the observations and technical vulnerabilities identified and can also be trended over time.
- It allows for documentation and tracking of comments from business owners along with rationale used in sustaining the observations.

Standard Reports of the ISRA Module

The standard reports include

- system inventory report (lists all asset items associated with system under review);
- system observation report (lists all observations , threat source, threat description, threat actions);

- observation current controls, planned controls, and combined controls report (lists all observation/control pairs for current, planned, and combined);
- impact analysis report—remediation (lists observations along with ranking for each attribute—financial, regulatory, operational, confidential, integrity, and availability along with impact rating, percentage of risk mitigated, percentage of residual risk, and adjusted impact rating);
- recommendation report;
- ISRA report;
- control report;
- specific control report;
- legend report (lists all ratings and scales used in the process);
- executive summary report;
- methodology report (defines the methodology used in the process);
- test plan report to include complete and incomplete reports; and
- technical evaluation plan report.

Further Development of the ISRA Module

The module will be further developed to

- customize reporting process to include additional reports as needed;
- conduct additional work on test plans and activities required to test controls;
- provide automatic integration with CVEs;
- develop an easier way to choose from lists to autopopulate records;
- provide better writing capabilities, spell checking, etc. inside certain fields; and
- provide better linking to documentation, diagrams, etc.

Mitigation of Information Security Risks (MISR) Module

Purpose of the MISR Module

This module is utilized to track the mitigation efforts of the findings found in the risk assessments. This module integrates with the ISRA to allow for automatic updating in the ISRA module in future and ongoing assessments.

Benefits and Use of the MISR Module

The module

- tracks mitigation plans, providing dates, status, classifications of mitigation, and assessments to which mitigation applies; and
- allows for updates of mitigation plans for easy review.

Standard Reports of the MISR Module

Standard reports include

- outstanding mitigation report;
- pivot table reports to include mitigations that were completed and those that are still outstanding, providing the number of high, medium, and low mitigation efforts for each of the risk assessments; and
- MISR summary report that includes details such as ranking, department involved, plan, and related assessment.

Further Development of the MISR Module

The module will be further developed to

- automatically update MISR from ISRA module and referential integrity capabilities; and
- provide additional reporting options.

Vendor Management (VM) Module

Purpose of the VM Module

This module provides a tracking mechanism for all of the organization's vendors. It follows the requirements specifically laid out in NCUA Part 748 review of service providers; however, it can be modified for any other industry regulations on third-party service provider reviews and specific company policies.

Benefits and Use of the VM Module

The module

- allows for easy identification of critical and active vendors and vendors dealing with sensitive data;
- provides ranking of the vendor criticality to the organization;
- provides descriptions, contract dates, maturity dates, reminder dates, notices, contract types, vendor types, provider types, and business owners in an easy-to-read format;
- provides a review form for each vendor that specifically follows the FFIEC "outsourcing technology services" guidelines for evaluating vendors (as stated before, this can be modified to include industry-specific regulations); and
- is able to copy and paste specific contract terminology that documents the agreements with the vendors related to protecting sensitive information.

Standard Reports of the VM Module

The standard reports include

- vendor report sorted by business owner, classification, and review dates; and
- vendor review report to identify easily the areas that have been or need to be reviewed for each vendor.

Further Development of the VM Module

Future development will include automatic self-assessment reporting capabilities.

Incident Management (IM) Module

Purpose of the IM Module

This module was developed to standardize the format following the NIST SP800-61 recommendations on incident management. This step-by-step module conforms to the organization's policies on incident handling.

Benefits and Use of the IM Module

The module

- identifies all required questions that need to be answered following a security incident being identified;
- provides a checklist of notification and a walk-through of current policies regarding the notification process;
- provides areas for incident details and status of incident; and
- provides areas for incident handler comments and ease of use of tracking incidents.

Standard Reports of the IM Module

The incident tracking report will satisfy the NIST recommended review format.

Further Development of the IM Module

Future development will include automatic incident management reporting capabilities.

Business Impact Analysis (BIA) and Business Continuity (BC)/Disaster Recovery Plan (DRP) Module

Purpose of the BIA and BC/DRP Module

This module was developed to assist the information security manager in conducting a business impact analysis and preparing the organization's business continuity/disaster recovery plan. This step-by-step module conforms to the organization's policies on having a business continuity and disaster recovery plan implemented that is effective, comprehensive, and updated on a routine basis.

Benefits and Use of the BIA and BC/DRP Module

The module

- provides a step-by-step method to conduct a BIA on the organization that includes the collection of all assets, list of business functions, employee contact list, list of service providers, and other important records required for continued business operations;
- provides a standardized survey and questionnaire to all department heads;
- provides automatic risk calculations; and
- assists in writing a comprehensive business continuity and disaster recovery plan.

Standard Reports of the BIA and BC/DRP Module

The standard reports include

- complete business impact analysis;
- critical business functions;
- critical assets;
- critical records;
- employee contact list;
- vendor contact list;
- critical facilities;
- secondary functions; and
- standardized business continuity plan and disaster recovery plan.

Further Development of the BIA and BC/DRP Module

This includes capabilities for automatic business continuity plans and disaster recovery plans and enhancement of testing and tracking.

Web References

AFCEA International www.afcea.org

Alta Associates www.altaassociates.com

American Council for Technology (ACT) and Industry Advisory Council www. actgov.org

American National Standards Institute (ANSI) www.ansi.org

ASIS International www.asisonline.org

Cisco www.cisco.com

Computer Security Institute www.gocsi.com

Computing Technology Association (CompTIA) www.comptia.org

ECRYPT: European Network of Excellence for Cryptology www.ecrypt.eu.org

EEMA—The European Association for e-Identity and Security www.eema.org

European Information Society Group (EURIM) www.eurim.org.uk

European Network and Information Security Agency (ENISA) http://enisa. europa.eu

Executive Women's Forum www.infosecuritywomen.com

High Technology Crime Investigation Association (HTCIA) www.htcia.org

Information Security Forum (ISF) www.securityforum.org

Information Systems Audit and Control Association (ISACA) www.isaca.org

Information Systems Security Association (ISSA) www.issa.org

Information Technology Association of America (ITAA) www.itaa.org

Infragard www.infragard.net

Institute for Information Security Professionals www.instisp.com

International Association of Privacy Professionals www.privacyassociation.org

International Federation for Information Processing www.ifip.org

International High Technology Crime Investigation Association (HTCIA) www.htcia.org

International Information Systems Forensics Association (ITFSA) www.iisfa.org

International Information Systems Security Certification Consortium, Inc. (ISC²®) www.isc2.org

International Security, Trust, and Privacy Alliance (ISTPA) www.istpa.org

International Society of Forensic Computer Examiners (ISFCE) http://www.certified-computer-examiner.com/

International Standards Organization www.iso.org

Internet Assigned Numbers Authority (IANA) http://www.iana.org/assignments/port-numbers

Internet Security Alliance www.isalliance.org

Internet Storm Center isc.incidents.org

Jericho Forum www.opengroup.org/jericho/

National Academic Centers of Excellence www.nsa.gov/ia/academia/caeiae.cfm

Packetstorm Security www.packetstormsecurity.org

SANS Institute www.sans.org

Security Content Automation Protocol Checklist (SCAPC) http://checklists.nist.gov/

Security Industry Association www.siaonline.org

TrueCrypt www.truecrypt.org

CISSP Related Links

General

http://www.ansi.org/
http://www.cccure.org/
http://www.cissps.com/
http://www.ethicalhacker.net/
http://www.ieee.org/
http://www.isc2.org/
http://www.iso.ch/
http://www.nist.gov/
http://www.nsa.gov/
http://www.sans.org/
http://www.searchsecurity.com/

CBK Domains

Access Control

http://www.cert.org/advisories/
http://www.symantec.com/securitycheck/

Application

http://www.ansi.org/
http://java.sun.com/
http://www.phase-one.com.au/

Architecture

http://whatis.techtarget.com/
http://www.tech-faq.com/

BCP

http://www.bci.com/
http://www.disaster-resource.com/
http://www.drj.com/
http://www.dr.org/

Crypto

http://www.cryptography.com/
http://www.homenethelp.com/
http://www.howstuffworks.com/
http://www.techtarget.com/definitionalpha

Law, Investment, and Ethics

http://www.cert.org/
http://www.iab.org/
http://www.ietf.org/rfc/rfc1087.txt?number=1087
https://www.isc2.org/cgi-bin/content.cgi?category=12
http://staff.washington.edu/dittrich/forensics.html

Management

http://www.microsoft.com/technet
http://www.rcmp_grc.ca/tsb/pubs/index_e.htm
http://www.securityauditor.net/

Ops

Most material in this domain is covered in other domains. Use many of the resources already listed.

Physical

http://www.asisonline.com/
http://www.security.org/dial-80/links.htm

Telecom

There are too many to list. Use many of the resources already listed.

Index